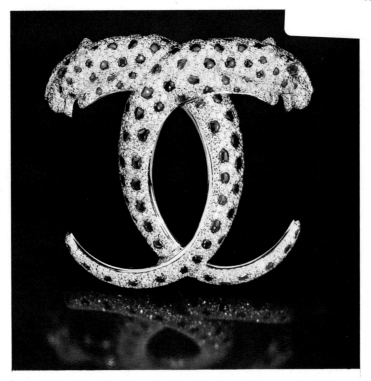

CARTIER
THE LEGEND

Gilberte Gautier

ARLINGTON BOOKS
LONDON

CARTIER — THE LEGEND
First published in this edition 1983 by
Arlington Books (Publishers) Ltd
15–17 King St, St James's
London SW1
Reprinted 1988
Originally published in 1980 in France
by Julliard under the title
Rue de la Paix

Text © Julliard 1980
English translation © Arlington Books 1983
Photographs © Gilberte Gautier

Typeset by Inforum Ltd, Portsmouth
Printed and bound in England by
Billing & Sons Ltd, Worcester

British Library Cataloguing in Publication Data
Gautier Gilberte
Cartier — the legend.   2. Jewelery trade — France
1. Cartier (Family)
— Biography
I. Title   II. Rue de la Paix. English
338.4′773927′0944   HD9747.F8

ISBN 0 85140 619 X

FRONTISPIECE: *Mystery Clock of rock-crystal, onyx and black enamel. Cabochon turquoise motifs, with a yellow gold and ebony base. The hands are rose-cut diamonds on platinum (1925, Cartier collection).*

To Robert Hocq, always a friend.
To his daughter, Nathalie.

Contents

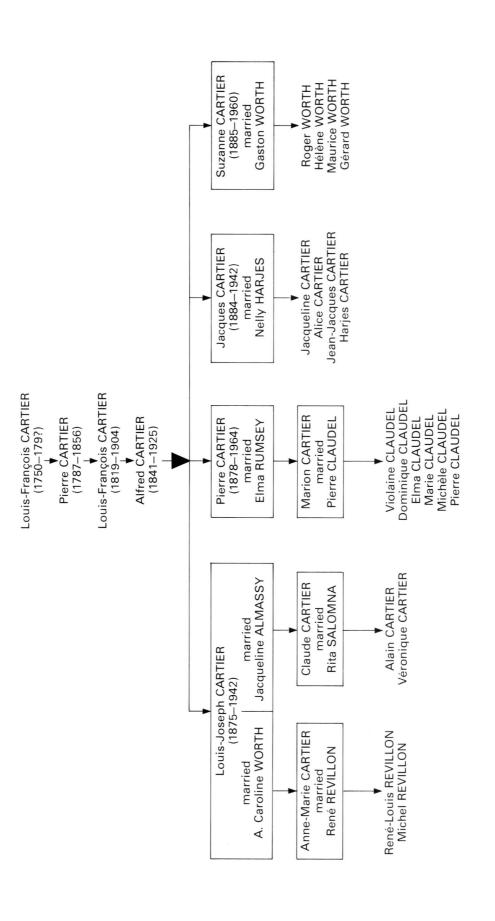

Louis-François CARTIER
(1750–1792?)

Pierre CARTIER
(1787–1856)

Louis-François CARTIER
(1819–1904)

Alfred CARTIER
(1841–1925)

Louis-Joseph CARTIER
(1875–1942)
married
A. Caroline WORTH
married
Jacqueline ALMASSY

Anne-Marie CARTIER
married
René REVILLON

René-Louis REVILLON
Michel REVILLON

Claude CARTIER
married
Rita SALOMNA

Alain CARTIER
Véronique CARTIER

Pierre CARTIER
(1878–1964)
married
Elma RUMSEY

Marion CARTIER
married
Pierre CLAUDEL

Violaine CLAUDEL
Dominique CLAUDEL
Elma CLAUDEL
Marie CLAUDEL
Michèle CLAUDEL
Pierre CLAUDEL

Jacques CARTIER
(1884–1942)
married
Nelly HARJES

Jacqueline CARTIER
Alice CARTIER
Jean-Jacques CARTIER
Harjes CARTIER

Suzanne CARTIER
(1885–1960)
married
Gaston WORTH

Roger WORTH
Hélène WORTH
Maurice WORTH
Gérard WORTH

Acknowledgements

This book could not have been completed without the friendly under-standing of the late Robert Hocq, former president-director general of Cartier, who authorised the examination of the Society's archives, and the interviewing of past and present collaborators for Cartier-Paris, Cartier-London and Cartier-New York.

Special thanks are due to Marcelle Decharbogne, Charles Jacqueau, Annette Worth, Brunneheimer (curator of the Museum of Decorative Arts), Jessie MacNab (curator of the Metropolitan Museum, New York), André Denet, Gérard and Hubert Desouches, Gaston Cusin, Edouard Dermitt (adopted son of Jean Cocteau), Roger Worth (great-nephew of Louis Cartier), Georges Walther (Consul at the French Embassy in Budapest), Daniel Alkouffe (curator at the Louvre Museum), Doctors Kestlei and Dubrocki, Lucien Lachassagne, Georges Remy, René Genette, Robert Thil, Enrique de Meneses, René-Louis Révillon (grandson of Louis Cartier) and Jacques Cartier (grand-son of Jacques Cartier), Alain and Véronique Cartier (the children of Claude Cartier), Jean Marais, Pierre Galante, Véronique Ristelhueber-Guilloteau (documentalist for Cartier-Paris), and Danielle Pittée (documentalist for Cartier-New York).

The author would also like to take the opportunity of warmly thanking all the participants in the diverse Cartier departments: jewels, stock, manufacture, administration, photography, etc.

A posthumous tribute to Jeanne Toussaint who allowed us to understand better, and to know, Louis Cartier, an inspired creator, but quite simply, the man.

INTRODUCTION

Birth of a Dynasty

SARAGOSSA, 1808

Pushing forward those in front of him, pressed by others from behind, a young man, twenty-one years old, waited like all his French companions, to be shot and then incinerated in the oven of a bakery designed specifically for this purpose.

Ever since Joseph Bonaparte had become king there had been revolution in Spain, and during the past three years Pierre Cartier had seen the death of many of his companions in arms. He knew from experience that, at the hour of death, extraordinary images both joyous and painful could arise through a blur of memories. Memories of his own parents suddenly rose in his mind. Once again he saw them, hands tied behind their backs, just as he was today, crowded into the cart with the other prisoners, destined for the scaffold.

In order to flee from Paris his aunt had disguised him as a girl. He had felt ridiculous and terribly offended, a small six-year-old boy, dressed in girl's clothes, arriving in the streets of Sarcelles where a joyless childhood awaited him. He forced himself to follow his aunt's advice: to forget certain good manners and that he was the son of Louis-Francois de . . .?

The absurdity of the situation made Pierre smile briefly and sadly. He had totally forgotten what names and what title his father had possessed when he was arrested in 1790 as a suspect, like so many others, while working as a metallurgist at the Louvre Museum. Having escaped the guillotine by no longer being his father's son, only to die, incinerated at Saragossa as a soldier of the Empire under serial number 8649, seemed to be the height of absurdity! What did it matter that he had gained a reprieve of fifteen years – of which three were particularly exciting, when he had been attached to Napoléon's personal guard, and had learned how to handle arms, to swear and to pick up girls. It was from an old man, long ago, that Pierre had learned the special art of working

*Pierre Cartier
(1787–1856), former
soldier of Napoléon,
craftsman specialising in
powder horns and the
ornamentation of muskets.*

with leather, soldering metals, shaping crystals, and had become a
virtuoso in ornamental engraving on the clasp and butt of a gun.

Pierre was jostled, and in turn pushed against the man in front;
suddenly, the line of prisoners disintegrated; there was the sound of
cannons, the smell of gun-powder and blood, the clamour, the stam-
pede . . . Could this be the French assault which had been expected for
so many days?

Pierre obeyed an instinct which advised him not to flee with his
companions. He caught sight of a door on one side and climbed into a
loft. He was now free of his bonds and, seeing a trunk, he lifted the lid to
find that it was full of dresses and trimmings. He dressed himself as a
Spaniard, knotted a scarf under his chin, and fled, travelling by night

and lying low during the day, a plan which was as good as it could be in the circumstances. God willing.

That night, as he left the bakery, now deserted by both torturers and their victims, Pierre suddenly realised that it was through the expedient of disguise that he had twice escaped death. Thus began his belief in his good fortune.

He still believed in it when, after five days of hunger and thirst, he stopped, exhausted, and was challenged by two English sentinels.

He continued to believe in it when, after a horrific voyage in a ship's hold, he arrived at Plymouth where he was to be detained for six years.

At the end of the Napoleonic wars Pierre Cartier found himself back in France. Three years later, in 1817, he married a young girl from the provinces whose dowry enabled him to buy a studio in le Marais.

In 1819, when he was thirty-six years old, they had a child to whom he gave the first name of the father he had hardly known. Louis François. This late arrival of a son made a different man out of Wellington's former prisoner. He was astonished to discover enthusiasm when he had believed himself to be blasé, ambition when he had supposed himself to have realised the futility of the desire to contol and dominate.

Ambition tempered with prudence, enthusiasm with cunning; it was the lot of Pierre Cartier to control his destiny by utilising his many virtues: gambling sometimes with skill, moderation and artfulness, sometimes with arrogant daring, he had the wind in his sails.

Pierre was to bequeath to his dynasty this taste for the paradoxical, a certain art in directing life according to circumstances.

CHAPTER ONE

Louis-Philippe to the Third Republic

1

In 1847, on the first floor of the studio in the Rue Montorgueil, the craftsmen of the jeweller Picard were passionately discussing the flight of Charles Louis Napoléon Bonaparte, who had just escaped from the fort of Ham, disguised as a stonemason, and was reported to have taken refuge in Belgium. After the previous defeats of Strasbourg and Boulogne, could there be one last attempt to overthrow Louis-Philippe?

François Cartier, who was engaged in carving a wide-petalled dog rose, listened without joining in; he refused to involve himself politically, a trait inherited from his father. Similar in this to many artisans' sons of his generation, he had been profoundly affected by the wave of violence of 1830. He was then eleven years old and already working as an apprentice beside his father who had taught him how to blend metals, handle leather, and sculpt in ivory.

At eighteen years old, he had joined Maître Picard in order to acquire all the techniques of jewellery-making. A skilful designer, he learned simultaneously moulding, pressing and mineralogy, and by the age of nineteen had become a craftsman of extreme ability, combining a perfect mastery of taste and of judgment with the diversity of his talents.

A few months hence, François Cartier was to become the proprietor of the Montorgueil studio, Maître Picard having decided to cease business. Pierre Cartier provided one-third of the funds, his wife's uncle a third, and the remaining third François hoped to reimburse in rapid stages.

In the studio the discussion continued with increasing fervour. François listened to his companions' alarm at the grave international climate; riots in Galicia and Cracovie, revolts in Milan, Pope Pius IX had fled Rome disguised as a curate. Maître Picard tried to calm them. He knew that the politics of Louis-Philippe and of Monsieur Guizot exasperated most French people, but France was stable compared with England, where many people were undergoing considerable deprivation and hardship; new machinary was bringing about a fall in hand-made goods, work conditions, already deplorable, were made worse by the influx of Irish immigrants to the cotton mills. Even seven-year-old children were working fifteen hours at a stretch.

François, knowing that his son, Alfred, would be seven in two years' time, hoped to build him a future in keeping with his own ambitions – if politics did not thwart his plans. Having become a master-craftsman in his chosen profession, aware of his talents and proud of them, François

Louis-François Cartier (1819–1904), son of Pierre, who was to set up the first shop at 9 Boulevard des Italiens and attract the patronage of Princess Mathilde.

Cartier was determined not to be hindered on his way to success. He felt an enormous thirst for money and power, and when the workers again talked of England, of the reduction of the price of cotton, he felt scant pity.

His wife, Antoinette, whom he had chosen upon his father's advice, was the daughter of small shopkeepers who had fled Auvergne during '*La Terreur Blanche*' and the Restoration. She was prudent, shrewd and knew how to keep their accounts. François understood that she had a great wish to become middle-class, but was unaware that she did not always understand the contradictory aspects of her husband. Full of crazy ideas, he could be like a boy expressing himself in the delicate shades of his paintings, and also an implacable man, tough in business, concerned about the future and tight with his money.

Calm returned to the studio, and Maître Picard reminded his workers that all of them, goldsmith-jewellers, enjoyed the privileges to which they were now entitled because of the corporation to which they belonged. Also, they were middle-class and among the 'Six Corps de Marchands de Paris', the principal channels through which all the commerce of the great city flowed. Indeed, since the 'Six Corps' consisted of such long-established professions, they were not only middle-class, but the élite of the bourgeoisie. Secretly François approved. He was oblivious to the growing confusion and uncertainties in the world. He had inherited from his father a strong sense of discrimination between practical and frivolous adornments. Even in periods of great deprivation, the goldsmiths carved jewels in metal, steel or iron, and for the more privileged there were ornaments even set in 'biscuit de Sevres'.

2

After two years recuperating with his parents-in-law, Pierre Cartier, wasted by illness and slightly bent, but still an amazingly elegant sixty-year-old, found himself, in 1848, once more in Paris. No longer were there soldiers in the Bois de Boulogne, and the Champs Elysées was crowded with noisy throngs of people, colourful with jugglers, acrobats, adventurers – and the unemployed. It was like a permanent fairground.

Following the violence on the 23rd February, his son had closed the shop, and on the 30th May, after the bloody riots of the 20th April and 15th May, François decided that his wife and their son must go and join the family at Clermont-Ferrard. Meanwhile, he waited in impotent rage, to resume business. Commerce and industry were paralysed in spite of the creation of national studios which had attracted to Paris a crowd of provincials who were barely able to subsist. The confusion deepened a little more each day. In a troubled political climate there were continuing confrontations between the extremists and the lukewarm republicans, and meeting after meeting took place. Politically it was essential to maintain the goals which had reassured the people since the beginning of the year, sustained initially by a number of small

The Boulevard des Italiens at the time of Louis-Philippe. The Boulevard des Italiens was then a fashionable thoroughfare leading to the Palais des Tuileries.

tradesmen, and particularly the clergy, who had upheld the first movement of the revolution. However, since then, the provisional republic, contested by the reds, no longer satisfied anyone, and anxiety grew.

Not only France, but the rest of Europe too was shaken by bloody riots. 1848 acquired a special place in history under the name of the 'year of revolutions'. The Chartist movement in England was strong, uprisings in Italy and Poland occurred, while Hungary and Berlin became prey to serious turbulence and the Emperor of Austria prepared to abdicate, still unable to decide whether his brother or his nephew should succeed him.

Pierre Cartier, walking along the Rue de Rivoli, contemplated the almost imperceptible nuances of how one should be able to safeguard stability for the future. There was no doubt that, since the bloody day of the 22nd June, organised by the extremists, the movement supported by the genuine workers was now mixed with adventurers and thieves, and would eventually be followed by severe reprisals.

The Republican enthusiasm which had caused the flight of Louis Philippe on the 23rd February, gave place to a great lassitude. Like a good number of the French, he thought that order would soon be restored. His son had gone to le Marais to look up old friends and colleagues, with the idea of reconstructing a solid team for Montor-gueil, which he wished to see back in business at the beginning of September.

At the corner of Rue de Castiglione, Pierre paused before one of the windows of an International Agency establishment and noticed some coats of arms and a sign stating that Arthur Smith, importer-exporter, would buy and sell anything in record time.

Pierre Cartier was well aware of the Smith legend. This empire was capable of acquiring and furnishing, at a moment's notice, apartments in the best city locations, castles in Touraine, wines from any of the provinces, jewels and toiletries. All this, they claimed, could be produced from the cellars of Rue de Castiglione. Their detractors, however, insisted that there was "no more kummel, English beer, gold, lottery tickets or furs than could be obtained from a neighbourhood tavern, money changer, boulevard or any good shop." Nevertheless, it was evident that Arthur Smith was gifted with an extraordinary sense of publicity, a king among intermediaries and high finance tricksters, and was in contact with all the celebrated go-betweens from the capital. "Arthur Smith is able to furnish not only a bedroom *à la Louis XV*, but also beautiful idols for your delight, *Messeigneurs!*"

In spite of, or possibly because of these misrepresentations, the upper-crust of Paris cosmopolitan high society adored these shops on the corner of Rue Castiglione and Rue du Mont Thabor, and Pierre Cartier, noting the way in which the clientèle eagerly sought access to this amazing emporium, saw a possibility for the favourable resumption of his own business. He did not hesitate and walked inside.

Like all who enter the fabulous world of an international trading company for the first time, he was dumbfounded by the massive array of objects available to buyers; bottles in strange shapes and colours, chairs of carved wood, pictures and furs, loose coins and wads of paper money casually displayed in wooden bowls.

The hubbub of conversation was dominated by the strident ringing of bells, and orders being shouted in French and in English. Pierre, overcome by a slight faintness, closed his eyes, and collided with a tall blond man who exclaimed "Damn!" The grating tone of voice sud-

Diamond pendant set in festoons on filigree platinum mount. In the centre is a mobile motif of diamonds with a pearl button (around 1905). OVERLEAF, LEFT: *Vase clock with Louis XVI décor. Blue marble urn with handle and base of chisselled vermeil. Enamelled discs with horizontal mechanism indicate the time (1904).* OVERLEAF, RIGHT: *Second Empire parasol made of ivory, black lacquer, coral, gold and diamonds (Cartier collection).*

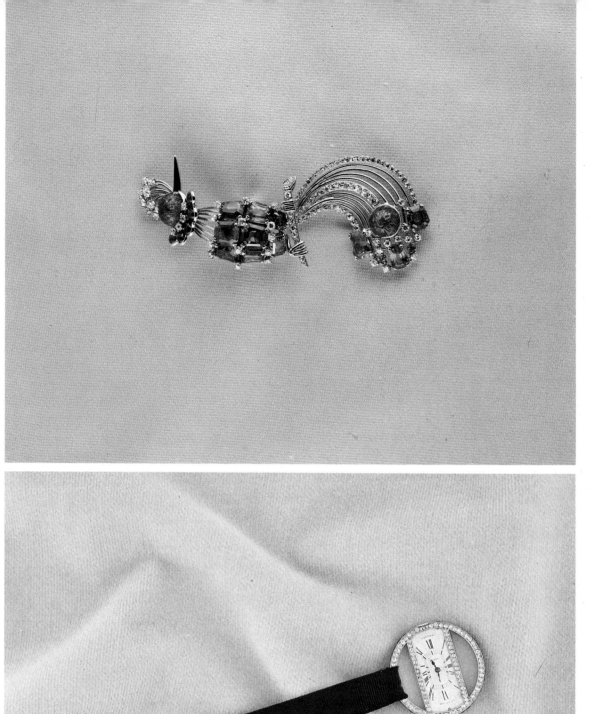
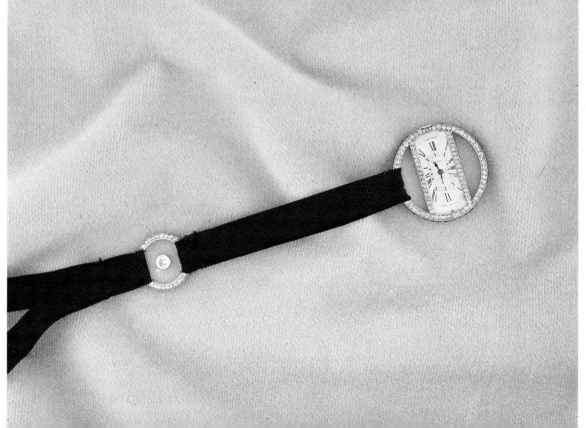

denly conjured up a brief and vivid memory of a day in the past; it was in the East End of London, near the Thames, children in rags, beggars asleep, old men scavenging amongst the rubbish, long staircases, frequent scuffles in Shadwell Street. By sheer chance, Pierre had found himself there in time to save David Hollman, who had been attacked by a gang of robbers.

It had been in 1843 when Pierre had travelled to England each month to do the accounts for Monsieur Picard. He thus learned to speak the language fluently, which helped him enormously in his contact with gem dealers. In the three years during which he travelled between London and Paris, he never omitted to visit Hollman. And here again, by chance, they met in Paris.

Later, installed in front of a glass of sherry in a café where customers were shouting from one table to another and exchanging magazines, *Le Robespierre*, *Le Tribunal Révolutionnaire*, *La Guillotine*, Pierre Cartier and David Hollman discussed at length the past two years. Pierre recounted his illness, the sale of his business, the installation of his son in Rue Montorgueil, and David told how, in eighteen months, he had become one of the most important aides to Arthur Smith.

Like a number of English commercial businessmen, Smith had set up in Paris after the Restoration. He was in touch with the great families of the world and was extremely well-informed on international politics. Thus Pierre learned that Louis Napoléon still had solid support in England and that he pursued his electoral campaign with the help of funds put at his disposal by a certain courtesan named Miss Edwards. Infatuated with an exiled Prince, Miss Edwards dreamed of installing herself as 'Imperial Mistress' in Paris. The political ambitions of the emperor's nephew were equally supported by his ex-fiancée and German cousin, Princess Mathilde. Louis Napoléon wished to defend the principles of order and stability, a comforting formula after the months of revolution, which according to the English had been led by the poet Lamartine, Victor Hugo and Madame Georges Sand. Everyone yearned for work and money.

TOP: *Bird brooch. Carved emeralds,* cabochon *sapphires, gold and diamonds mounted in platinum (1949, Cartier collection).* BOTTOM: *Watch-pendant necklace. Rose-cut diamonds on platinum (1913).*

It was a memorable day in the destiny of Cartier; without knowing it, Pierre had directed his son towards an important client. François had just decided to re-open the studio Montorgueil the following week.

On the 2nd December 1848, Louis Napoléon acceded to the Presidency of the Republic with a majority of 4 million votes out of 7 million ballot papers. For the most part, this success meant little to the French except that 'an adventurer supported by other adventurers' had succeeded. France and Paris were about to come alive again. Europe had to follow.

Europe did follow.

Within three years, there were important discoveries of gold deposits in California and in Australia which allowed an increase of exports in France and England. The first world-wide exhibition in London affirmed the industrial expansion of England. The French bourgeoisie breathed confidently at last and a certain dashing élite whirled to the waltzes of Johann Strauss.

3

"These dockyards are prodigious and overwhelming (there are six of which each is in itself a great port) and triple-masted vessels are aligned ship upon ship, their curved prows with breast plates of copper rising like gleaming fish. There is one from Australia of two thousand five hundred tons; others of a thousand tons or more, from all corners of the earth. This is the meeting-place of the world. A merchant watching the arrivals of spices from Java and shipments of ice from Norway told me that forty thousand ships come in here in a single year." So wrote Taine in *Voyage en Angleterre*.

Pierre Cartier, who had accompanied David Hollman to London to conduct some important business with Arthur Smith, threw a last look at the docks as he embarked at Tilbury for France. He had clinched a deal in the pearl market with which he was extremely pleased, and hoped to be able to acquire diamonds under equally favourable conditions. The pearls and precious stones were destined to be presented to Thérèse Lachmann shortly before her marriage to the Marquis Albins Francisco de Païva. There was gossip in Paris that the Marquis was practically ruined and that Thérèse had only married him for his title. Some alleged that the day after the marriage she had said: "You have given me your name, I have discharged my duties as an honest woman this night, but you, Monsieur Païva, you have married a mere tramp, you cannot introduce her anywhere, nor are you able to receive anyone; therefore we must separate. You return to Portugal, I shall stay here and remain a tart."

Pierre Cartier later recalled that she, known in Paris as 'La Païva', had a heavily lined face, an implacable glimmer in her dark eyes and a splendid body. She was of Russian origin and had fled from Moscow at the age of eighteen. Later she abandoned her French husband and their child in order to shock and seduce Paris (amongst others, the pianist Herz, whose considerable fees did not satisfy her formidable appetite for luxury).

Departing for a tour of America, Herz announced that he wished to break off the alliance. For La Païva this meant that she was deprived of everything: her carriages, furs, jewels, apartments, and was now confined to a small house. On the verge of suicide, she decided, as a last resort, to appeal to a friend of Herz, the poet Théophile Gautier, who looked after her and advised her to go abroad. Paris loathed outcasts and no protector would now be interested in her. Introduced to a go-between who procured funds for her, Thérèse left Paris for England having decided that she would succeed or die. She was armed with a flask of chloroform in case she failed, but secretly swore that she would one day return to do battle again in the Champs Elysées, in the most celebrated mansion in Paris. Soon after her arrival in London she went to a play at Covent Garden. She arrived alone and left on the arm of Lord Stanley.

That night, Pierre Cartier arrived in London. At Tilbury, in the falling dusk, he watched the girls, badly made-up and poorly dressed, sitting side by side in the shadows. In the pubs there were more girls drinking with the sailors and dockers. Along with tens of thousands of others, they were a part of the world of prostitution which had developed with accelerated speed from Brussels to London, from Chicago to Boston and New York. Pierre, tapping his leather bag, thought of 'La Païva,' a prostitute who had raised herself above her station, and who had inscribed her name in history.

On the 2nd December 1851 there was a coup d'etat, the principal instigator of which was the Duc de Morny, illegitimate half-brother of Louis Napoléon.

After the plebescite, which guaranteed ten years of absolute rule to the Prince-President, the severe repression of the rioting population of Paris and the '*senatus-consulte*' ratifying the plebescite, the Second Empire was established.

4

Within two years, Paris was transformed, not merely as a city, but above all there started a new way of life filled with frivolity, gaiety, festivals and grand balls.

The new prosperity of the European countries and their rapid development meant that rich families, seizing every opportunity, were emerging from the middle classes. The nobility were also profiting from the development of the industrial era, and with the luxury business rapidly expanding, François opened a new studio in the Rue Neuve-des-Petits-Champs and was well on the road to equalling the greatest masters of his profession. At thirty-four he felt in complete control of his life and of his artistic destiny in the creative fever which prevailed. Material security allowed him to work with a clear head, although he was annoyed sometimes at being conditioned by the dictates of fashion which did not always allow him to give free rein to his imagination.

The jewellery trade was extremely conservative and the art at that stage was considered no more than the job of slavish copiers. "Invent or perish," Michelet recommended, but the trends were still obstinately rooted in antiquity. Since 1748, with the Pompeien discoveries and the return to Renaissance forms of expression, the brilliance of the First Empire was fervently pursued.

The jewels created for the occasion of the marriage of the Emperor were equal in magnificence to those of the most brilliant Courts that Europe had ever known. The somewhat dismal period of Louis Philippe was giving way to a new era, and the recent creations of François tended towards originality. Faithful to Massin, he maintained that jewels must be competitive in the way they were presented; they were to be designed so that light radiated from the centre and this was achieved by placing stones in delicate and light mounts. François took account of these points, when he came to create for the Marquise de Mennelglaise – very much in favour in the Tuileries – jewellery which David Hollman was to deliver to him.

During a reception given by the Princess of Metternich, the Comte de Nieuwekerke noticed the jewellery set of the Marquise de Mennelglaise and enquired as to its source. François Cartier did not dare to hope for a personal visit from the Comte de Nieuwekerke, but when a carriage of white and blue livery with scarlet facings drew up before the porch and a tall figure descended, as the two men's eyes met, François recognised the man whom the photographers and caricaturists had popularised: the protégé of Napoléon III, appointed, to the indignation of many patrons of the Fine Arts, purely to satisfy the wishes of Princess Mathilde who was wildly in love with the handsome Nieuwekerke.

5

Alfred, son of François, at the age of thirteen already knew the art of filigree (the goldsmith's technique of working an object in an open pattern), and of soldering in gold, silver and glass, and even the art of champlevage which involves hollowing out the surface for cutting the object and encrusting it with enamel and precious stones. Each morning Alfred worked at Montorgueil under the strict eye of his father's deputy, and in the afternoon a student would teach him English, French and History.

In this year of 1854, France, together with England, Turkey and Piedmont, was engaged in the Crimean War against the Russians. The question of the Orient strongly pre-occupied Europeans, in as much as it appeared necessary to maintain the integrity of the Ottoman Empire rather than to see it destroyed by the aspirations of the Balkan people and the covetousness of the Turks.

Another matter claimed the attention of the French. This was the Universal Exhibition which was to open the following spring and for which the commercial building sites were already much in evidence on the Champ-de-Mars.

Alfred was hoping that his father would change his decision not to present his latest creations in the jewellery pavilion. François did not consider himself worthy of equalling great masters like Bapst and Meller, and had decided that it was wiser to await his hour; even the most exalted form of pride must be tempered with humility. Naturally, this disconcerted the young and enthusiastic Alfred who did not think much of humility. He felt that his father, who had recently worked officially for Her Imperial Highness, Princess Mathilde, equalled Fossin, Bapst and all the others in skill, and the adolescent boy felt immensely proud that his father now had access to one of the most important ladies in Paris.

It was inevitable that Princess Mathilde would captivate Alfred Car-

Alfred Cartier
(1841–1925), son of
Louis-François.

tier, fascinated as he was with the idea of his own future destiny being linked with a lady of such noble and romantic origins. Although the issue of a King and the Princess of Wurtemberg, with an empirical background, Mathilde was more proud of her connection with Napoléon than of the authentic blue blood that ran through her veins. She had twice failed to achieve the Imperial Crown; the first time was on her engagement to d'Arenberg, then the real Emperor. Exiled and madly in love, he asked her not to forget him, a promise given but quickly forgotten.

In 1840, at the age of twenty, she married the son of a powerful Russian family, Anatol Demidoff, Duc de San Antonio, to the extreme wrath of the Tsar Nicolas, who had wished to see her become the wife of his son, the Tsarevitch.

Mathilde, in fact, spent two appalling years in Russia, being beaten constantly by her husband who pursued women, spent his nights in clubs and drank too much. Finally the Tsar, himself, insisted on the divorce, ordering Anatole Demidoff to pay her an annual allowance of two hundred thousand francs.

Since the coup d'etat of December 2nd, Mathilde had become the most powerful woman in Paris, dazzling the Tuileries with her intelligence, her culture and her exotic whims. Enamoured of all forms of artistic expression, she patronised painters and aspiring writers whom she often lodged at her property at St. Gratien. Her salon at Rue des Courcelles was the most sought after in the capital. She had a great freedom of style and language, capable of the best and the worst, a woman of passionate friendships and devouring hates; she enraptured and disconcerted Alfred Cartier.

Nieuwekerke was a man, of whom Alfred's father had said that he was devoid of talent, a second-rate sculptor and a deplorable director of the Beaux Arts. However, he was a very handsome and appealing man. On reflection, Alfred vowed to mistrust love.

6

Paris, focal point of the diplomatic world, was savouring national pride, and celebrated the victory of Sebastopol (considered as a revenge for Waterloo) with a whirlwind of parties. The Treaty of Paris made up for the shame of the Treaty of Vienna. The Second Empire had never been so popular, never had Montorgueil and the workshop in the Rue Neuve-des-Petits-Champs throbbed with such activity.

In spite of his desire for innovation, François had succumbed to the current infatuation with the Renaissance, and was to some extent confirmed in this by the success of the Universal Exhibition of 1855, when visitors had been able to admire the Crown Jewels at the Louvre Museum (at last open to the public) and, above all, a unique Renaissance collection given by the violinist Sauvageot. Thus *Le Figaro* had commented wryly, "There is no end to the rebirth of the Renaissance."

However, François had resolutely decided to go against current trends and the success of his latest creations proved that he had been wise. Contemplating a recent creation, made for a friend of Princess Mathilde (which she had wanted to wear at a reception given by the cousin of the Emperor in honour of the ravishing Virginia de Castiglione), he experienced a great feeling of satisfaction.

The Empress harshly criticised Mathilde over this dazzling party in honour of a political adventurer, the instrument of Victor Emmanuel who (through Cavour's influence) was entrusted with gaining access to Napoléon III, by any means, in order to achieve the unification of Italy. However, in spite of dissensions within the palace (the Italian sympathies of Louis Napoléon and the antipathy of the Empress) the Tuileries had nevertheless welcomed – under the cold gaze of Eugénce – the Count and Countess of Castiglione. '*Le Tout-Paris*' was ready for the beautiful Piédmontaise. Aged nineteen, with the eyes of the Emperor upon her, no one could ignore her presence.

On the 29th June, during a party given at Villeneuve-l'Etang, the Emperor invited the Countess of Castiglione to take a seat in his barge. They lost their way on an island in the middle of the lake; she came back a little crumpled, "and the Empress let her vexation be seen". She regretted that she had given her Imperial husband a son three months before.

The incident of Villeneuve-l'Etang took on such an importance that the British ambassador believed it wise to inform Lord Clarendon, to whom he wrote a letter which ended in these terms: "Speaking politically, such things cause the Emperor infinite damage."

The apartment where the Countess of Castiglione lived was situated on the first floor on the road of the same name, at number 10. There was a rumour in Paris that 'a foreign agent' had been secretly charged by Cavour to find an apartment for Virginia and her husband, and the Englishman had skilfully chosen the Rue de Castiglione adjacent to his own establishment.

In the course of the next few months, François made various models for Arthur Smith, inspired by those which had totally enchanted the Comtesse de Mennelglaise, the Comtesse de Nieuwekerke and her Imperial rival, Mathilde. He longed to know if one of his recent creations was destined for Castiglione. But, either because he was excessively scrupulous or through genuine ignorance, David Hollman told him that he was not always party to the gods' secrets.

In the autumn of 1856 at a reception given by Princess Mathilde, Virginia de Castiglione wore a pendant of emeralds valued at 100,000 francs, an offering from the Emperor. "One day," prophesied Alfred, "we will sell precious stones to the great of this world."

7

According to a curious and superstitious law, great towns grew in the path of the sun; Paris developed towards the West. "Like flowing water, the town stretched on, searching for free spaces, skirting round obstacles that it could not instantly annihilate and could only clear away with time. But, being the work of man, Paris obeyed the rules of men; swarming along religious routes or markets, thronging around the commercial and administrative centres and filling the enclosures which gave it security." (*Guide du Vieux Paris*)

Paris was being transformed at an increasing rate, with the creation of new districts, including the Champs-Elysées. The purpose of the plans adopted by the Emperor corresponded to a strategic need to open up large areas in the crowded city in order to prevent insurrections.

The district of Notre-Dame-de-Lovelte was already renovated and had become fashionable again, and a great transformation had been achieved in the Place de l'Opéra. There was a wonderful wide road from which one could view the trees of the Tuileries, which ran through the Rue de la Paix and the Place Vendôme.

François, who wanted to install himself in the commercial and fashionable heart of the capital, at last realised his expectations. Thanks to David Hollman, he was able to purchase, for the duration of his lifetime, Gillion's the jewellers, situated at No. 9, Boulevard des Italiens. A porch separated Gillion's boutique from the celebrated Café des Anglais where young society bloods dined, gambled and flirted until dawn in the rooms of the Grand Seize, whose windows opened on to the Rue Marivaux, beside the Comédie Italienne.

Since the accession of the Second Empire, the Café des Anglais had become the temple of high-ranking Parisian alliances and François clearly foresaw what an important role the proximity of this establishment of pleasure (the most celebrated in the city) would play in his future expectations of success.

As François left No. 9 Boulevard des Italiens, equipped with all the papers which confirmed him as proprietor of the boutique Gillion's, he fondly recalled his father who had died three years earlier. He remembered the confidence bestowed on him, just as he was now placing his trust in his own son, Alfred, barely eighteen years old. Alfred had all the characteristics of an opportunist. He was gifted with a lively intelligence, able to grasp quickly the diverse aspects of a problem, although he had an unfortunate tendency to dissipation, tired easily and was somewhat unsystematic; however, his tenacity was to overcome his deficiencies. He was a good technician, a skilled designer and an adroit and passionate salesman.

As François had foreseen, the proximity of the Café des Anglais soon proved propitious for his business; the clientèle of the Boulevard des Italiens was not only composed of famous habitués of the Grand Seize (Gramont-Caderousse, Prince Napoléon and Paul Demidoff, nephew of Princess Mathilde), but also of the ladies of high society who frequented the Tuileries, and the bankers of the Petit Bourse.

Never would aristocrats nor the grand bourgeoisie cross the threshold of the Café des Anglais, reserved for revellers, actresses and courtesans. Nevertheless, they experienced a delicious and perverse shiver as they imagined the base acts which, supposedly, went on there.

The year 1860 began favourably under the auspices of ascending economic growth. Europe and America were industrialising with a speed which frightened many, but the financiers and stock brokers had never been so optimistic. Skilfully advised by one of them, François had made some important gains in the stock market. Then came the intervention of French troops in Italy and he decided not to speculate further.

An order for a set of emeralds and diamonds, abruptly cancelled, had been the prelude to the exile of the Comtesse de Castiglione. Since the attack in the Avenue Montaigne, the fifty-two-year-old Emperor was consumed with insatiable need for love and affection and chose his mistresses at random from society, the bourgeoisie and the demi-monde.

The liaisons between courtesans and the famous filled the gossip columns; *Le Gil Blas* and *Le Figaro* (to which Alfred's private tutor had recently contributed) made a merciless attack on society. It was *Le Figaro* that revealed to its readers the sensational liaison of the banker, Bianqui, with Anna Deslions, which led Bianqui finally to his ruin.

Anna, nicknamed Marie Antoinette by the habitués of the Grand

Seize, had a craving for jewels. Of all the courtesans of the Café des Anglais, Anna was now Cartier's best customer.

François was aware of her reputation. He knew she had started in the brothel, Les Deux Boules, from whence she had installed herself in the '*quartier des Lorettes*', at 43 Rue Saint Georges, where she lived on the same floor as the Goncourt brothers, who claimed that on the evenings of their receptions Anna asked their maid to allow her to look round the tables "to feast her eyes on a little luxury".

After several years, the half-starved gamine of the Rue Saint Georges had turned into a full-blown woman, with a rather heavy body, surmounted by a superb head, her swarthy face dominated by immense dark eyes, the sensuality of her delicate mouth sharpened by a beautiful nose with palpitating nostrils; her thick brown hair half hid her face and her expression appeared blank. François thought her nonchalant, a bit of a fatalist, and had a suspicion that she did not have such a promising career as a courtesan. Zola was inspired by Anna Deslions for the character of Nana.

Within the context of its own century, it is easy to understand that the philosophy of the Cartiers was impregnated with this particularly immoral period: luxury was prevalent alongside egoism and pleasure; a time when 'La Païva', queen of the courtesans, built her own mansion on the Champs Elysées. Scholl quipped that the rumour about 'La Païva' was renowned: "Whoever can pay goes there, the main item is there already – the street."

To demonstrate his recognition of François' skilful purchase of a gem to enrich his collection, Prince Demidoff invited him to share his table at the Café des Anglais. It was a different world which confronted François that evening; discreet lighting, walls lined with velvet, statues and paintings to the glory of the eternal female, framed the hubbub of the conversation, the glistening cascade of jewels on bare shoulders, doleful boredom on the faces of some, lasciviousness on others. No doubt in a brutal fashion, an artist's observant eye would have noted every last detail of the setting and of the actors in this strange festival.

Between the tables, two courtesans danced, closely entwined, one suddenly biting the shoulder of her partner; if some spectators seemed disconcerted at this scene, neither Demidoff nor François Cartier seemed to notice it. There was nothing lewd about the conversation between the Prince and the shopkeeper that night. Demidoff was not ignorant of the prudishness of the French petty bourgeoisie, and François was too well informed about the escapades of the Prince to venture into an area in which he would be out of his depth.

François was aware that people like Demidoff, both hedonistic and violent, were passionate artists and that the background bequeathed by their ancestors was one of the most illustrious in the world. He also knew that they were impassioned by jewellery.

The purchase of the coveted stone compensated for the recent disappointment of the Prince. One of the most celebrated diamonds in the world, Le Sancy, came into his family's possession in 1838, acquired for 500,000 roubles by the Princess, his mother. It was re-sold to a rich dealer in Bombay. It had once belonged to Charles le Téméraire and then to Nicolas de Sancy (who gave it its name); he pawned it to Henri de Navarre in return for 12,000 Swiss Guards and Henri (later Henry IV) repaid him by appointing him as Minister of Finance. The 53 carat diamond, having been taken from Switzerland, was sold to James I, King of England, who had it set into the Stuart crown. Henrietta of England, daughter of Henry IV, secretly took it back to France, and Mazarin joyfully integrated it into the French crown jewels. It disappeared during the revolution, re-appeared in the family of Don Manuel de Godoy, favourite of the Queen of Spain, was sold again, and pawned to raise funds for part of the Italian military campaign; (Bonaparte, when Emperor, had tried in vain to acquire it). Such had been the extraordinary and historical destiny of this most celebrated of diamonds. Demidoff was enraged to learn that the gem had returned to its original country. There is still an old belief that the most beautiful gems always return to the Indies.

François, like Demidoff, had often imagined the fantastic realm of Golcorde, this ancient region of Hindustan where the Sultans had amassed an incalculable number of precious stones: the Grand Mogol of 280 carats, the Koh-i-Noor, had belonged to the Mongols.

François learned of Demidoff's admiration for the Shah diamond, 93 carats in the quite extraordinary form of an elongated prism, of which only half the facets had been worked. He heard that the treasure of St. Petersburg possessed, among other marvels, a cut diamond of 194 carats with Indian engraving, the diamond of the Empress Eugenie, a stone of 53 carats which had belonged to Catherine the Great, the Nizam Diamond of 277 carats discovered in 1835 near Golconde and, of course, the celebrated Brazilian diamond, l'Etoile du Sud, discovered in 1853.

Crinoline days.

The beau monde *at 9 Boulevard des Italiens.*

It was just at this moment when the Prince asked François, no doubt sarcastically, if the fascination of South America had incited the Emperor to intervene with French troops in Mexico, that the jeweller noticed one of his very good customers, Gramont-Caderousse, enter accompanied by an astonishingly beautiful young woman. Tall, slim and dressed in a red velvet gown with a border of squirrel fur, she wore a net of the same colour on her thick, glossy black hair and a yellow rose pinned on one side emphasised the dark intensity of her stare. The young woman struck the room with her dazzling presence and there was a shiver of excitement. Demidoff told François that she was the favourite of the celebrated blood, Gramont-Caderouse, and that she had very rapidly become the possessor (like all his previous mistresses) of an apartment in the Champs Elysées, a carriage, furs and jewellery.

While admiring the young woman, now installed at the centre table beside her protector, François felt slightly uneasy and thought that Gramont-Caderouse lacked that certain vigour required of a libertine. But then Demidoff had a great weakness for beauty, was supremely cultivated, a lover of all forms of art and equally a *debauchée* whose exploits gave pleasure to many of the more depraved of society. Wasn't this perfectly reconcilable?

Once the Prince, while at Chez la Farcy in the middle of the night, had summoned a young girl, demanded that she be "pure white and dressed completely in black" and gave instructions that she be taken to the Café des Anglais for a particular diversion. The most renowned pedlar of human flesh in the capital chose the most intractable of her lodgers, and took her, dressed all in black, to the carriage stationed in the Rue Joubert. Rather anxious, the prostitute had asked, "Is anyone else coming?" to which Demidoff's messenger replied, "She has arrived already." In the back of the hackney was a negress dressed all in white. What the particular diversion was, is best left to the imagination.

When they parted, Demidoff predicted to François that Barucci, insolent and pulpy though he was, would soon be one of his best clients. François agreed, but even he could not imagine what an important role Barucci was to play in the destiny of Cartier some years later.

8

Imagine the life of a shop in the Boulevard des Italiens, in this year 1863, with dazzling fabrics, the rustle of crinolines, the murmur of conversations, rumour and scandal.

The rhythm and frequency of customers was regulated by their activities. In the morning, stock-brokers and bankers with their wives, in the afternoon, society people from the Tuileries, and later in the evening courtesans and revellers, among them stock-brokers and bankers, but at this time accompanied by the female friend of the moment.

Frequently, ladies of high society encountered the courtesans in the houses of these tradesmen, at the races or at the theatre, and, of course, the carriages of the *demi-monde* often rivalled and surpassed in their sumptuous harnesses, outfits and jewels, those of the respectable ladies of the Tuileries. There was a triumphant inpudence in the attitude of the kept women, which, in turn, only heightened the contempt of the ladies of society. Certainly, some great courtesans held salons for famous artists and politicians. *Le monde* and *le demi-monde* were aware of this, but no respectable lady was capable of lowering her eyes to a high-flying prostitute and, even less, of addressing a word to her.

One afternoon, the Princess Metternich stopped her carriage in front of Number 9, and then gave an order to her coachman to drive off immediately. The landau of Marguerite Bellanger (mistress of the Emperor) was drawn up in front of the Café des Anglais. The Princess returned an hour later, angry for various reasons – signet rings, for instance, seemed to be an exorbitant price! She found it extraordinary that, although the *habituées* of the Tuileries had established the shop-keepers' reputation in the first place, they had become the victims of the publicity thereby created for them. She mentioned how, at the races recently, the Empress had asked her if her crinoline had come from the studios of Alexandrine, Vignon or La Ferrière. The Princess had answered that her dressmaker was Monsieur Worth, and the Empress had asked for his address. Princess Metternich supposed that henceforward Monsieur Worth would never again make a dress for 300 francs.

François offered the Princess a signet ring studded with a mauve stone and she left delighted, declaring that she would continue to sing his praises.

François, with a certain amount of irritation, thought for a long time about this Monsieur Worth with whom all of Paris was now infatuated.

The success of the English couturier would have left him indifferent, had not, during the preceding week, one of his buyers snatched from under the jeweller's very nose, a batch of feathers and signets by paying more for them than their true value.

He must meet Worth. Watching Alfred, all smiles, engrossed with a customer, he knew how this would be achieved. Worth, like Smith, was English. David would be the perfect liaison and, as Alfred would soon be celebrating his twenty-second birthday, François would give his wife a dress from the couturier of the Empress.

The next day, he learned from David that Charles-Frederick Worth, born in Lincolnshire in 1825, had been very young when he left his village of Bourne in order to set himself up in London with his sights set high. He had started at a draper's shop with a salary of five shillings a week, and had spent his leisure hours visiting museums, admiring women's dresses. Following this he had entered the House of Allenby, the courturier, where he amassed a small nest egg and then decided to try his fortune in Paris. Worth had confided to his friend, Smith, that it was in front of a portrait of Queen Elizabeth I in a brocade dress that he had first become aware of his gifts. After a spell at the house of the couturier, Gagelin – where his very original ideas had frightened them, but where he had found some alluring English women and also a Swedish associate – he had installed himself at 7 Rue de la Paix and become a success overnight.

Worth was above all an innovator, a courturier of the elite. It was he, for example, who had introduced the first female mannequin (previously dresses and fabrics had been presented on wicker models). He married one of his saleswomen, young Marie, who wore his latest creations with incomparable grace at the races and at the theatre. Worth's evening dresses were of exceptional beauty. Smith said that he would soon be employing more than 700 workers and that his business turnover was just under 20 million francs per annum. Worth had two sons who were to follow in his footsteps. Smith felt sure that a man of the calibre of this couturier must inevitably form an alliance with François Cartier. Rich in unusual ideas, always original, they were both equally anxious to escape from routine. The fashions and ideas of Charles-Frederick and the trend that François wished to give to jewellery, were totally complementary forms of expression for both arts.

François, himself, recollected a lyric of Martin, the private tutor and old friend of Alfred – on the subject of art. Referring to Voltaire, he

Yellow gold cigarette case. Mother-of-pearl lid encrusted with Chinese décor. Thumb-piece of rose-cut diamonds.
OVERLEAF, LEFT: Crystal Mystery Clock. Twelve-sided crystal mounted in a portico. Two crystal columns, with an onyx and gold base. Billiken (Anglo-Saxon god of Happiness) is at the top, made of crystal (1923).
OVERLEAF, RIGHT: Sphere-shaped watch in pale blue enamel and rose-cut diamonds. White enamel frame in a silver setting, with yellow gold and pearl chain (1909).

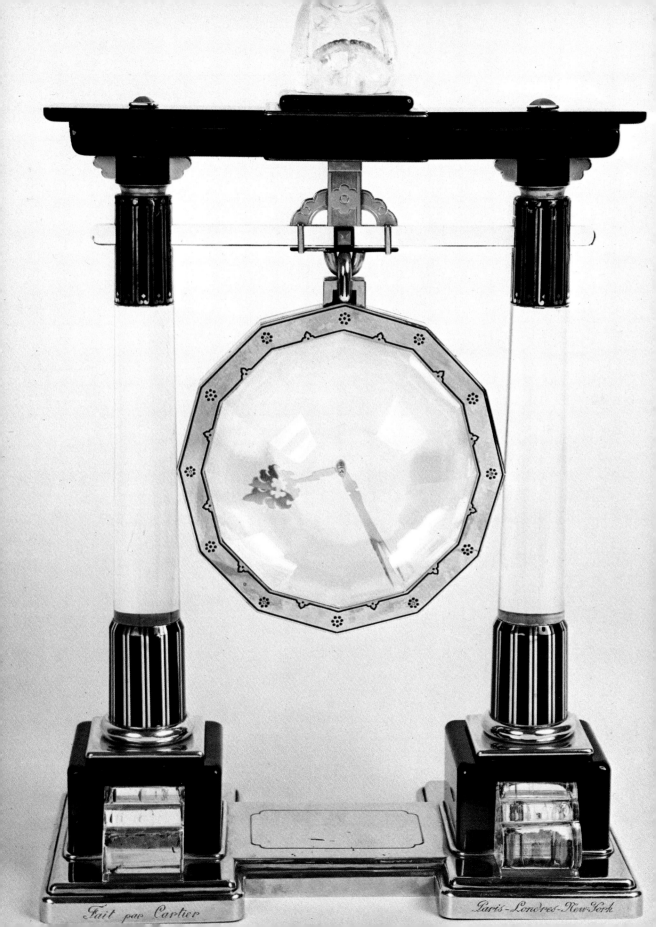

proclaimed that all artists are brothers, each carrying his own inspiration to others.

As for François, he thought that art called for instinct, not necessarily intelligence. In the service of creativity, the artist had to unite his inventive genius with all his accomplishments. Knowledge and skilful technique in the process of design, were what gave the feeling of beauty. François decided to visit Worth the very next day.

Thus Antoinette and François Cartier entered into the astonishing world of Charles-Frederick Worth. "After the freezing cold of the street, the heat was agreeable and sumptuous, scented, too, by floral decorations of camellias and plants which bloomed on the staircase and landing and squeezed up against the 'mannequins' of the great couturier, invariably wearing a chignon or a dress which would be launched upon the world of tomorrow. On the left, there was a suite of rooms furnished with oak tables on which were displayed pieces of silk and satin, forming a background for the most beautiful artificial flowers in Paris. On the fourth floor they were able to admire some of the latest creations of the master; dresses ready to be delivered, shown in the way that a painter in his studio displays a painting destined for a salon or the academy. They were there, these marvellous dresses, lined up in threes or fours, subtly lit against a mirror in which only the centrepiece could be seen, the fall of the bodice, the deployment of the train. Composed with great care, as elaborate as a five act play, their value had nothing to do with the price of the materials from which they were made. The genius employed in their creation and execution was what counted. The salon of light had hermetically sealed windows and the walls were palely papered. In the flickering gas light, obscured by lampshades, ladies could be seen trying on the dresses that they would appear in at the Tuileries the next day." Such was the elegant beginning of the House of Worth.

TOP: Black enamel vanity case in yellow gold with rose-cut diamonds, onyx thumb-ring and black silk tassel (1920, Cartier collection). BOTTOM: *Bracelet with 342 baroque pearls. In the centre, an oval sapphire set in yellow gold. Openwork motif of rose-cut diamonds and pearls. Platinum mount (1915, Cartier collection).*

Thanks to the recommendation of Arthur Smith, Antoinette and François Cartier were received by the Master in person. Worth, whom the Empress Eugénie had named "the tyrant of fashion", the man who was to give them international elegance for decades to come, received them in an office, papered in green almond velvet. He sat draped in a vast beige great-coat bordered with otter, a fur hat at an angle on his head. He had a round face with an astonishing blue stare – half merchant, half Venetian doge.

The Master chose the colours for them, the material and the style of outfit for Antoinette, after which, in a raucous voice, in perfect French but with a terrible English accent, he questioned François about his work, appearing flattered (not, however, without a certain condescension) that the jeweller of the Boulevard des Italiens would make some jewellery to adorn the dress created by the Master, in this instance, in plum coloured crêpe de Chine and grey lace. François envisaged the earrings – fine pearls and garnets, a matching necklace, the buckle of the belt in carved gold, enriched with garnets.

As they prepared to take their leave, two young boys came rushing into the office, followed by their nurse. Worth became surprisingly tender and gentle in introducing his sons: Jean Philippe, seven years old, and Gaston, aged ten. Antoinette was struck by the intensity of the blue-eyed gaze of the children who smiled at her. Many years later, François was to recall this first meeting and was always moved by the memory of their smiles. How could he have foreseen, at the end of that afternoon in March 1863, that he had met the children who were destined to unite the houses of Cartier and Worth?

At present, however, Alfred was not interested in marriage and when Antoinette became worried François reassured her, knowing that their son was not ready for such responsibilities. He had led a pleasant and relatively affluent childhood which, naturally, he was reluctant to give up. Alfred did not wish to risk becoming the prey of any adventuress, and he was certainly too clear-sighted and too querulous to let himself be carried into a costly liaison. His current lady-friend was a young working-class woman who was content to be of modest help, accompany him to soirées at Ba-ta-clan, on a trip to a Bullier dance, to festivals or for a meal at the gilded Maison.

Antoinette and François were accompanied to the first-floor landing by the Master and his sons. The Cartiers likened the principal staircase to Jacob's Ladder, an angel on each step, and emerged to face the street – congested with horse-drawn carriages and pedestrians. As evening fell, one could see the silhouettes of scaffolding on the Palais de l'Opéra, the construction of which had begun two years previously. The Place de l'Opéra was to be finished the following year.

François admired the shop window of Meller, next to the English pharmacy, and was delighted by their successful visit to Worth. He did not tell her the reasons that had motivated his decision but he had a feeling that he had played a trump card in a game governed by his own rules, and that delighted him.

Once more, he realised how much he liked the Rue de la Paix, the street of luxury, of jewellers, of haute couture. He stopped outside No. 13 to note how the allure of the district changed with dazzling rapidity when one observed the scaffolding of the Place de l'Opéra beside the Boulevard des Italiens.

Martin had told him that the Rue de la Paix had been opened up on the ancient site of the convent of Les Filles de la Passion, and that Madame de Pompadour was buried there, in part of the crypt of the Trémoille (the Princess of Talmont had said that the bones of the great, which lay in the Trémoille, must be uncomfortable to feel that they were near the bones of a *Poisson*). François asked if he had not been fooled, and whether the bones of Madame de Pompadour (née Poisson) really lay in this place.

9

Some months later, François was summoned to the apartment of Desirée Valois by the banker S., protector of this *demi-mondaine*.

The room was decorated in purple silk, the ceiling a deeper shade than the walls, with Persian carpets, 18th century mirrors inlaid with marquetry, glass-cases sparkling with gems, jewels and precious objects, displaying a certain vulgar luxury, tempered also with a certain refinement: rare books and paintings of quality. François recognised the touch of S. who had been, until recently, one of the masters of the establishment, and was finally led to his ruin by women and gambling. The bad luck of S. eventually made him the laughing stock of Paris. Gortschakoff, Chancellor to the Tsar, stooge of pleasure to Prince Demidoff, remembered that S. was a living refutation of the proverb 'bad luck at cards, lucky in love'. The beautiful Désirée was preparing to abandon him for Prince Napoléon – so said Plonplon, the brother of the Princess Mathilde, to whom Girardin had recently introduced her. The controversial Girardin was very friendly with Prince Napoléon, and Scholl, a client of François, detested both Girardin (whom he had nicknamed the pimp of Plonplon) and the Prince.

François was aroused from his reveries by the entrance of S. into the room. He scarcely recognised him; he was thinner, his complexion waxy, his hands trembling – in a few weeks he had aged several years. In the course of conversation, S. expressed his gratitude to François for

Charles-Frederic Worth, called "the tyrant of fashion" by the Empress Eugénie of Montijo.

having given him discreet financial support on numerous occasions. He told him of his forthcoming departure to the provinces, and how he would be arranging to repay the enormous debts contracted during a deplorable year by closing his business and selling a property in Le Loiret. In compensation for the sums kindly lent, he gave François some shares in the Suez Canal project and pre-emptive rights in the Monceau district over three separate pieces of land. This was an unexpected proposition and quite pleased François who had helped S. out of genuine sympathy.

That evening, at a reunion meal attended by the men – Alfred, Martin and the new chief at the Studio Montorgueil – François discussed the exile of this dethroned financial monarch. This allowed Martin to observe that Maître Cartier had thus renewed the ancient tradition of collaboration between goldsmiths and royalty which had existed since time immemorial. Delicate mention was made of Saint Eloi, patron of jewellers.

François moved on to Jacques Coeur, the great gold and silversmith to Charles VII, who had financed the Royal Artillery, thus assuring victory over the English armies and the conquest of Picardy and Normandy. It was comforting to recall the importance of the role played by goldsmiths and jewellers in public life; to remember that many changes in the fortunes of the realm had been saved by the guarantee of the crown jewels. "You others, jewellers, merchants of all, merchants of nothing", was no more than the mollified bitterness of a thwarted courtesan.

In this year, 1863, the death of Horace Vernet provoked numerous articles, and all the gazettes reproduced his Academician's sword which François and Alfred studied in detail. They noted the mixture of styles of Charles X and Louis XVI, and were amused at the symbolism which paid homage to the non-conformity of Vernet, expressed in the hunting horn (favourite instrument of the romantics) beside the head of Socrates smoking a pipe. In contemplating the sword of the warrior painter, François thought that Vernet (descendant of a long line of painters – an unbroken family tradition) would transmit to his son and even his grandson, a great artistic promise. And, of course, the day would come soon when Cartier would make Academician's swords.

10

After buying a sweet box, crest and a pendant, Hortense Schneider ordered two belt buckles and Alfred insisted on delivering them personally, which made the salesmen gossip and irritated his father.

François knew his son to be a realist, dependable and also well-informed by the daily press. Nevertheless, he experienced a certain anxiety. Alfred had, on several occasions, been to applaud the actress at Bouffes d'Été, and never missed a chance to speak her name or comment upon her milky white skin, her coquettish eyes, her retroussé nose, her admirable legs and her incomparable talent. He knew all about Schneider: how, engaged by Offenbach at two hundred francs a month, she had demanded two thousand francs eight years later to create *La Belle Hélène*. He knew of her adventures with Berthelier, Offenbach and so many others, and also of her affairs with Gramont-Caderousse, who had gaily squandered a colossal fortune (two hundred thousand francs annuity) upon her.

Gramont-Caderousse had been the idol of all Paris. His popularity arose not only from his sheer physical charm, but from an exquisite personality, composed of a mixture of gallantry, pride, humour and sarcasm. Some had said of him that his English grooms, his carriages, his dogs and the occasional scandal maintained his prestige, but Rochefort affirmed that he had spirit and almost genius, was possessed of a tender sensibility and soul, one of those delightful men who pursue their career of love and pleasure fervently when they are young, knowing that in the future they would have time to devote to important matters.

Gramont-Caderousse died at the age of 32 in the arms of Hortense Schneider, leaving her an annuity. There is some doubt about this and it was rumoured that this lover of fancy dress balls bequeathed only one Breton costume, a costume of Louis XIII, a costume of Henry IV and a domino 'outfit' to her.

Recalling the death of Gramont-Caderousse and the scandalous life of the celebrated Schneider, François Cartier watched his wife bent over an account book and realised that he was not far from sharing her anxieties. It was time for Alfred to take a wife. In the past three months he had refused two suitable and pleasant girls with comfortable dowries. François feared he would be equally casual at a meeting organised by Marie Worth the following month. The wife of Charles-Frederick strongly appreciated the friendliness and sense of humour of Cartier's son and, since their first meeting in the rooms of the great couturier, an excellent relationship had developed, which ran parallel to their fruitful artistic and commercial connections. The growing fashion for sewn jewellery allowed for close co-operation between the doyen of haute couture and the jeweller from the Boulevard des Italiens, for the production of sumptuous outfits. The most famous of these was a creation for the Empress who had honoured François with her custom since the beginning of the year.

Faithful to his belief in innovation, François worked with an open technique, dear to his master Massin, and had just completed, for a close friend of the Viceroy of Egypt, a tiara of flowers interlaced with fruit and leaves that Worth found wholly admirable; high praise coming from a man who always expressed his enthusiasm in measured tones.

The inauguration of the Suez Canal brought a considerable amount of work to the goldsmiths and jewellers: frequently the Viceroy himself made a visit to the jewellers and diamond cutters. He had just ordered a table service of forty-two pieces of gold cutlery enriched with precious stones. Each piece was valued at 60,000 francs, and the value of one of the trays alone was one and a half million francs.

Alfred came back late that night, astonished to find his father still working on some original sketches. François replied that the form of expression of jewellery was in full evolution and that the arts, which obeyed a natural law, must adapt to the new tendencies, emanating from all branches of human activity. François told him of the magnificence of the table service being created by Fontenay for the Viceroy. Alfred told him in turn that Offenbach's favourite prima donna was equally in favour with the Viceroy of Egypt. His own admiration was essentially of an artistic order. Hortense was decidedly too expensive for his purse, he added.

11

In the little parlour of Duke Georges de Mecklembourg-Strelitz (son-in-law of the Grand Duchess Helene Pavlovna), François waited for his client so that he might show a baroque pearl of 140 grains. Through the half-open door, the jeweller shared in the scene which was taking place in the salon: soft pomp of purple satin; ladies in velvet and silk appearing and disappearing, sparkling in a flash of jewels. The orchestra, concealed under a curtain of greenery, played Offenbach, which was currently being hummed by the *Tout-Paris*. François observed the actors in the scene and recognised in the group, Rouher, Minister of State for Napoléon III, from the Auvergne, with whose family his wife was connected. It was through Rouher, customer and friend, that François was up-to-date with the undercurrents of politics. Thus he knew that certain members of the Imperial entourage were anxious about the isolation of France, because of the inability of the Emperor to face the problems from every angle. Many thought that the nephew of Napoléon I still tended towards evasiveness and conducted his politics in a somewhat conspiratorial manner.

His recent talks with Bismarck irritated the entire world. Queen Victoria judged France severely: "That country will never be tranquil. It assumed it could re-draw the map of the world. It is the eternal troublemaker, it really is monstrous." At the same time the Chancellor of the Tsar, on a private visit to Paris after the Franco-Russian tension, had this warning: "You others, the French, remain so unconcerned with misplaced vanity that you refuse to be conscious of the political aberrations of your Emperor."

And in the parlour, where the jolly echoes of Offenbach resounded, François realised, with an uneasy feeling, that he also belonged to this majority of French people who were satisfied with the superficial politics of Napoléon III. In sixteen years France had been proud to achieve the victories of Sebastopol and Solferino; the Chinese expedition alongside the English had allowed the installation of the French in Cochinchine; and, since 1860, the acquisition of the counties of Nice and Savoy had enriched their territories. Mexico remained a delicate point. It was just as well that Maximillian of Austria had been pronounced Emperor, at the instigation of Napoléon III, but there were rumours that the French and Austrian armies were the victims of continuous guerilla attacks.

After waiting for two hours, François was finally received by the Duc de Mecklembourg, accompanied by Gortschakoff, and, once more, the jeweller had to admire the Russian passion for gems and pearls, delighting in giving technical explanations. The pearl submitted to Mecklembourg had come from the Persian Gulf (the colour of pearls varies according to the depth and part of the ocean that the oysters come from) and was composed of a mixture of carbonate of lime and aragonite prisms. A pearl is formed when a secretion, emitted by the oyster, combines with an irritating body. A cross-section resembles something like an onion. The unique quality of the pearl is provoked by luminous rays which traverse the concentric layers of shell and come to the surface.

Gortschakoff engaged François in conversation and recalled the splendour of carpets destined for the tomb of Mohammed. He spoke of his admiration for the collectors for the Maharajah of Baroda. He was ecstatic about the irridescent sheen on millions of pearls he had seen in the incomparable Orient, where velvety tones of blues and pinks mixed with creamy white, dark violet and black pearls.

Mecklembourg praised the Empress Eugénie for having brought

The Empress Eugénie of Montijo.

natural pearls back into fashion, and said that he had authorised Fabergé, jeweller to the Tsar, to do whatever was necessary for the purchase, if the opportunity should one day occur, of the admirable Regent Pearl offered by Napoléon I to Marie Louise. François replied somewhat diffidently that if the old Empress, now Comtesse de Bom-belles, did one day decide to part with this pearl of 337 grains, he too would be pleased to acquire it. In fact, in 1926, it was Pierre Cartier, François' grandson, who was to buy this pearl from the Youssoupof family, who had bought it from Fabergé.

Recalling today the fabulous pearls of yesteryear is an extraordinary experience. Should François, for example, be questioned by Russian aristocrats concerning the necklace of Madame Thiers? Indeed, was the jeweller of the Boulevard des Italiens instructed by Thiers to collect the pink pearls destined for the creation of the famous necklace?

The Russian lords certainly learnt nothing from François. He cared little, in truth, about knowing for which of the '*trois Dosnes*' the pink pearls that all the world's jewellers were searching for, had been reserved.

Like most Parisians 'in the know', Francois knew all about the life of Thiers (who was Balzac's inspiration for his *Rastignac*), how he had become the lover of Madame Dosne, married to a stock-broker, who owed his fortune to skilful property speculations. The formidable ambition of Madame Dosne had been focused directly upon the career of the 'great little man', whose marriage to her elder daughter she had arranged. On the 6th November 1833, *Le Constitutionel* had published a paragraph stating: "Yesterday, Mademoiselle Dosne, daughter of the Receiver General des Finances de Lille, reached her fifteenth birthday, and yesterday the ceremony of her engagement to Monsieur Adolphe Thiers took place. Mademoiselle Dosne is said to be very pretty and very rich and her dowry is estimated at two million francs."

In his mansion in the Place Saint Georges, Adolphe Thiers lived in perfect harmony with his wife, his mother-in-law and the second daughter of Madame Dosne, who became his mistress!

12

An artist should have the privilege of working in peace without having to worry about the problems of politics, but when that artist is also concerned with commerce, there are certain considerations which he is well advised to take into account. François wanted to be able to dedicate himself entirely to the creation of jewellery for the Universal Exhibition of 1867, for which the foreign pavilions were already being built in the Champs-de-Mars, but the gravity of international events deterred him from working with the necessary enthusiasm. He foresaw a sombre future.

Dark rumours were circulating about the political evasiveness of the Emperor. After the victory of the Prussian armies over the Austrians at Sadowa, certain reports tended to confirm that the neutrality of Napoléon towards Austrian affairs suggested a secret agreement with Bismarck. Napoléon's great plan was to annexe Belgium and the Grand Duchy of Luxembourg. It was from a minister that François heard that, after the discussion in Biarritz, the envoy of Guillaume de Prusse had concluded, "Napoléon III disappears into his own dream – one does not know where – in a cloud of smoke."

Bismarck often came to Paris and, on most occasions, he was received at the house of 'La Païva', who had become the mistress of the fabulously wealthy Silesian, the Comte de Donnesmarck. The gossip columnists taunted them in their articles, calling her 'the Jewish prostitute' who delighted in playing a political role that identified her with Castiglione. La Païva had just moved into the sumptuous mansion at No. 25 Champs Elysees, thus fulfilling the prophesy made to Théophile Gautier, when she was at her lowest ebb and had left her hotel room, "to begin again in England, Theo, and start from scratch."

The work on this mansion lasted six years and cost the Comte de Donnesmarck ten million francs. The scarlet damask covering the walls had been specially woven at Lyons, the imperial staircase was of onyx, the ceilings were painted by Baudry, and on the walls, in successive frescoes, epics of the celebrated courtesans were depicted. A novelist climbing step by step in admiration of the frescoes announced, "Like virtue, vice has its points."

Henckel de Donnesmarck was so in love with his mistress that he bought her the estate of Pontchartrain, where the fine flower of the intelligentsia and a number of politicians were invited.

Yes, an artist should be able to work in peace and François, who was not satisfied with his two recent creations, remembered his father, Pierre, with his over-riding optimism, who liked to claim that it was vital to work for the future without encumbering oneself with details. François also tried hard not to think too much of the tortuous politics of the Emperor, of the deceitful ambitions of 'La Païva', or of the menace of Thiers who, it was now known, frequently received Castiglione in his own mansion at the Place Saint Georges. François had to concentrate all his vital energy on the Universal Exhibition. The international acclaim that was to result from it would make the capital shimmer with its lights aglow, and the shop in the Boulevard des Italiens would benefit beyond François' most ambitious hopes.

It was raining and cold on the 16th May 1867, when the Empress Eugénie and her husband opened the exhibition – tiptoeing along the improvised planks thrown over gaping ruts. Nothing was finished. But on the 22nd May, the international gathering praised the exceptional success of the event at the Champs de Mars. The exhibition extended to the Iéna Bridge and the Military School. Its circular layout was so bold as to disconcert, and even alarm some of the visitors. It enchanted many others. It was a sort of monster sphere, giving the illusion of a perpetually rotating dome bristling with standards and flags of all nations.

Tsar Nicholas, the Viceroy of Egypt, the Prince of Wales, the King of Belgium, Bismarck and various Maharajahs were among the distinguished visitors, all guests of France. "Louis XIV and Napoléon I would not have been able to imagine such a reunion," exclaimed one ambassador.

People from the provinces invaded the capital, jostling each other amongst the multitude of international stands, discovering English cottages, dens from Lapland, Mexican haciéndas. The French people were able to sample the products of many nations, served by authentic nationals from their own countries. They were able to see all the latest discoveries: looms, ploughs, photographic devices, ironwork, the art of perfumery, clothes and jewels; the indispensible and the superfluous were side by side. The stands were vibrant proof of the incredible prosperity of the Second Empire. Paris was again a focal point, with a whirlwind of fairs and brilliant receptions, and a gaiety which for many, however, was no more than a mask. Parisian fashion triumphed, and there was a way of life that fascinated foreigners, with its incomparable luxury and the launching of new trends.

Worth was established as the king of international haute couture. The subtlety of French taste was imposed, the shop windows of the jewellers confirmed the prestige of Bapst, Sauvent, Massin and Vevier; two young houses also joined the ranks of perfection and good taste: Cartier and Boucheron.

It was an evening in July when Alfred Cartier made the acquaintance of a provincial couple accompanied by their daughter, an adolescent of fifteen who wished to take home a jewel from Paris as a souvenir of the exhibition. Invited to give his advice, Alfred felt gauche and annoyed with himself for being shy and nervous under the piercing blue-eyed gaze of the young woman. He could not understand it and surprised himself by stealing a glance at her, noting the slimness of her figure, her bust already blooming, her matt complexion accentuated by the tender green of her outfit. He noted the fullness of her mouth and her oval face, framed by heavy ringlets which escaped from under the very small hat on the side of her head. He thought that she was extraordinarily beautiful.

After the departure of his last clients, François observed to his son that, at twenty-six years old, he was at times a simpleton, and this attitude gave lie to the theory that his recent visits to England and Holland had apparently added to his maturity. Understanding his son's feelings, François knew that sometimes chance events work out better than organised ones. This had already occurred to him when, at Worth's last reception, Alfred had refused to court the young girl with a rich dowry, whom his parents had planned as a future wife for him.

Alice, daughter of Griffeuille, a rich tradesman from Roanne, certainly seemed to have made a strong impression on Alfred. She was rather young but, if all went well, within three years Alfred would be twenty-nine years old and she would give him beautiful children. The Griffeuilles visited the Cartiers on three further occasions before they returned to the provinces, having enjoyed living amongst seasoned Parisians, in a capital that entertained and pleased them. The Paris of the Exhibition of 1867 had never so truly justified its reputation of being the capital of one of the more frivolous and more spirited countries.

The announcement of the re-embarking of troops for Mexico troubled only the minority (the Emperor Maximillian was to be shot at Queretaro on the 19th June); Paris lived for the hour of the International – the hour of Hortense Schneider also. All the leading lights of Paris were invited to the exhibition held in honour of Hortense, who had triumphed in *La Grande Duchesse de Gerolstein*. It became fashionable to visit her dressing room at the variety theatres. The Tsar, the Kings of Prussia, Greece, Belgium, Spain and Portugal, the Sultan of Turkey, the two Louis' de Bavière, the Prince of Wales and Bismarck – all were unanimously delighted by the audacious satire of Meilac and Halevy, and by the music of Offenbach. Even Bismarck roared with laughter.

Alfred, always a fervent admirer of Hortense, went and applauded at the Palais Royal, where she was appearing in another of Offenbach's operettas, *La Belle Hélène*. He understood, as later did Hortense's biographer, that the operetta reflected frivolous contemporary society and that Schneider was the incarnation of its own parody in luxury, in gaiety, and in irreverence. At a time when many ideas, old and new, were subject to derision and change, Hortense's tiny feet danced and stamped on what, officially at least, were respected aspects of society: the government and the army. "Hortense, who represented the Imperial background in its entirety, made, without knowing it, the first kick against the Empire."

The star's glory was such that, when arriving at the official entrance of the Universal Exhibition, in her landau of grey and red, she replied insolently to the guards who demanded her identity, "I am the Grand Duchess of Gerolstein," and they stood to attention and let her enter.

The *affaires* between Schneider and the international élite were irresistible food for the gossip columnist. A frustrated actress made a joke soon to be taken up by the gossip columnists, "Decidedly, this Schneider is the gateway for Princes."

13

François Cartier, having decided to keep himself more in the background and delegate some responsibility to his son, entrusted Alfred to make a visit to La Barucci's house, as she had requested.

The young man paused for a moment in the hall and gazed up at the vast staircase of white marble, the ebony negroes with their teeth of blue-tinted enamel under coral lips, the topaz of their round eyes reflecting the light diffused from the torches which they brandished in their raised arms.

In the boudoir, there was a profusion of knick-knacks in the enamelled and partitioned niches, a vast round seat, XVIth century mirrors, and tall Japanese vases. On a marquetry table there stood a globe containing a silver cup which shone with enamelled leaves, Renaissance style, and on the velvet pedestal was the letter 'N' in gold, surmounted by the Imperial Crown, homage from Napoléon III for a night of love. On a nearby console was a vermillion cup, upon which were piled visiting cards which bore witness to the quality and number of friends of the much-courted Barruci. Her latest scandal had delighted all Paris. Invited by the Prince of Wales to a meal among close friends, she had exhibited her bottom to excuse her lateness, and before the dumbfounded expression of the Prince had exclaimed, "I have allowed you to see the prettiest part of me and you are not happy?" The Prince had to burst out laughing.

La Barucci was stretched out on flowing lace upon a crimson sofa and Alfred noted that the face of the russet-haired beauty had grown thinner. La Barucci seemed tired. There was no longer, in her attitude, that superb insolence which had captivated men. The courtesan spoke in a husky voice, her stare was abnormally bright and her hand shook as she removed a very small gold key from its chain. With a movement of her head she indicated a precious wooden chest encrusted with lacquer. Alfred took from this case a gold bracelet set with turquoises, made the previous year. As Julia Barucci had grown thinner, it was necessary to adjust the jewel. Between two nervous coughing fits, the great courtesan asked if Cartier was able to conceive the creation of cups enriched with jewels. Alfred replied that anything was possible. Obviously Julia had not ignored the fact that 'La Païva' had recently had some vases made for her property of Pontchartrain in this style.

Alfred prepared to leave but Barucci made a sign for him to sit down again. She suddenly felt a need to chat with him and to tell him about her past. She recalled her native Piédmont, recounting the stages of her rapid success. How, from the brothel of La Farcy, she had very soon become a protegée and then a courtesan, adding that she sometimes experienced nostalgia for her native Italy where her parents still lived in poverty. She told him that she helped them sometimes in her dreams, that her real name was Giula Beneni, it was a bawd who had named her 'La Barucci'. It sounded triumphant.

Vaguely disturbed by this outpouring of confidences, Alfred noticed the abnormal pallor of her hands, the red of her cheeks, the sweat on her face which she dabbed nervously with a handkerchief of embroidered lawn decorated with her initials. With a clumsy smile she excused her feebleness, confessing, after a moment of reflection, that her state resulted from a sort of inner anguish in facing the future about which she had terrible forebodings.

Then, with a dismissive gesture, she pulled languidly at the plaited cord of gold and red velvet and a maid appeared carrying on her arm a sumptuous dress of grey satin, a model inspired by a creation of Worth. Since the couturier of the Rue de la Paix had decreed the death of the crinoline, a new style had been born, all movement and fluidity. Women were at last ceasing to resemble moving cages.

On his way back from the Champs Elysées to the Boulevard des Italiens, Alfred was obsessed by the pathetic expression on the beautiful face of the courtesan, moved also by this sudden trust with which she had confessed her worries.

14

The supper at Tortoni's house finished pleasantly; it had begun in the Gymnasium where the Cartiers had invited the Griffeuilles who were spending a few days in the capital. Léonide Leblanc, star of the Gymnasium, had arrived surrounded as usual with glittering companions, talking loudly and showing off. She waved to the jewellers, and Madame Griffeuille admired her jewels, recently created by François (a topaz with a mount of old silver), which greatly enhanced the sobriety of the Worth dress.

The outfit worn by Antoinette had also been created in the Rue de la Paix; deep mauve taffeta decorated with ruches and bows of beige satin. Antoinette, in full bloom, secretly observed the young Alice; she judged her to be still basically provincial, but Paris would mould her, if their plans were realised.

The young people did not displease each other; the important point was whether Arthur Griffeuille would consent to a large dowry for his daughter. For his part, François had decided to allow his son to become a partner, and to give him sole ownership of the vacant property under construction in the Monceau district.

Observing Leblanc, Antoinette explained to Madame Griffeuille the shamelessness of the courtesan. Alfred listened patiently to his future father-in-law who was anxious about the decline of the Emperor's health. Griffeuille, a confirmed Bonapartist, maintained that Louis Napoléon's lamentable physiological state was solely responsible for the errors in a political policy which was becoming more and more unpredictable. He was anxious about the growing vehemence of Napoléon's beliefs and about the recent triumphs of the opposition, despite a flourishing economic situation. Alfred agreed absent-

Brooch for a corsage made from diamonds on platinum. The part forming the pendant is detachable (1913).

mindedly and looked at his father, who smiled through the conflicting opinions, and he realised increasingly how much he had inherited from his father over the passing years. Alfred now maintained a total distrust of politics, although by the very nature of his profession, politics cropped up daily in the form of confidences from his singularly well-informed clientèle.

For his part, François, who enjoyed the charm of the vast room with its faded gilt, decorated with academic paintings and statues, would have preferred to listen to the music and admire the sparkling jewellery of the women; but it was important to listen to Griffeuille, who continued to assess the year 1869. And so François resigned himself to listening to an account of the assassination of the journalist, Victor Noir, by a distant cousin of the Emperor. Griffeuille was astonished at the extraordinary violence which had taken place and was indignant at the result of the elections confirming the triumph of the opposition. François confided to his son's future father-in-law that the Emperor was conscious of the strength of the opposition and had charged Emile Ollivier to form a Ministry which would symbolise the new governmental policies. Griffeuille grumbled that that told him nothing worthwhile. The French were utterly unreliable, in his view, and seemed to have forgotten so quickly that proud moment when world-wide praise was showered on France at the time of the inauguration of the Suez Canal.

François suggested ending the evening somewhere where there was dancing. Antoinette approved, but imposed her own conditions. She wanted to know if the place was 'quite proper'. "Certainly," replied François. Monsieur Griffeuille appeared to be almost disappointed.

By a crushing majority, the May plebescite approved the liberal reforms of the new Constitution, and Alfred could imagine the enthusiasm of the Griffeuilles (who had returned to their province). They would be back in Paris in July for the betrothal. The house in the Rue de Prony would be ready for the young couple in 1871, and Antoinette was already making arrangements at Bon Marché, the Louvre and at Magasins Réunis to choose all that was necessary. Alice's mother had given her carte-blanche, and Antoinette acquired with these responsibilities an assurance and confidence which made her suddenly far more attractive to François, as he observed her leaning over her embroidery frame.

In spite of his optimism, François was not able to quell his anxiety.

Crystal Mystery Clock. Turquoise enamel and rose-cut diamonds, numeral surround. Chinese statuette. Vase and chimera are of white jade. Coral tree onset with pearls, with nephrite and onyx base (1930).

The news reaching the editorial offices was heavy with foreboding. Queen Isabel II of Spain, having been hounded from her throne by a military coup in 1868, announced her official abdication. For thirty-one months the Spanish government had tried to find a Prince worthy of assuming the responsibilities and, after many attempts among the European courts, they finally chose Prince Leopold d'Hohenzollern-Sigmaringen. The King of Prussia agreed to this, and the news was very soon to be made public.

François and Alfred had heard the day before, from a close acquaintance of a Minister of State, how grave and far-reaching the consequences of this choice might be. Many felt it was a great offence to install a Prince of the House of Prussia on the throne of Spain. And the conflicting feelings of the French people in the days which followed confirmed their anxiety.

On the 4th, 5th and 6th July there were violent reactions from the press, which proclaimed that France was experiencing a deep feeling of humiliation at the announcement of the successful candidate from Hohernzollen. After a passionate speech from the Minister of Foreign Affairs, Adolphe Thiers, replying to Grammont, exclaimed before the Legislative Assembly, "You must throw down your gauntlet, gentlemen, in front of a man, to oblige him to duel with you."

The other European courts, however, did not share either the indignation or the fury of France, and Napoléon III, mindful of the supremacy of the Prussian army, refused to enter into a conflict with the lamentably few forces that were left to him, the outcome of which would almost certainly be fatal. He turned towards the King of Belgium and Queen Victoria in the hope that they would intercede in the withdrawal of Hohernzollen's candidature.

William of Prussia, however, did not want a war with France and, on the 12th July, in his position as head of the House of Hohernzollen, he obtained the renunciation of the candidature of Prince Léopold to the throne of Spain. This decision of appeasement, paradoxically, satisfied only a minority, and the result of the compromise was only to stir up further passion and argument. The press disapproved almost unanimously of this peace, as being half-conceded. *La Gazette l'Opinion Nationale* spoke of "the sadness, despair, disappointment and anxiety of the French people." The newspaper, *La Presse*, affirmed: "If the Prussians refuse to fight, we, the rest of the French, will compel them to do so by putting the butts of our rifles in their backs, by re-crossing the Rhine and clearing the river to the left bank."

On the Boulevard des Italiens, the crowd cried furiously their espousal of an ardently defended cause: the supremacy of France in the role of International Affairs. A collective hysteria was seizing Parisians who dragged the government through the mud. It became necessary to expunge the Prussian affront with war.

Before all this sabre-rattling and without the knowledge of the Emperor, the French Ambassador in Berlin had demanded an appointment with King William concerning the formal renunciation. The old Prince was resting at Baden-Baden. The whole incident was getting out of hand and becoming an infernal nuisance; he charged his aide-de-camp, Prince Radziwill, to discuss the matter with Ambassador Benedetti. Bismarck, who had been thinking of resigning, seized on the situation to make public the discussion which was to become infamous under the name of 'The Ems Despatch'. This despatch which, in reality, was an article which appeared in the *Deutsche Allegmeine Zeitung*, said that the French government was trying to humiliate the ageing King William by demanding 'formal guarantees', in spite of his support of the renunciation. A defamatory text. Unfortunately, this diplomatic error was compounded due to a bad translation: Benedetti, Ambassador of France, was described as 'the warrant officer of the Empire'. A new collective fever overtook the Parisian crowds. On the 14th July the roads to and from the capital were invaded by a crowd of demonstrators shouting "To Berlin, to Berlin."

In spite of the intervention of Thiers, Parliament voted for the war with a quasi-unanimity. Between the ultimatum of the 6th July, the withdrawal of the candidature of Hohernzollen and the intervention of the Minister of Foreign Affairs at Ems, just three days had passed. Nine days before the declaration of war, a telegram reached the Boulevard des Italiens. It was from Griffeuille and said: "Because of the gravity of events, we must postpone our plans. Alice sends her best remembrances to Alfred, and the expression of her affection to Madame Cartier and to you, dear François. I join with her in sending you my esteem. May God protect France."

15

The foolish enthusiasm which prevailed during the first days of August was maintained by false reports which told of the inexorable crushing of the Prussian army: a manoeuvre intended to keep prices up on the stock market. France awoke in a stupor to learn of the defeats at Forbach and Reichshoffen, the retreat at Mac-Mahon and of how the Emperor, who had left the Tuileries on the 28th July after conferring on Eugénie the regency, waited at Châlons, in company with the Imperial Prince, aged 14, to take a decision concerning the offensive at Metz. Bazaine assumed general command of the armies while the Emperor, with little strength remaining, a worn-out old man with made-up cheeks, sat painfully on his horse to inspect the troops who lacked the bare essential means for combat.

On the 1st September, Antoinette's maid learned from Melanie, an employee of Dr. Evans, dentist to the Imperial family, that the surgeon had decided to save the Empress and organise her flight. On the 2nd September, surrender was announced. Bismarck, exasperated by the somewhat sly diplomacy of Napoléon III, demanded that peace negoti-ations begin immediately. On the 4th September, the Boulevard des Italiens was invaded by a huge crowd. Paris had been told of a capitula-tion, but the French indignantly refused to believe it. François Cartier was awaiting the return of his son who had gone for news. Antoinette anxiously paced the apartment, noting how the crowd was becoming denser minute by minute.

Two hours later, Alfred, in the company of Martin, confirmed the presence of the German armies at the gates of Paris. The Tuileries had been invaded, the Imperial insignia uprooted, the eagles stamped upon. *La Marseillaise* was unceasingly sung and resung, resumed and acclaimed; the crowd rushed to the Hôtel de Ville and then to the Palais Bourbon. When François heard that the republic had been proclaimed – whilst under his windows the crowd still cried "Long live Trochu" — he realised that a régime had been abolished without a single drop of blood being shed. The unpredictable Parisians.

In Paris, on the evening of the 4th September, all the flower-girls were selling red carnations.

The winter of 1870–71 saw France involved in war. There was the incessant sound of cannons and artillery to bear, the cold and soon the hunger. Like all the jeweller's fraternity, François had closed his premises; the gunsmith was the only dealer still active in the Boulevard des Italiens. The jeweller found comfort in the knowledge that his wife was with her family in Auvergne, for the lives of the women and children still in Paris were becoming more and more miserable. Loaded with packages, pitiable souvenirs which they refused to abandon to the Prussians, they ran from the bombardments.

The Parisians were rationed to 400 grammes of bread; a fresh egg cost 1.25 francs and chicken wings sold for 9 francs; but the population showed an admirable *sang-froid*. The infrequent reports from the battle-fields spoke of horror, bravery and also of shame. The heroism of some, the slavishness and greed of others; there were many who became servile to the occupying armies and extracted ransoms from the French soldiers.

People get to know each other better in difficult times; François noted, without bitterness, the collapse of his early ambitions. He was now a resigned fifty-year-old, who was concerned only for the life of his son.

Alfred was a lieutenant in the National Guard, and was nicknamed 'the Marquis of the Moleskin' because he wore black moleskin boots during the rigorous winter. He often came to visit his father and each week, in the back of the shop, he would sort out the accounts. It was from his son that François learned of the bargaining at Versailles and how Belfort was left to the French in return for the entry of the Prussians into the capital, where the Emperor, William, insisted on holding a ceremonial review of the troops.

When the Prussian army went on parade in the Champs Elysées on a cold early morning in March, all the shutters were closed, save those of 'La Païva'. The big windows of No. 25 were open, and the crystal chandeliers which were lit in every room, threw sparks of light into the gloom outside.

Eighteen days later, the Commune was established, the National Guard having refused to deliver to the Germans the 227 cannons acquired by conscription. Paris, simultaneously dazed and vehement, was settling into a civil war. The Gare de l'Est and of Saint-Lazare were crowded with people fleeing from the capital; the Retreat sounded from Montmarte to Belleville, and during the night of the 29th March the alarm bells rang without interruption, dominated always by the great bronze bell of Notre Dame. The red flag fluttered on the Fort d'Issy, and the rattle of arms and the bursts of machine-gun fire seemed louder than at the time of the siege of Paris by the Prussians. Even Neuilly was not spared; nothing, it seemed, could escape the whistle of high shells from Versailles, where cannons were installed on the former Prussian fortifications.

Soldiers made their encampments on the Worth property of Suresnes. The veteran and his family had left for Switzerland. The superb house was still intact. But for how long, François wondered, as he waited at the Place Vendôme, mingling with the crowd and observing the construction of scaffolding for the Column of Vendôme (the bolts were removed the following day).

On the 15th May, François, having had no news of his son, waited at the headquarters of the National Guard and was able there at last to find him. Alfred had his arm in a sling; he looked feverish and his cheeks were hollow. "A simple sprain," he explained, "a clumsy fall, an accident, I couldn't find it in me to fight against other Frenchmen." François was not surprised to learn that, at that moment, no-one trusted anyone else. Alfred, like him, had one wish only: that this nightmare might cease. Each experienced an immense weariness with the burden of their French nationality.

Then, once more, the alarm pealed out, repetitive and clamouring; and again there was the sound of drums and trumpets. The night of the 21st May was the start of a bloody week: barricades and fighting in the streets; incendiaries in the Rue Royal and in the Tuileries, in the Cour des Comptes, the Palais Royal, in the Hôtel de Ville, the Gobelins and the docks of La Villette; and on the morning of May 27th, François, woken at dawn by two colleagues, learned of the loss of Martin, the student, close friend and ardent journalist, who had died fighting at the Père-Lachaise.

One after another they were forced to the last bastions. The Commune controlled the area between the Faubourg du Temple up to the Rue de Belleville. A young girl who fell in the street, struck in the chest by a bullet, was immortalised by Jean-Baptiste Clement in the song, *Le Temps des Cérises*. On the 28th May, Alfred, mixing with the other guards, read the proclamation of Mac-Mahon, that "Paris had been delivered by the French army who had come to save the people; that the soldiers had, in four hours, recovered the last positions occupied by the rebels, the struggle was over; order, work and security would soon return."

It was through smoking streets, with the sinister sound of crumbling houses and the sporadic echo of occasional gun fire, that Alfred returned to the Boulevard des Italiens. On hearing of the death of Martin, he remembered a phrase which had been uttered the day before by a guard who had been witness to the shooting: "This is the brutal result of pure force." A few hours before the end of hostilities, Martin had fallen victim in an absurdly complex situation.

Three months later, London was the venue for the sale of the jewels of Giula Beneni, known as La Barucci, who had died of tuberculosis. Alfred was there as the official expert. The commission, thus obtained, allowed the Cartiers to start building up a new stock of jewels and to await the recommencement of business in a capital which still had to recover from many wounds before it was ready to return to the world of luxury.

On the boat that brought him back to France, Alfred recognised some famous faces. A good number of Royalists and Bonapartists had fled from Paris at the fall of the empire; now they were returning. At the centre of a group of admirers, as usual, was Léonide Leblanc. She smiled at him. He acknowledged her discreetly and listened to her talking of her hatred of the Bonapartists.

She commented that if the Emperor had permitted a son of Louis-Phillipe's to gain access to the throne, the whole stupid war would never have taken place. She claimed to have been told by the Duc d'Aumale that foreign courts were in favour of a French presence in Madrid, which seemed to confirm the rumours, according to which the Duc d'Aumale had followed Talleyrand, Clemençeau and many other men in the actress' bed.

Alfred was invited to join Léonide's table. She teased him throughout the meal, unaware that François' son must know what a prime specimen of greed and prostitution she was. He was amused to hear her catalogue Parisian vices, telling tales about La Païva in faintly prudish tones, recounting how Gambetta and Bismarck had met in the Jewish prostitute's mansion to discuss aspects of the peace treaty. La Païva's estate in Pontchartrain was the only one left untouched by the Prussians; she was preparing to leave France, and had confided to her close friends that she had sworn that, before leaving, she would acquire the Empress Eugénie's necklace for her own beautiful neck.

In bitter tones, Léonide said that La Païva's wealthy lover would no doubt be made a Prince as a result of the services he had rendered to William of Prussia, adding that it was really unbearable to think that the bitch should end her days as a Princess in her Silesian palace, wearing an Imperial necklace round her throat.

In a discreet reference to Léonide and the Duc d'Aumale's affair, Viscount Neuroy commented that France still had eligible princes and that there was plenty of hope left for clever women. Léonide, however, wanted to keep Alfred's interest and requested an end to bedroom gossip. She wanted to know whether it was true that fabulous new diamond mines had been discovered in South Africa.

Yes, Alfred confirmed that inordinately large diamonds had recently been discovered on a South African farm worked by some poor brothers – the de Beers.

Replying to a deluge of questions, Alfred said he did not share other jewellers' concern at the reports of new and particularly pure gems reaching Europe; his father would soon go to South Africa to study how best to make use of this new opportunity; for the time being, it was impossible to do more than speculate.

Léonide continued her questions, and Alfred told his fascinated audience all about the history of diamonds. How, before Alexander the Great's invasion, diamonds had been found only in India, and how they had gradually been discovered in Greece, Egypt and the Roman Empire. He mentioned the Orloff, the Kohi-Noor, the Southern Star and the Dresden diamond. When asked all kinds of technical questions, he explained how, in most cases, a diamond started life as a crude lump, how it was then cut roughly (using another, finer diamond); the stone was then placed on a turntable (previously covered with a paste made from diamond powder and olive oil) which went round at 3000 revolutions per minute so that it could be cut. According to what criteria was a diamond judged? The essential ingredient was the cut: this was a real work of art which required hours, months even of patient work, depending on the juxtaposition of differing layers within the stone. The smaller the stone, the more delicate the task.

Viscount Neuroy, recalling the ostentation of the age of Louis XIV, asked whether it was true that the Duchesse de Berry had worn the Sancy diamond. Alfred had no idea, but found himself describing in minute detail the dress the Duchesse had worn for her wedding to the Prince de Conti, which was made of gold cloth dotted with seed pearls and diamonds; her hair was entirely covered with diamonds belonging to the Crown Jewels, and lent to her by Louis XIV: they alone were worth 18 million francs.

Yellow gold cigarette case with lapis placage, agate sides and a central Hindu style motif of 'Taurus' in emeralds and cabochon rubies. Hanging .ing of yellow gold (1925).
OVERLEAF: Grey jade carp clock, mother-of-pearl and red enamel on rock-crystal. Base of obsidian, gold and coral. Rock-crystal screen with hands and numbers in rose-cut diamonds.

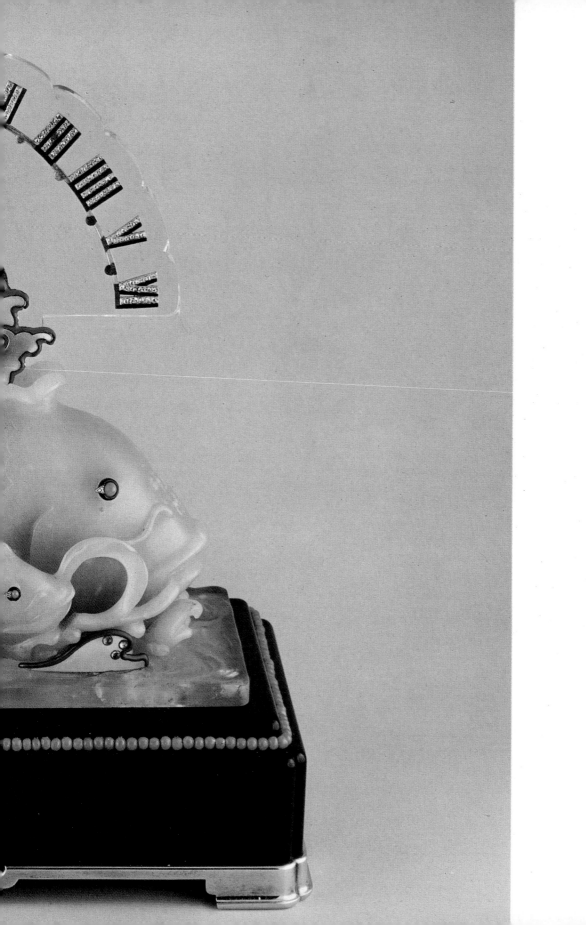

16

On his return from London, Alfred was pleasantly surprised to meet the Griffeuille family, and to learn that Arthur and his father had come to an agreement which opened the way for considerable expansion to their business, as well as enabling them to re-build the Rue de Prony premises which had been destroyed during the Commune uprising. Griffeuille was to lend the Cartier family a large sum of money in exchange for a life annuity; he had also increased the size of his daughter's dowry.

Alfred and his father became partners at the beginning of 1873; Alfred and Alice were engaged six months later, and early in 1874 the wedding took place. The ceremony was discreet but elegant. The ladies were dressed in creations by Worth, whose son, Jean-Philippe, was Alfred's witness. David Hollman was there too, a little sad at leaving Paris for London where he was to take over his father's business after his recent death.

That night in the smoking-room, the gentlemen discussed the relative merits, in the context of a largely royalist National Assembly, of the Comte de Chambord, of a Bonaparte heir and of the Comte de Paris. Chambord's intransigence was likely to spoil his chances of becoming king; his haughty condescension had upset his supporters in the Assembly. (He had said: "I am unwilling to accept compromises or solutions.") He was demanding, among other things, a return to the use of the fleur-de-lys on the French flag. Commenting on the royalist majority, Thiers had delighted even his enemies when he had said: "Gentlemen, there is only one throne in France, three men cannot sit on it!"

Eight months after the wedding, Alfred and Alice Cartier told the family that a child would be born to them between May and June. François was surprised by the emotion which filled him when he heard the news. On 6th June 1875, he announced: "So here is Louis-Joseph Cartier, the heir to the dynasty!"

Louis-Joseph took after his great grand-father Pierre: under childish features, he had a proud expression, supported by a wilful chin, a high forehead, a delicate brow, intense blue eyes which could be tender and forceful at the same time. When he started to learn to walk, his every gesture expressed a will to charm. Alfred claimed that Louis would not be an easy child, but that he had the measure of him. As for Griffeuille, he claimed that his grand-son, born with the Constitution, was a lot

TOP: *Tiger bracelets. Sapphire, diamond, emerald eyes, mounted in yellow gold.* BOTTOM: *Small, grey agate clock with cabochon sapphires, white enamel, silver and yellow gold rim. The hands are diamonds (1914, Cartier collection).*

stronger than the Third Republic, voted in as it was by royalists and ultra-royalists. Alice's father kept inveighing against the Amendment, which had been voted in by 353 votes to 352: "This joke republic would never have been founded had some confounded Deputy not turned up late!"

Despite the many pessimistic predictions and manoeuvrings, the Third Republic, founded by men without any belief in it whatsoever, bore witness to a determination to start anew which astonished the whole world. War wounds were healing, and if Paris had not yet returned to its former glory, when it attracted the cream of international society, there were hints that wealthy foreigners, longing for glamour, would soon return to burn their fingers in a capital unlike any other in the world.

The Rue de la Paix was teeming with people again. Worth, Guerlain, Vever and Meter were, as they had been under the Second Empire, the meeting point of the international élite. Charles Frederick Worth had added to the number of his home-based sewers; his agents kept the world informed of his latest creations, and the old man's sons followed in his footsteps with dignity, Jean-Philippe as designer and Gaston as administrator.

More than ever, Worth's influence proved beneficial. Alfred, whose competence as a dealer now crossed international frontiers, was sometimes made the intermediary for dealing with certain purchases destined for the rich clients of the famous couturier. This worried François a little, for he could see signs of fear on the part of the wealthy and he called their buys panic purchases, refuge purchases, made as a safeguard against the future. The newly-born republic had made privileged people wary of showing off their wealth. The Faubourg Saint-Germain was unable to forget the Commune. Hence there transpired a stagnation in the development of taste; inspiration seemed to have abandoned the jewellers. Their creations were lacking in any originality: typical jewellery still consisted of brooches and hair ornaments in the shape of a crescent or a star, or else bow-ties or multiple-stranded necklaces popular during the Second Empire.

A new development, meanwhile, augured a different future. A new class of buyer began to flock to the capital – Americans from both North and South who paid considerable sums for gems of exceptional size and quality. The market was looking up since the exploitation of South African mines. Diamond jewellery had become fashionable, and

Alice Cartier, née Griffeuille, wife of Alfred, in an evening dress created by Charles-Frederic Worth.

gold objects were limited to powder compacts, card-holders, umbrella handles and handbags. François felt they expressed a feeling of melancholic yearning for the past, and he was irritated by this lack of imagination. The combined influences of Etruscan, Oriental and Greek styles still applied, as well as a revival of Medieval art. Nothing new had happened and the Cartiers had to follow a fashion that did not exist, but was simply a movement evolved from previous movements.

François maintained that it was necessary to take account of the influence of the American jeweller, Tiffany, although most of his colleagues had refused to take him seriously when he settled in Paris in the 1850s. He represented the trends of a new world on the march, with a particular vision of artistic creation, and his new conceptions were to shake a traditionalism which had become obsolete.

In the year 1878, the republic was beginning to settle down, although Griffeuille was one of the many people still speaking out against the government, questioning the monarchist and conservative majority in the Senate, and the presence of Mac-Mahon at the head of the government. However, in spite of turmoil and discussion, France returned to work, wanting to regain pride of place in a totally different climate from that of recent times. François came to regret the classy insolence of a Gramont-Caderouse, the zest for living of Demidoff and other great Russian dukes, all those who had contributed to the fabulous life-style under the Second Empire and – why deny it? – to his success. This was a rather defeatist view for a man who had always been prone to optimism, and the sentiment was all the more contradictory in that in the past he had often condemned the scandals of a system on which he was dependent.

When he confided to Charles Frederick Worth, the Englishman had comforted him thus, "We live by and for luxury, any question we ask ourselves is superfluous, we must assume our role and that is all there is to it." Alfred, whose realism was not tempered with metaphysical anguish, had decided to follow Worth's advice and the father recognised in his son the ardour which had animated himself until the year 1870, a year which had broken him.

He tried to muster up enthusiasm for helping his son with preparations for the International Exhibition, considered by its organisers as a democratic challenge to the Imperial Exhibition of 1867. His daughter-in-law confirmed that their next baby, like the first, was due in the spring. She hoped for a sister to Louis, and the family hoped that this next birth would allow Antoinette, the grandmother, to escape from the world of fantasy in which she had been living for a year, shut away with the family at Roanne. "An illness of the soul," said the doctor at Guermonprez, who had not been able to cure Antoinette's lassitude, which was characterised by violent headaches that left her haggard, with a fixed stare, remaining prostrate in isolation for long spells. Her apathy and silence expressed refusal to participate in life. She was apparently determined to live by herself in a world to which all, even her family, were denied access.

François reflected on the blossoming Antoinette of former years; 1867, his pride in the International Exhibition; 1873, the engagement of his son; 1874, the marriage of Alfred; 1875, the birth of Louis . . . Would Antoinette be conscious of the birth of Alfred's second child and would she see the Universal Exhibition?

In a riot of colours, noise and flags, the rediscovered music of Offenbach rung out (the Variety Theatre had brought back their production of *La Grande-Duchesse de Gerolstein*) and the crowds thronged haphazardly into the pavilions spread over forty-two hectares. The entire world was witnessing the extraordinary economic recovery of France. Large and small businesses alike benefited from the new inventions and the technical progress. Jean-Phillippe Worth, standing by the side of Alfred, recalled the words of Zola: "The climate is towards science, and artists are necessarily dragged along by the profound necessity for an exact study of actual facts and things." Tradition was about to be disrupted and the creators were being irrepressibly directed towards the future.

The future was expressed in the realism that impregnated the new literature. In sculpture, Rodin still alarmed the Academiciens; Impressionism, ridiculed by many, including Eugenie de Montijo with a tap of her fan some years earlier, began to impose itself; Pissaro, Sisley, Monet, Boudin and Degas would be recognised one day as masters by these same detractors – Alfred and his father foresaw this.

Statistics confirmed the enormous transformation taking place. During the year 1878, the railways were extended from 17,740 kilometres to 19,796 kilometres, and a further 9,000 kilometres of development were planned for the years to come. The modernisation of sea ports was on a par with the improvement of the navigable canals: thanks to the building of the Suez Canal, the tonnage of the fleet went from 52,835 tons to around 157,250 tons; steam traffic quadrupled; the propeller replaced

Princess Mathilde, cousin of Napoléon III. She introduced Alfred Cartier to the Imperial Entourage.

the paddle, and the construction of ships benefited from the replacement of wood by iron. Gramme, the inventor of the alternating current motor, created the first industrial dynamo; the Russian physicist, Joblochkov, perfected the electric lamp; then Edison, on the basis of Charles Cros' work, prepared to launch the gramophone on to the international market. The hydro-electric industry was in its infancy, but it was possible to foresee the future of hydro-electric power. As for the first images achieved by Niepce and Daguerre, they now belonged to past history: Nadar had just taken his first instant photograph.

Wandering aimlessly among the 5,235 stalls set up on both banks of the Seine, Parisians and provincials commented on the figures and documents, and were stupefied to note how techniques had evolved in just eleven years. But, paradoxically, artistic development – in spite of the wish to display originality – remained locked in the traditional forms of expression. Orientalism continued to triumph: beside the Trocadéro, the Japanese and Chinese Pavilions experienced a success which even surpassed the predictions of the organiser. The educated as well as the philistine had only praise for the finish and technique of the objects exhibited, marvelling at the jade, clusters of coral, incrustations of gold, of rock crystal and of enamelling; all these were used in a profusion of artistic flowers and animals – a flirtation of nature with art and exoticism.

During a visit to the Champ de Mars, François, holding his grandson by the hand, met Princess Mathilde, who was accompanied by Méada, the Commissar General of Japan and by her new lover, Popelin, the enameller, who had become Mathilde's biographer. For some time, the jewellers of the Boulevard des Italiens had been in touch with Popelin, who had promised to introduce them to two German enameller friends of his who wished to establish themselves in France. In exiling the Protestants, who were supreme masters of the art of enamelling, Louis XIV had made the glory and the fortunes of many societies of Central Europe, where these exiles had taken refuge. Popelin and François frequently deplored the cruel blow which the revoking of the Edict of Nantes had dealt the art of French enamelling.

Popelin confirmed that the Borteny brothers would soon arrive, which delighted François. As for Mathilde, she was ecstatic about the periwinkle blue of Louis' eyes. Then with her usual vivaciousness, she proceeded to recount her astonishment, her enthusiasm and her scorn for certain contemporary creations; she made a rendezvous with François two days ahead, teasing him because his caskets were no longer ornamented with 'her' crown nor 'her' title. "Alas, Princess," answered Alfred's father, "it is necessary to yield to the laws of the Republic." Mathilde burst out laughing and Louis Cartier never forgot the quality of that engulfing laugh.

Born at Chaton, in August 1878, in the villa rented by his father for the summer months, Alfred's second son was christened Pierre. As his grandfather had foreseen, Antoinette refused to undertake the journey from Roanne.

At the end of 1881, Jean Philippe Worth told Alfred that a brief liaison he had had with one of his father's models, had turned out to have heavy consequences – the young girl was expecting a child. A man of honour, he had told his parents about the situation. After the inevitable storm was over, the grand old man of fashion made the only decision which seemed possible to him – the Worths would bring up the child and Dorothy, its mother, would be substantially compensated for the sacrifice – if it was a sacrifice – to which she had consented. And, at a time when the conventions of the so-called bourgeoisie were most strictly upheld, Charles Frederick, King that he was, had decided that his own son would be an unmarried father: "Better not to marry than to marry badly."

Some months later Andrée-Caroline was born. She was slight, with an engaging face; fair and graceful, she enjoyed her first childhood games in the immense park of the property at Suresnes in the company of Louis Cartier, six years her senior. It was on Andrée-Caroline that Louis started to practise his gifts as a born charmer, liking in turn to protect and dominate her.

17

François could not resign himself to living in the country with a companion who was only a shadow of a wife. On the other hand he judged his presence to be superfluous in Paris, and so he decided to dedicate himself to a project that he had had in mind for a long time: to travel and to paint. He was also convinced that he could be more useful to his son in finding inspiration through chance discoveries and it therefore seemed all the more important to involve himself with a world in motion, as the jewellery world seemed to be content with its present state of stagnation.

It was a form of second youth that made him, at the age of sixty-three, follow, in reverse, the road taken in adolescence by Carl Fabergé, son of Gustav, jeweller to the Tsars, who had decided that his heir should travel the world to find inspiration.

Alfred did not dissuade his father: he understood the reasons for his decision. François was more affected by the illness of his wife than he

Rock-crystal, onyx, rose-cut diamonds and seed pearl pendant on a plaited pearl necklace, consisting of 1157 seed pearls (around 1915, Cartier collection).

dared to admit; he had become aware, too late, of the importance of her role in their past, and no doubt reproached himself for not having always been cognisant of her understanding and tenderness.

He had given in too much in the past to his desire for power; it now seemed necessary to him to distance himself from others, to renew himself: the world was waiting for him. Alfred was both satisfied and disconcerted at having to assume sole responsibility for Cartier and Son. Henceforward he was very much taken up with the business, and he had less time to devote to his family. The gap in Louis' life was filled by his very close attachment to Jean-Philippe Worth, the unmarried father of the young Andrée-Caroline. The little girl's nanny often came to look for him to take them to the Monçeau park, and Louis also accompanied his mother to the workshop in the Rue de la Paix, where he loved handling the materials, and admiringly watched his friend, Jean-Philippe, cutting, giving orders, trying new dresses on the models. "One day," he said, "I shall be a couturier." This enchanted Jean-Philippe and made Alfred curse.

Once a month, the Cartiers were invited by the Worths to their estate at Suresnes, which was frequented by all of Paris society. On several occasions, Louis had the pleasure of meeting the Princess Mathilde, who, with her usual casualness, would arrive unexpectedly on a whim.

The young boy was fascinated by the astonishing atmosphere in this enormous house, decorated with the old man's coat of arms; each time he stopped before a wrought-iron gate to look at the cornflower and the snail, "Why snail?" he would ask. "He takes his house with him, probably an emigré's motto," would come the reply. "Why cornflowers?" "A delicate flower, the flower of a poet, grandfather's favourite flower."

The profusion of trinkets surrounding Madame Worth, amazed Louis, an emotion which he could not have realised was shared by others – among them Edmond Goncourt, who noted in his journal on 9th September 1882:

Brooch with pendant watch, made of gold, blue and white enamel with rose-cut diamonds and pearls (1905, Cartier collection).

> *One can have no idea of the insane trinket mania in this house. They are everywhere: on the walls, on the plates, from all ages and all countries. Madame Worth says that there are 2500 of them. And everywhere, even on the backs of the chairs, in the crystal drops. The place is a delirium of bits of porcelain and carafe stoppers. You feel as if a kaleidoscope of shining glass is continually being shaken before your eyes and you leave this house,*

where crystal salad bowls are encrusted into the tiles, taking with you the sort of nightmare that you bring out of some mad fairy-tale. The owner returns home in the evening, incapable of eating or of enjoying the astonishing building, with a headache from all the aromas and perfumes of the great ladies whom he has spent the whole day dressing.

Business became difficult in the year 1883, as a consequence of the crash of the 'Garantie Nationale', which had ruined a good number of the *petit bourgeoisie,* and at Cartiers the drop was particularly felt by the goldsmiths and in the newly set-up bronze art departments. In contrast, 1884 marked a recovery for the jewellers; conscious of Republican unease, Royalists and Bonapartists displayed anew a need for luxury and a desire for parties. Americans flowed into Paris and the shop in the Boulevard des Italiens saw its clientèle grow to include foreigners not only keen on precious stones of quality, but equally anxious to acquire bracelets, necklaces, tiaras, as well as watch chains.

On the 4th February, 1884, Alice was born of the long-awaited little girl who was christened Suzanne; thirteen months later a third boy, Jacques, was born. From the birth of Louis to that of the youngest child, ten years had gone by; a decade which had seen the Third Republic governed by Thiers, Mac-Mahon, and at present Jules Guevy.

Gambetta, who had cherished a certain idea of France, had died in 1882 in circumstances that were as mysterious as they were fantastic; the world continued to be disturbed by the manoeuvres of international intriguers, endeavouring to unite England, Russia and other European states against France.

Greece had just acquired Thessaly and Epirus; the Russians, governed by the son of Alexander II, who had been assassinated in 1881, took possession of Turkestan; France had acquired Moorea and Tahiti. The army of 'the revenge' astonished Europe. The 14th July, which had become a day of national celebration, had enabled the Parisians to admire Spahee and light cavalrymen from Africa who, after Algeria, had just conquered Tunisia.

And from 1886, a look at the names in Cartier's visitors' book serves to illustrate the background to some particularly tumultuous years in the life of France.

In February 1886, Leopold de Hohenzollern-Sigmaringen ordered a romantic set of topaz on chiselled gold, to be delivered to Madame de Bonnemains, Rue de Berri.

In December 1886, the Comtesse de Saint-Priest, accompanied by a very beautiful blonde lady with brown eyes, advised her friend on the choice of a pendant, and the following month, one of General Boulanger's aide de camps took delivery of a necklace and pendant. The Viscountess de Bonnemains – after her brief idyll with Léopold de Hohenzollern – entered into the life of the General. Léopold, brother of King Carol of Rumania, went on to other *amours*.

Carol of Rumania was married to the *Infanta doña* Antonia of Bragance, daughter of the King and Queen of Portugal. The family was singularly honoured in France this year: the jeweller's craft was sought on the occasion of the marriage of Marie-Amélie, daughter of the Comte de Paris, to the heir to the throne of Portugal. The marriage took place on 16th May, and the level of luxury flaunted on this occasion was considered provocative and aroused an outcry from the opposition. The law which banned reigning families came up again in Parliament, to be made binding on 23rd June.

And the Duc d'Aumale – who had favoured the ascension of General Boulanger – was one of the first to be affected by the new decree. Louis Cartier (then eleven years old) recalled later the astonishing silhouette of Louis Philippe's fourth son: "From my window, I could see the hero of the conquest of Algeria, his deeply-lined face still with a proud expression, smoking his pipe, which he told me one day he had christened 'the brave'. I also saw Léonide Leblanc at his side, and I was proud to be able to say to myself that the son of a King lived in a house built on the land of the jewellers of the Boulevard des Italiens."

The decree banishing the reigning families reinforced the popularity of General Boulanger, and through some of his well-informed clients Alfred learnt that this growing popularity alarmed the world, particularly Bismarck, who considered a war with France was imminent.

The spring of 1887 was a dangerous period but after ten days of grave crisis, following an incident at the frontier, Bismarck recognised that the French protestations were well-founded and the enthusiastic people interpreted the German attitude as a submission to General Boulanger.

On the 30th June, Alfred Cartier delivered in person to the mansion where the General lived in the Rue Dumont-d'Urville, a silver snuff box and a signet ring. In August 1887, a necklace of seed pearls reached the Hotel de la Belle Meunière in Royat; the General, stationed in Clermont-Ferrand, had gone there to meet his lover again.

In September, a new client, Madame Limouzin, took delivery of a

butterfly brooch, and of a tortoise-shell comb enriched with amethysts.
A month later the Wilson scandal broke out. The traffic in embellish-
ments organised by David Wilson, son-in-law of the President of the
Republic, was revealed and Parisians were dismayed to discover that
compromises and underhand deals were not the sole prerogative of the
Second Empire. Madame Limouzin, who was an accomplice, gave the
name, among others, of General Boulanger and although there was
nothing very compromising against the former Minister of War, he was
nevertheless arrested and detained for thirty days on account of the
insolence he displayed in his telegram of protestation.

The Wilson scandal exasperated the French, who demonstrated, and
on 2nd December 1888, Jules Grévy resigned and was succeeded by
Sadi Carnot. General Boulanger became the chief in the line of *malcon-
tents*, on the right as well as on the left, and the political career of the
soldier who wore a red carnation and rode a black horse grew trium-
phantly, funded by three great clients of Cartier – the Duchess d'Uzès,
Prince Napoléon and the Comte de Paris.

And yet, despite his crushing majority win in the Départment of the
Seine, Viscountess de Bonnemain's lover refused, on the evening of
27th January, to sanction the coup d'etat which the people were
clamouring for: "Why should I take power illegally, when I am persuaded that in six months I shall be given it unanimously?"

Early in 1889 Alfred, although aroused by the Boulanger affair, had
other matters on his mind – on the one hand, the preparation of new
designs for the Universal Exhibition, on the other, he was wondering
whether or not he should re-sell his assets in the Panama Canal. There
were disturbing rumours circulating among his clients on the stock
market, but he was unable to forget the considerable gains realised by
his father owing to assets in the Suez Canal made over to him by the
banker.

Was Ferdinand de Lesseps still worthy of the confidence of thousands
of subscribers? Were stockbrokers, who had become anxious because of
the considerable number of assets bought, wrong to panic? On the 4th
February 1889, the French heard that the Universal Company of the
Interoceanique Canal had filed its bankruptcy petition. The crash of the
Panama Canal caused a good number of suicides. Alfred Cartier, who
had lost a lot of money, threw himself courageously into the preparations for the exhibition, christened 'the anniversary' in homage to the
revolution of 1789. Republican France wanted to demonstrate through

this universal exhibition of art, of industrial techniques, the considerable achievements of two decades.

The official opening took place on the 6th May. The Exhibition's star attractions were the gallery of machines and the Eiffel Tower, built two years earlier: at 7,000 tons, 300 metres high, the tallest building in the world. The colonial annex aroused much enthusiasm, and coming into contact with the Cochin-Chinese, the Indo-Chinese, the Senegalese and Tunisian sections, the French got the feeling that they were establishing closer ties with this overseas world.

The 'wondrous electricity' inundated the esplanade of the Tuileries, the gardens of the Trocadéro and the Champ-de-Mars, and Louis Cartier observed everything intensely, fascinated, as his father had been in former days, by the enormous transformations affecting the world's activities. If his main interest was now for jewellery, he remained no less concerned with dress fashions which were extremely becoming in this spring of 1889: tunics with pointed panels at the front and with full sleeves, pleated in the same way as the skirt. Pastel colours were especially favoured. There were also watered-silk capes enriched with rubies, decorated with flowers, with a matching band on the belt – Jean-Philippe Worth had surpassed himself. He had created models of stunning grace, with mini-reproductions for his daughter, Andrée-Caroline – now eight years old – who wore her outfits with the ease of a seasoned model. The elegance of the child, the luxury with which she was surrounded, sometimes irritated Alice, who said that the man who married Jean-Philippe's daughter would have to work blood, sweat and tears to be able to allow her to continue living in the style of a child princess. "Outrageous luxury!" she said to Louis.

Andrée-Caroline was the idol of the Worths – father, grandfather, uncle, aunts, cousins (if Jean-Philippe was resigned to being single, Gaston was married with four children to bless the union) and Louis Cartier shared this idolatory. With her maternal intuition, Alice had noticed the change in the relationship between her oldest boy and Jean-Philippe's daughter. Formerly the dominant one – fourteen years old – he was totally subjugated now by a young girl who was precocious and conscious of her power to attract.

When the exhibition closed its doors in 1889, both organisers and contributors congratulated themselves on its success: contrary to that of 1878, the exhibition of the anniversary was revealed to have been beneficial.

Worth, Pacquin and Laferrière had scored a huge success, and an evening dress due to the collaboration of Worth and Cartier had attracted the attention of King Léopold of Belgium and his following.

In the autumn, Louis and his brother went back to school. The Boulangist danger had gone away, the 'General of the Revenge', after travelling from Brussels to London, was now a refugee in Jersey after his condemnation in absentia on the 14th August.

18

On rediscovering his family after his travels, which had led him to Central Europe and Scandinavia, from England to New York and San Francisco, François Cartier realised how much absence and the desire to distance himself had sharpened his perceptiveness. It was with emotion that he recognised Louis as his favourite grandchild, and discovered the secret antagonism of the younger child for his older brother. Louis and Pierre were as different in physical appearance as they were in personality. The former was graceful and a dreamer, often inattentive, giving the feeling that he wanted to escape from reality, and yet able suddenly to consider a problem with total concentration, and to sort out questions with a remarkable synthesis of mind. Pierre, on the other hand, had less grace, his features revealing an extraordinary will-power and a complete refusal of half-measures or prevarication, yet he had an ability to achieve an admirable degree of control when he wanted to gain someone to his cause. Louis radiated an extraordinary magnetism, whereas Pierre had a kind of charm which came more from a certain art in human relationships, than from a physical and intellectual attraction like Louis who used it ruthlessly.

To celebrate the return of the grandfather, Alice organised a reception to which the Worths were invited. In the course of the evening, François was able to observe his grandson confronting his father or his brother Pierre, and afterwards being very meek and willing to adopt unconditionally the ideas of Jean-Philippe. François understood that Louis was at an impressionable age, profoundly divided between the rigorous conceptions of his bourgeois education and Jean-Philippe's dizzy world of fantasy.

His view of the photographs taken by Nadar in the course of the last months confirmed François' impression. One was able to admire

Jean-Philippe at the foot of cardboard pyramids, disguised as a general of the Second Empire, as a Neopolitan singer with eyes of velvet, a guitar across his shoulder, as the Sultan, or even as a languishing Egyptian dancing girl. What Louis admired in Jean Philippe was his aristocratic disdain of what was said of him, which Louis would have liked to emulate but could not, unable as he was to shake off the strait-jacket of his origins.

Louis and his grandfather met in the adolescent's bedroom, and François, pressed with questions, recounted his discoveries, expressed his enthusiasm, his astonishments and his disappointments. He evoked memories of America, describing how it teemed with building sites and mechanical diggers, gigantic cranes raised towards the sky. He spoke of the insane luxury of the great families of Boston, Philadelphia and San Francisco (all of the ladies dressed by Worth) and how the major part of the colossal fortunes were built up – through skilful speculations, sometimes compromises, but always opportunism. He also said that those who had dared put their faith in fate now had power – the majority of millionaires had started as travelling salesmen, had cleared land, marketed livestock. He recalled some exceptional careers in which success was due to an ability to exploit the opportune moment, the circumstances and the people.

Cornelius Vanderbilt helped his farmer parents from the age of eleven and, at sixteen, with a borrowed hundred dollars, he bought a ferry boat which was the beginning of his fleet of merchant ships. The Vanderbilts (Cornelius, who died in 1877, had had thirteen children) now possessed a dozen fabulous houses, of which seven were on Fifth Avenue. One was like the Chateau du Blois, another an exact copy of Jacques Coeur's house at Bourges.

John D. Rockefeller, the son of a hawker of pharmaceutical products, had begun as an accounts clerk at the age of fourteen.

Carnegie had been a messenger boy at a telegraphic bureau in Pittsburgh at the age of fourteen. At eighteen, the future steel emperor entered the Pennsylvania Railroad company, working for a salary of thirty-five dollars a month which he then judged to be enormous.

François also told of the all-powerful Morgan, the John Pierpoint Morgan, who made Wall Street tremble, and would be called upon to help financially the government in difficult moments. How could François, speaking then of Morgan, have realised that his grandson would marry the daughter of the 'god' of Wall Street?

All the American millionaires, he added, had adopted the saying of Cornelius Vanderbilt: "The law, the law, what does it matter to me . . . haven't I got power?" And François concluded: "America, America, there is the future," after which he showed Louis some water-colours and also drawings of jewels, explaining that new openings were being offered to creative people who dared to make their jewels out of diverse materials. A young designer who had formerly worked for him had understood this perfectly. Lalique, whom he had supported and encouraged, was someone who had perfectly assimilated the lessons of Tiffany: "He attaches importance to keeping the spontaneity of the artisan. In the jewels that he designs the metal is always worked by hand and the stones that Tiffany mounts easily as studs are chosen above all for their form rather than their market value."

To which Louis replied that, in spite of his contempt for the value of stones, Tiffany had nevertheless bought most of the Crown Jewels put on sale by the Republican Government, some years earlier. The grand-father was intrigued by a nuance of contempt in his tone. Was it from his friends at the Lycée – it was well-known that students got politically involved – or was it the influence of Worth, the Worths who sent each term a bouquet of purple violets to the ex-Empress, and did not hide their Bonapartist sympathies.

François looked at his grandson and noted his elegant bearing and the defiance of his smile. How much Louis resembled his own father! His father, an intrepid adventurer, smelter of precious metals, genial gold-smith who had devoted his art to the making of fire-arms; his father, orphaned at the age of six and of whom one knew little in spite of the research carried out. Had his forebears been guillotined or had they fled, leaving the sister in Sarcelles in charge of bringing up the child?

Why the devil did François, who had never judged it necessary to reveal to his son the secret confided by Pierre Cartier at the moment of death, find it necessary to speak about it to the adolescent? No doubt – as he was later to confide to Gaston Worth – because he understood Louis' present difficulties, his ambivalence, his agonising struggle, and he had decided to whip his pride by giving him a lesson in humility. Louis must accept his social milieu without blushing at being the son of an artisan-jeweller.

This confidence, coming after praise for Vanderbilt and Rockefeller, seemed all the more precious, and it would be up to the oldest in the third generation to prove that he had been the descendent of Louis

François of . . . of . . .? François no longer knew, he had never really known, any more than his father, a former soldier of the old guard of Napoléon, who, when all was considered, had never taken very seriously the stories of his aunt at Sarcelles.

Louis would never forget this interview, giving praise many years later for the perspicacity of his grandfather, who had understood his difficulties and put him on the path which would be his henceforward.

The bourgeoisie was to acquire predominance and he would be proud to be a bourgeois even and, above all, if he had the slightest drop of blue blood in his veins – and he promised himself that he would obtain proof of that one day.

CHAPTER TWO

The End of the Century

1

Having gained his Baccalaureat a year previously, Louis Cartier was initiated into the techniques of the profession with a frenzy of learning and an understanding that astonished his colleagues. Although lacking in discipline, sometimes dreamy, with a tendency to nonchalance, he nevertheless managed to overcome these deficiencies. He worked hard, always hoping for the birth of the unexpected 'idea'.

The workmen in the Mazuchetti studio, who soldered links in long chains with blowlamps, frequently saw Louis' tall figure bent over the stretching machines in order to observe all the operational phases in the melting of gold and in the creation of jewellery.

He soon knew all about Picq and Lavabre, how craftsmen created contemplative Buddhas, firebirds and pots of flowers set with agate or onyx, decorated with coral and fine pearls.

A pupil of Messonier, initiated into pictorial techniques, Louis quickly developed a love for painting, although unable to draw correctly; his teacher thus concluded that he had the hand of an engineer but drew like a technician.

A follower of Bourdelle convinced Alfred that his older boy had the talents of a sculptor, so Louis was sent to Greece where he was soon joined by Pierre. Louis recalled:

> There were some happy moments; we discovered that we could dislike each other cordially, even at times exchanged blows, but we would be reconciled and in complete agreement when it was a question of jewellery or business: we were the Cartiers. Our father was unaware that we had secretly made the same oath: to become the greatest in our profession. In his thirtieth year, Pierre secretly took courses in Political Science, and told me that he dreamed of this career. I confided in him that I was doing law courses without our father's knowledge; this complicity enchanted us.

Boni de Castellane (1867–1932).

On the 13th February 1894, Louis experienced great sorrow on learning of the death of his best friend. He was one of the twenty-one victims of the bomb attack at the terminus at Saint-Lazare. The waves of anarchism reached Lyons and Marseille, and Alice, who lived in terror of violence, begged her sons not to leave Paris for London where they were to be sent in the spring.

François returned from Russia just as the Dreyfus Affair began. He was stupefied at the atmosphere reigning in Paris but more astonished still to discover at Roanne, where he had been called urgently, that his wife's sanity had deteriorated.

People became gripped by the *affaire*. France was divided between those for and those against Dreyfus. All this seemed absurd at a moment when he was on the point of concluding a commercial agreement with Carl Fabergé, jeweller to the Tsar, who wished to make large objects in hard stones for his client, under the protection of Cartier-Warembose. The agreement between Fabergé-Warembose-Cartier was concluded five years later.

Louis and Pierre questioned their grandfather: was he for or against Dreyfus? To which François replied that he detested generals, Jewish or not, that military history was unseemly. Boulanger, who had failed to reverse the regime in 1889, committed suicide three years later at Ixelles, on the tomb of Marguerite de Bonnemais, dying as he had lived, as a sub-lieutenant (citation Clemençeau). Families were torn to pieces, friends detested each other, and all for the sordid history of a bill. François refused to take part.

It was at Roanne, by the bed of the dying Antoinette, that François heard of the assassination of Sadi Carnot, fourth president of the Third Republic (after its remarkably tormented adolescence), that Casimir Perier was to succeed Sadi Carnot. He resigned six months later.

For the first time the Cartier son was invited to the bi-annual council, when designers and jewellers gathered under the presidency of Jean-Philippe, to discuss the coming spring fashions. Louis, taking notes, made alterations to the sketches. He was irritated with a dress of Jean-Philippe, destined for a fabulously rich American, Fanny Read: "The shining circles on the shoulders annoyed me, they were like a contradiction, a sort of nonsense, injuring the harmony of the model. I envisaged a geometric cut, long and fine."

The idea of the *diamant-baguette*, one of Louis' innovations, was born and applied with much success some years later.

The studios of couture and jewellery lived in a fever, inspired by the creation of dresses and jewels for those invited to the marriage of the century, which was to grip the entire world. Boni, the impertinent Boniface de Castellane, who represented at the end of the century what Gramont-Caderrouse had been under the Second Empire (minus his fortune), was to marry in the spring. His wife-to-be was Anna Gould, ugly, but incredibly rich; her dowry, at sixty million francs, was estimated to be the largest in the world.

In Paris, many knew of the extraordinary rise of her father, Jay Gould, son of a New York State farmer, who had left home at the age of twelve to create a fortune in an America which was being built at breath-taking speed. Extremely gifted in dealing with money, Jay Gould was able to boast, eighteen years later, of being a multi-millionaire; he founded 'Goldborough', a town bearing his family name. At forty years old, Gould possessed a bank account as large as Vanderbilt's, he had created the main railway lines and had provoked a fight (with his own weapons, the railways) with a competitor, who refused to allow him certain routes which would make possible a junction between two rail networks. The locomotive duel between Jay Gould and his adversary, machine against machine, followed. Once more Jay Gould triumphed.

The Goulds considered the marriage of their daughter, Anna, and a ruined noble with pleasure; the alliance of money and nobility satisfied their snobbishness. Boni, although penniless, was still the most desirable bachelor in Europe, linked to the Talleyrand-Perigord, Potocki, Sagan and Radziwill families, and no American in high society could ignore the fact that one of Boni's ancestors, Vice-Admiral Castellane-Majestre, had perished beside Lafayette in the War of Independence.

It was in Fanny Read's drawing-rooms that Boni had chosen Anna, a puritanical and unbecoming girl. The Duchess of Gramont, invited to New York for the ceremony, was to write in her memoirs that Anna was said to be ugly by the aesthetic rules of Paris but perhaps not in her own country: "I have always pictured her as the commanding chief of the Iroquoise indians, her head surrounded by long eagle feathers. She was small and lean, her face entirely taken up by a big nose and two enormous black eyes. Bands of hair in the shape of propellors, made her seem even shorter and her back was strewn with black hairs."

In view of the wedding of the century, the pearl stringers worked for a week towards creating a five-strand necklace, which was to be a present from the Castellane family; other designs had been submitted to

Howard Gould and consisted of a brooch in the shape of a bow-tie, enriched with coloured diamonds, and a 200-diamond chain (Alfred had given a pearl dealer in New York one hundred exceptional diamonds for this chain), offered by Frank, brother of Anna, who was later to build a house in Juan-les-Pins.

On the 4th April 1895, Anna Gould, dressed in white satin enriched with pearls, was married. An orchestra of sixty musicians played under the direction of the head of the metropolitan opera. All of the American journals and certain European newspapers gave a description of the wedding casket, which was made up of a diamond tiara, pearls, emeralds and rubies, a heart-shaped brooch decorated at its centre with the celebrated Esterhazy diamond, a chain of two hundred diamonds, a bow of blue, pink and white diamonds, a necklace of ten strands of fine pearls, and a horse-shoe of diamonds.

Louis Cartier was to become an intimate of Boni de Castellane, the man who married and almost squandered part of the greatest fortune in the world. The passion for the style of the eighteenth century, furniture and paintings, was drilled into him by this amateur connoisseur from whom he had bought a number of pieces of furniture and objets d'art. That Boni had fascinated this boy, seven years younger than himself, is easy to believe. He was dazzled by the dandy whose scathing words would be quoted and peddled by Paris society: "The first time I saw Anna, I thought she was not too bad at all, considering her dowry." And later: "I have been the first representative of the Fauberg Saint-Germain to marry a rich American." Or yet again the famous reply of Boni to his neighbour at Maxims, when his cousin, le Duc de Talley-rand (who had just married Anna after their divorce), passed in front of their table without any acknowledgment: "You have not said good-day to each other, don't you know each other?" "Yes, Madame, and very well, we served in the same regiment." A certain physical resemblance encouraged Louis to identify himself with Boni, this Boni of whom the Duchesse de Gramont said had "the complexion of a sixteen-year-old Swede with the light of dawn and the profile of Louis XV as sculptured by Caffieri."

For a long time, the alluring blondness of Louis was to suit Boni's style of dressing admirably. He wore, according to his mood, a hand-kerchief or a cornflower, sometimes a carnation, in his buttonhole, and in moments of reflection would bite the end of his fine moustache imperceptibly, stroking his nostrils slowly with his index finger. Haughty condescension, sometimes irritating, and a certain art of mockery was to remain the mark of Boni.

Consuela Vanderbilt, the Duchess of Marlborough: "Bejewelled and harnessed, I was thought worth being presented to well-to-do English society!"

The year of 1895, during which New Yorkers were gripped by the union of dollars with nobility, saw the crowning of a matrimonial association almost as spectacular: that of Consuela Vanderbilt – descendant of the Commodore – and the Duke of Marlborough. In her memoirs Consuela Vanderbilt recalls, not without humour, the important role of jewels in social climbing:

Jewels seemed to be a necessary addition to my trousseau. The fashion was chokers, mine were of pearls and consisted of nine strings with a diamond clasp which scratched my neck. My mother had given me all the pearls she had received from my father and, among others, three very beautiful strings that had formerly belonged to Catherine of Russia and the Empress Eugenie, so there was a necklace that I was able to wear around my waist. My father made me a present of a tiara of diamonds surmounted by stones cut in the form of pearls. Certainly, these jewels were beautiful but they never gave me pleasure, and the heavy tiara invariably gave me a headache, while the choker gave me a scratched neck. Nevertheless, bejewelled and harnessed, I was thought worth being presented to well-to-do English society!

2

On returning from a journey to Anvers, the eldest Cartier expressed his conviction that the exploitation of South African mines would bring about a transformation of the market. It appeared, however, more necessary to foresee the future in terms which the new clientele was affirming for itself: the élite of the bourgoisie wished to confirm their rights to luxury at last.

Louis was persuaded that the infatuation with semi-precious stones was declining and that the doleful era of industrialism was succeeding to a more luxurious era, one needing the inspiration of a former epoque that was above all sumptuous: the eighteenth century, when certain goldsmiths had tentatively experimented with platinum but to no great consequence. For three years, however, Tiffany's had been considering using it again, as demonstrated by certain jewels created for the Gould-Castellane wedding.

Some Parisian studios had been tempted for a while to research into this matter, and Louis had decided to be the first to make it fashionable. The use of platinum was increasing all the time, a white metal, malle-

Cigarette case. Yellow gold and black enamel with old-cut diamond motifs set in platinum (1925, Cartier collection).

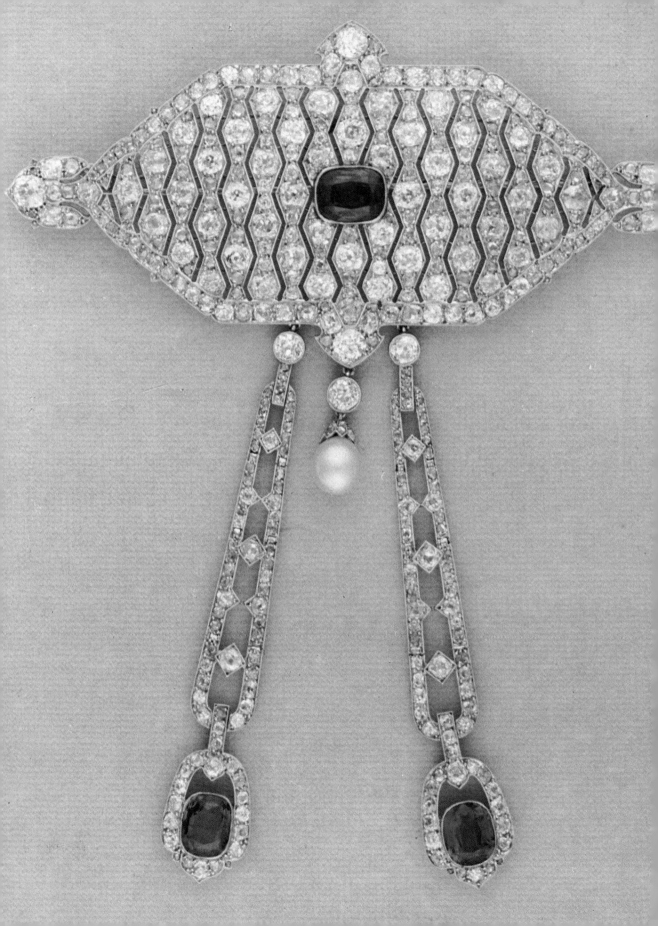

able and ductile, that never oxidised, resisted all acids and allowed the creation of light settings of an infinite suppleness. The reign of precious stones had arrived – sparkling sapphires and rubies, emeralds from South America – and success was dependent on abolishing as much as possible the claws that held the stone in place, so that the mount was almost invisible.

Some months later, the Countess of Breteuil sported a dress whose front was embroidered with platinum, diamonds and sapphires; then, at the Palais de Glace, the beautiful Otero made Liane de Pougy jealous by sporting, on a velvet choker, a pendant in Louis XVI style presented by the Duc de Guiches, and bearing the signature of Cartier.

The veteran Charles Frederick Worth died at his private house in La Rue de Berry in 1895. The ex-Empress sent violets. François, who had not been away from France since the funeral of his wife, followed the mortal remains of his old friend. As if in mockery, the couturier of the élite, the man who had made the law at the Tuileries, whose creations had been the pride of the entire world of elegance, was buried in a communal grave. This angered François. "Very soon I will order a vault which will be worthy of Cartier," promised Louis, to which François retorted, "There is no immediate hurry on that point." Although seventy-five years old, he still had an immense appetite for life, knowledge and influence, and was convinced that he would live to see the marriage of his favourite grandson.

The grandfather had observed the behaviour of Andrée-Caroline Worth and Louis, and had concluded that they were troubled by each other. At the same time, it was clear that each was endowed with a strong character, almost too strong. Unlike the young girls of the bourgeoisie, Andrée was not an innocent young thing. She was able to give an opinion and to express disagreement. Jean-Philippe was delighted that his daughter had a perhaps somewhat puritanical personality and not that of a silly goose with obstinate blinkered eyes; she was a girl after his own heart.

Corsage decoration which transforms into a brooch and earrings. It is made of diamonds, sapphires and seed pearls, set in platinum (1921, Cartier collection).

François was not unaware that his son looked kindly on the idea of an eventual union between Cartier and Worth and, if there were a feeling for such a marriage, then coupled with the considerable financial advantages, it would suit Alfred very well. The death of the founder of the Worth dynasty would make his sons inheritors of the immense fortune, which Marie, his widow, possessed. Jean-Philippe richly endowed his daughter who, because of her humble origins, was excluded from marrying a member of the upper classes. She was the child of an unmarried father, and ravishing and fortunate as she was, could therefore not be admitted into society. After having talked for a long time with Alfred, François questioned his grandson, who answered evasively, "She pleases me and disturbs me."

Madame Worth senior had an interview with Andrée, who steadily held her grandmother's gaze, directly and proudly, with her immense eyes and said that she did not wish to hear talk of marriage for the moment. Louis was a childhood friend, a good-looking boy, and that was all. They had an agreement to let time pass.

Louis, for his part, continued to work intensely, his passion for the eighteenth century fast becoming obsessional. He would visit libraries and second-hand booksellers, in his quest for knowledge. Late into the night he would study, taking notes. This irritated Alfred, who was sorry to see that his son spent so little time in the shop, apparently with only slight concern for the practice of selling.

The Duchesse d'Uzes had asked him to design a brooch in platinum decorated with a red carnation. He replied without grace that rubies were certainly not the best stones for the carnation of Madame la Duchesse.

Alfred repaired the insult of that disaster. Louis, reprimanded by his father, rebelled. He had, undoubtedly, great sensitivity in his contacts with clients, but also a personal feel for stones that the clientele understood straight away.

There were signs of an important market in emeralds in South America. Before his departure, François said that this would be his last journey and advised his son to let Louis act as he wished: "He is full of talent, swarming with ideas, have confidence in him!"

At the end of the year Louis submitted to his father and his colleagues a project for a different line of new clocks, based on those masterly creations of the eighteenth century, when clocks, travelling clocks and watches had been made by incomparable artists, chisellers and craftsmen.

With the development of techniques and the influx of less refined clientele, the nineteenth century had seen the utilitarian and functional aspects become more important than artistic ones. The twentieth century announced a triumphant future which necessitated a revision of values in which it was necessary to re-impose the notion of aesthetics on clockmaking.

Alfred rebelled. He had to fulfil the demand for bronze or marble mechanisms which he obtained from Jura or Switzerland. But what Louis envisaged was no less than a revolution, and Alfred's good Auvergian sense found arguments which Louis opposed with the brilliance of Bueguet. Sometimes it took seven years to make one clock – but what a clock! The genius of a Caron, Caron the most prestigious of them all, the one he most admired without limitation. He reminded him that if Caron had not been double-crossed by the vile Lepaute, clockmaker to the King, who copied his model, then Caron, the protestant, would never have become a Beaumarchian.

Louis repeatedly rejected mediocrity and insisted above all on the opportunism that had allowed him to foresee the inkling of change in the contrary whims of others: in the jewellery revolutions, like in platinum, they must be the first. It was not only a question of prestige but also an exceptional financial opportunity, the only language that Alfred cared to hear.

The following weeks were dedicated to setting up a plan made by the elder of the third generation. Visits were paid to l'Ecole Horlogere of France, where most of the craftsmen's children studied and were taught all the techniques from clockwork mechanisms to basic astronomy; within five years future graduates had to present the judges with a clock made entirely with their own hands, including the casing.

Then came a trip across to Switzerland where Louis was disappointed. Before coming back he made a detour through Epernay, to attend a meeting that would transpire to be of exceptional importance. In the Estienne workshops he made the acquaintance of an Alsacian-Loraine, who had fled from his native province after the Treaty of Belfort. Edmund Jaegar, the proud-faced blond, whose first care in reaching Epernay had been to have a funeral vault built, said: "I have left Alsace which has become German, to live in France where I am sure to be buried." This displayed foresight and good sense that Worth had lacked.

Edmund Jaegar told Louis of his scorn for modern fashions. His passion lay in buying models, soaps, in filing, cutting, taking apart and transforming the complete mechanism. "As soon as you can, come to Paris," insisted Louis, which was already Jaegar's intention. The obstinacy of the eldest Cartier, and the chance meeting, had made it possible for one of the most spectacular collaborations of the twentieth century to come into being on La Marne at the end of 1895.

Alfred gave his agreement, in principle, to organise a new line in clocks, but adding, in his crafty fashion, that nothing was very pressing. Louis accepted the compromise, all the time continuing to do his research and investigations. He began to recruit qualified staff, and to make more frequent appearances in the shop, to prove to his father that he was just as capable as his brother Pierre. It was thus that he received the Marquise de Belboeuf, who wished to have a *bague-chevaliene* made according to a sketch she had traced out and which she submitted to Louis with evident satisfaction. When he saw its originality, he did not really appreciate it: "Too virile for my taste," he objected. The Marquise left, half-amused, half-incensed. Louis would learn from his father that the Marquise de Belboeuf, a notable lesbian, sister of the Duc de Morny, loved to claim that her brother and herself, between them, had had all the most beautiful women in Paris!

Louis was called up for a year's military service. However, due to a weak heart and wishing to pursue his studies, he was deployed to the Secretariat de l'Intendance de Versailles, and was therefore not to be subjected to the rigours of a discipline that he abhorred. While there, he was able to continue his research into the organisation of a Department of Clockmaking.

3

Back in civilian life, Louis was excited to discover a different Andrée-Caroline. She had grown taller, and seemed very sure of herself. The light beige of her outfit sharpened the clarity of her blue eyes, and she looked radiant in a dress of velvet trimmed with embroidery and ruched with lace.

Louis, perplexed, considered the imposing number of buttons and buttonholes (Baroque pearls): back, elbow, dress front, and asked himself, with an emotion that turned his cheeks scarlet, how much time an amorous man must have to devote to undressing a lady before being offered the joy of embracing her naked and consenting body.

The young people walked in the park, conscious that the two families were deciding their future. The Worth-Cartier alliance, productive since the Second Empire, would be consolidated by their union. Louis' projects of renovation merited effective help from the top couturiers in the world. In 1898 the premises at 13 Rue de la Paix would be vacant, and thus Worth's clientele would have only two blocks to travel to reach Cartier, which would allow an exchange of clientele and much closer co-operation than in the past.

Madame Worth added two hundred thousand francs to supplement the dowry furnished by Jean-Philippe. And so the affair was concluded: Louis had time to go on his course and the date of the marriage was set for the end of March 1898, on condition that Alfred and Louis became associates. This agreement replaced that of 1872 between François and his son.

After the meeting when the agreements were discussed, Louis came back to Andrée: "It is all settled, we can get married!"

He felt transported, intoxicated, experiencing total joy – and was not aware of her sudden reserve, distant and immovable. The drama which followed was undeniably the result of his clumsiness. He did not explain very well to the girl the reasons for his enthusiasm: he spoke not of happiness nor their future together, but of development, new structures, commercial disruptions and his creative objectives. "I could already see him in Rue de la Paix, associated with his father, imposing his style, introducing daring techniques, revolutionising horological ideas," confided Andrée-Caroline.

The lovers gave precedence to ambition, and the daughter of Jean-Philippe would never forget it. However, in the months that followed, she was to be an agreeable fiancée, mischievous, sometimes coquettish, and if Jean-Philippe had any forebodings of the difficulties of his daughter, he did not seek to question them at this time. Persuaded of the attraction which Louis held for his daughter, he found it useless and ridiculous to dwell on the thought – almost indecent to consider – that 90% of the bourgeois marriages only came into being by virtue of the interests of both parties.

In the spring of 1897 there was renewed activity in the commerce of luxury. The grand season was exceptional, with brilliant receptions being arranged in the salons close to the capital by the aristocratic élite and the great names of cosmopolitan society.

To be affable towards Cartier, the Comtesse de Breteuil sent an invitation to the opening of the Charity Bazaar which would take place on 3rd May. Madame Gaston Worth and her niece were also invited by the intermediary of S.A.R., the Duchesse d'Alencon, sister of the Empress of Austria.

For twelve years, the Charity Bazaar had been one of the great events

Cartier, Paris (Rue de la Paix, 1898).

of the season. At the end of the century, the great passion of the people of the world was for Charity.

To the pleasure of altruism was added the far from negligible pleasure of buying all sorts of articles at a low price, sold by great ladies of society, and to exhibit jewels and outfits in an unusual way, in circles usually concerned with protecting their prerogatives.

Madame Worth, the mother, being unwell, kept Andrée-Caroline and her aunt at her bedside. A lackey, sent to Rue de Prony, took a message to Alice Cartier asking her to go to the Charity Bazaar by herself; the Worth ladies would join her if the doctor considered that the attack was not dangerous. Alice Cartier left in a cab at ten past four.

Arriving at the Avenue d'Autin, the taxi-driver noticed a thick cloud of smoke rising above the roofs; an unusual traffic jam was blocking the way and an infernal smell had spread over the neighbouring streets.

A few moments later Alice learnt that the Charity Bazaar was no more than a mountain of cinders. The room used for the cinematograph had burnt like tinder, and the fire had spread to all the stands, around which two hundred guests had gathered.

Ever since 1870, Alice had always been extremely frightened of fire and she was to confess later that, at that moment, she had been unable to co-ordinate her actions and thoughts, dwelling on the one idea that the wife of Gaston Worth and her son's fiancée might be in the fire. Although the most elementary logic implied that Andrée and her aunt could not physically have been at the place before her, Alice, petrified with horror, found herself mixing with the desperate crowd, and witnessing a terrifying spectacle. A journalist later said: "I have covered the war of 1870, assisted at eighty capital executions, witnessed fifty catastrophes but I have never seen anything similar."

The morning headline in *Le Figaro* was: '125 dead, 100 victims,' and the reporter, Andre Dayot, who had taken part in the rescue, wrote: "There is a lamentable concert of cries and sobs rending the air: the smoke disappeared little by little and in the charred debris one began to see shrivelled limbs, burnt bodies, the heads of the dead, white and grimacing; under the action of the fire, bodies were shrinking, stunted, skulls and stomachs had burst."

Alice Cartier went home reeling with horror. Physiologically afflicted since the birth of her fourth child, she would never be able to overcome the shock of this fatal afternoon of 4th May 1897.

After his return from South America, François Cartier was awoken by sobs. Alice was moaning: "The fire, the fire," and François had a discussion in the morning with his grandson, recalling Antoinette, his wife, and the mists which sucked her down in the last years of her life, as she refused, like a ghost, to accommodate herself to reality. He expressed doubts, spoke of leaving, confided his beliefs, which threw a shadow over the hopes put into the success of the third generation.

Louis was to dispel his alarm, using arguments which would have appealed to a younger François, who pretended to rediscover the spirit of his youth so as to be able to believe and to understand – or to make it seem so.

Alfred's eldest son, at twenty-two, was handsome and from a race of conquerors. He was marked with a kind of genius, and was able easily to reassure his grandfather. Everything about him – his tone, his smile – was worthy of attention.

He gave inspiration, and was of great comfort to the old man, who was pleased to have been reassured.

In truth, the recent alarms in the family had added to the burden of his widowhood and were not solely responsible for the personality disarray of François who, typical of his contemporaries, was divided between contradictory aspirations. To quote Jacques Clastenet:

> *The hundred years which had passed had been marked by revolutions in all domains, industrial production had increased formidably; railways, steamboats and the telegraph had abolished distances; political regimes and intellectual fashions jostled each other. But successive disillusions dispelled dreams, pessimism had succeeded optimism, the renewals of enthusiasm were colourless, one believed less in the virtues of the future. A wave of scepticism broke out, shortly to be coloured with a troubled mysticism. This epoque, later described as beautiful, appeared to be very decadent, anxious and struck with neurosis.*

As we have seen over fifty years the evolution and sometimes the contradictions of François Cartier, we will know in future the singularities of the man, he had a tremendous drive and vulnerability; he was a materialist, an artisan who ascended into the bourgeoisie. He was an opportunist who dared to question himself, ceasing to play the game of ambition, dedicated to painting and to travel, and, in the twilight of his life, affected by a metaphysical anguish about the future of his grandchildren in a world where everything moved too fast.

Under the presidency of the widow of the founder of the Worth dynasty and of the Cartier grandfather, the engagement of Andrée-Caroline and Louis proceeded in the normal way with the signing of the contract in the presence of the notaries of the two families.

As foreseen, the Dreyfus affair conclusively divided the country. With the adventure of the Marchand mission, Fachoda fanned the flames of anglophobia in a nation that was paradoxically anglophile, it being fashionable to pepper conversation with English expressions. With Russia, Franco-German relations improved and the future was shown to be more peaceful.

At the age of thirteen, Jacques, the youngest Cartier, showed himself to be the most gifted designer of the three sons. Louis, with an attention and tenderness that was not his usual manner, decided to supervise his jewellery education. Jacques learned one of the oldest arts in the world, that of working with gold and silver, with enamel and eventually precious stones. The invention of the method of cutting stones with thirty-two facets – called the re-cut – gave its special expression in the measure of perfection, in cutting stones which had a capital interest or jewels of which the gem stone became the central attraction.

The nineteenth century had been conditioned by too much diversity of style, influenced by the Renaissance period, the Mauresque, Egyptian, Middle Ages and Louis XV, but François Cartier and then Alfred – as Mauboussin, Mellerio, Linzeler, Clerc, Janesich, Vever, associated with Bapst in 1879, Morel, to whom Chaumet had succeeded in 1884 – had marked their epoque with a wish to escape from traditionalism. The end of the century represented an important turning point, the changing of forms in the art of designing jewels and in the ways of creating them. Lalique, who worked for Cartier for a long time, had a most remarkable influence upon the profession. He knew how to put poetry into naturalism, contrary to some whose work seemed most daring. Louis would not allow the liberation of jewels in the extreme interpretation of flowers and animals, and he persuaded Jacques that if they appeared to impose a style, it was in a form of innovation which must always take into account a certain classicism.

In the course of the years that followed, Jacques came to perfect his understanding of the mysteries of a method in which he later excelled, but the rudiments of the first formative influences, the visits to the museums of Europe in the company of his brother, Louis, were determining factors. Thirty years later, commissioned by the British Government, he wrote for an English Encyclopaedia a treatise on the art of modern jewellery, which is still referred to today.

On the 30th March 1898, in the church of Saint-Honore-d'Eylan, Louis Cartier married Andrée-Caroline Worth. The young couple went to live in a private house where Andrée-Caroline amused herself playing hostess. Marriage made her yet more ravishing, but Louis could see that his adorable child-wife was nostalgic for Suresnes. The Worths missed her terribly and he was frustrated at not being able to express his strong feelings of tenderness for a wife who lingered complaisantly in a state of adolescence.

She detested his anger, he hated her tears; they would tear each other to pieces and then become reconciled.

Preoccupied with the management of the premises of 13 and 14 Rue de la Paix (where Alfred had rented a place for the jewellery service, a studio for design and the administration services), Louis was not able to live with his head in the clouds, as Andrée wished. She would have loved to visit Egypt or Venice, but her universe remained limited to the Rue de la Paix, l'Avenue Marceau, and Suresnes, to where she frequently returned.

The marriage had inflamed the passion of Andrée for her father and gave birth to jealousy at Lous' friendship with Jean-Philippe.

But the couturier, stimulated by the important appearance of Paquin, Doucet, Jean Lanvin, worked intensely to prepare for the Exhibition of 1900, and Louis no longer had the time to linger over the state of mind of a young girl, too complex for his taste, complaisant with the languor at the end of the century and the romanticism of cheap society.

Andrée felt double-crossed and confided to her aunt: "One day I shall end up hating dresses and jewels." No one in the house of Worth took the jest seriously.

It was understandable that no one attached extreme importance to the feelings of a young married woman, whose emotions appeared trifling in this particularly eventful year of 1898, which began with the ringing article of Zola in *l'Aurore* about the machinations of the anti-Dreyfus people and, following this, the added risks of war. Recalling the Marchand mission had calmed spirits, but the Franco-English tension was still alive. Captain Marchand was celebrated as a national hero, those who were preoccupied with this knew the other side of the boulangiste affair.

At the end of November, the Worths were cruelly struck by the loss of the old man's wife. Andrée was very affected by the death of her grandmother and Louis became more tender towards the young woman, allowing her to travel in the autumn of 1900. This was an indication that his ambitious thirst was not only a desire for power, but that he also desired to create an existence which dignified her. She was a descendant of the greatest couturier in the world; she would be the wife of the greatest jeweller in the world. All seemed perfectly logical.

Andrée had the good taste to play the game. She was persuaded that her husband would become the greatest in the world, and she knew, too, that he was a minor expert in the art of psychology. She realised that his will for power was based upon an implacable pride and extraordinary gifts which some considered genius, but she also knew that she had only a small role in his life. Her husband could never be her ideal partner – of this she was now convinced.

On the 17th February, the French heard of the sudden death of

President Felix Faure. The press had a field day covering the story. Well-informed sources knew of the liaison of the head of state with Meg Steinheil, the wife of the painter. The beautiful Meg had for several years held a salon frequented by the smart set. She loved clothes, furs and jewels, and her painter husband was not yet in a position to satisfy her taste for these luxuries: so she converted her favours into cash.

Alfred had occasion to meet her at Ronsin and at the shop where she frequently went. She was one of those whose lucrative and showy liaisons launched her into the world. Recently, she had had made a head dress, adorned with a crest of diamonds, for a reception to which she was to accompany the Prince of Gaul in person (and certainly incognito said the gossips), owing to the frictions between Paris and London.

And then President Felix Faure died in the arms of his muse, holding between his shrivelled fingers a strand of red hair; he died through love, having taken too many stimulants to keep up his virility.

The press was to cover the story in such minute detail that *La Chambre de Deputes* had finally to intervene.

A small guilloché *enamel clock, created in 1900 for the Royal Family of Orleans.*

It was revealed that President Faure had shortened his interview with the Prince of Monaco, who wished to discuss the Dreyfus affair, the visit of the Prince having been preceded by that of Cardinal Richard, Archeveque de Paris. The chronicler, Gabriel-Louis Pringuet, was to explain that the feelings of the President lacked passion, and it was therefore necessary for him to take two stimulants before his lover's interviews:

> *A particular bell at the palace announced the visit of the intimate. On the day that was to be his last, the President, waiting for his beautiful friend, took two pills. Alas, it was the Cardinal. The President walked the length and breadth of his cabinet, and the Cardinal finally left. The bell rang again, he took two more pills, the lady entered, but unfortunately the President was dying.*

At a time of great international tension it was apparent that with the East revolting against the Russians and Europe exasperated by the British pretensions, the importance of a particular sector, combined with the morbid undertones of the Faure affair, was considered as salvation by some and abhorrent to others.

CHAPTER THREE

La Belle Epoque

1

At the beginning of this century, Louis Cartier, assisted by his brother, Pierre, was responsible for No. 13 Rue de la Paix. Three salesmen of international standing, who had previously worked for Worth, were appointed by Jean-Philippe in order to strengthen the team on the Boulevard des Italiens.

A Cartier salesman had to be bilingual, fully conversant with the subtleties involved in the creation of a jewel, from mineralogy to design. He had to be a gentleman, holding his own at receptions, attending races – complete with top hat, frock-coat, grey spats and patent leather shoes – and was expected to know the head porters of Europe's most prestigious hotels so as to be kept informed of the arrival of top people. Each salesman trained a secretary who, once he had mastered the knowledge, would in turn become a top salesman.

With his remarkable business flair, Alfred Cartier managed to convince his new associates that Cartier & Sons had a brilliant future, and that they would be well advised to invest in the company. Some of them trusted him with their savings and retired fifteen years later, having made their fortune. After the early uncertainty, the father's worries gave way to broad optimism; he was now convinced that his eldest son had gifts. He was able to discover talent and flair in other people, and could even detect creativity in those who were totally unaware of it themselves. He knew instinctively the mistakes to avoid.

At the beginning of the century, Louis Cartier's activity was essentially devoted to the establishment of the clock-making department. The first small enamelled clocks were created for an English peer and the d'Orléans family, but Louis, with greater foresight and ambition, had decided that Cartier creations would equal those of Bréguet. It was with that goal in mind that he began to cultivate the Couët brothers, whose father had been one of the first craftsmen of Bréguet. "I'll offer

Alfred Cartier and his three sons, from left to right: Pierre, Louis, Alfred and Jacques.

them such a vast amount of money that they will have to give in," he said. As indeed they did: in 1915 they joined the firm.

He had also decided to restore the fashion for convertible jewels (some attempt had been made in the eighteenth century without much success); when he finally managed to produce an acceptable design, he showed it to Jean-Philippe who remarked that Louis, after having been called the 'couturier' of jewel-making, would soon deserve the title 'technician' of jewel-making. The design was for a platinum bodice ornament: brilliant stones of a surprising geometrical shape for the time, embellished with cushion sapphires and a baroque pearl, to which were attached two diamonds set in platinum, studded with sapphires. These could be removed according to the lady's whim, and transformed into earrings – three jewels in one. Using the same methods, Louis had some diadems made, which could be worn as bodice ornaments by removing part of the ornamentation. The first of these convertible diadems was created for Andrée-Caroline who was expecting a child. "My son will be born with the new century," said Louis, very attentive towards his young wife, despite having to spend almost all of his time designing jewels for the Universal Exhibition.

In preparation for this even Parisians had witnessed major reconstruction which, for some years, had been transforming the city: the first underground railway line between Neuilly and Vincennes, the *Grand* and *Petit Palais* built on the site of the *Palais de l'Industrie* and the *Pont Alexandre III*, which had been built with its single arch of 108 metres, ornamented with 'gilded sculptures that offended some but delighted many more. Other recent innovations were the *Grande Roue* (the Big Wheel) and the *Gare d'Orsay*. At last a clear view of *Les Invalides* was possible, and on April 14th Monsieur Loubet inaugurated the exhibition which was to open to the public one month later. The ceremony was attended by two monarchs: The Shah of Persia and King Oscar of Sweden and Norway.

The exhibition was, as expected, enormously popular. In the foreign section, the Monaco and German buildings and the Boer farm attracted large crowds. Louis was particularly interested in the Russian building, and studied carefully the huge map of France made out of marble and jasper studded with precious stones, presented by the Tsar. "A magnificent example of the jeweller's skill which provides a definition of our craft, the jeweller as creator of works of art from precious materials."

The latest discoveries prompted gatherings of eminent scientists and, unlike many of his fellow citizens, Louis refused to believe in the 'failure of science'. He was delighted to be living in an age which had seen the birth of radio-activity, X-rays, liquid air and the wireless. The car industry was entering a period of rapid growth. The Duchess d'Uzès had shocked society eighteen months earlier when she obtained a licence to drive a car propelled by petroleum gas. Aviation was in its infancy, and it was during a reception organised by the Baron Deutsch de la Meurthe, that the friendship between Louis and Alberto Santos-Dumont began.

Physically they were very different – the former had dark hair and a dark complexion, the latter was fair with blue eyes – and the same applied to their personalities. Louis never openly admitted how much he admired the free and easy manner of the extremely rich Brazilian who had conducted his life with total disregard for conventions, while Santos, sometimes ironical, liked the distant guardedness of a man whose great talent he appreciated.

It was for his mistress (Baroness Belle de Neuilly) that Santos ordered an ultra slim gold watch, encircled with rubies and engraved inside: "To B.N. from A.S.D." Louis delivered the gift personally – a great distinction – to the extraordinary flat at No. 150 Champs-Elysées, which had been specially designed by Santos. Alberto, with his passion for heights, had had his tables fixed two metres from the floor; the same applied to the chairs which had to be reached by way of stools. Louis was amazed by this unusual décor. "The more I can escape the feeling of gravity, the better I feel," explained Santos.

During that visit, Louis was privileged to be shown the secret plans of the ovoid dirigible balloon which Santos was to pilot the following year, winning the competition and a 100,000 francs prize offered by the Baron Deutsch de la Meurthe. Santos celebrated his victory at Maxim's; and it was in the early hours of the morning that, looking at his pocket watch, he told Louis that it was not very easy for him to time his performances when at the controls of his air-balloon.

An enthusiasm for craftsmanship and a love of sport strengthened the friendship between the two men, and six years after that first meeting, Louis Cartier was there to applaud Santos' record flight of 60 metres. Thirteen months later, on November 12th 1907, when Santos stepped out of his plane after a 220 metres flight, he knew, by looking at his wrist-watch, specially designed by his friend Louis, that he was the holder of the first world record, having travelled the distance in 21 seconds. The first wrist-watch designed by Louis Cartier for Santos-Dumont, is exhibited at the São Paulo Museum in Brazil.

Drawing inspiration from some examples of the eighteenth century – ladies' watches attached to the wrist with a twist of real pearls, precious stones or velvet ribbons – Louis Cartier, combining expert knowledge with meticulous craftsmanship, created the fashion for wrist-watches.

June 1900 saw the birth of the long-awaited child, a girl who was given the name of Anne-Marie. Louis was hoping that motherhood would transform his spoiled wife, and when she asked if he was not too disappointed, he lied, replying, "No."

The planned journey to Venice had to be delayed as a wave of anarchy was sweeping through Italy. King Victor-Emmanuel had come to power after Hubert I's assassination. And, while the nationalist uprising of the Boxers in China continued to make the headlines – attack of the international concession, murder of the German consul! – Russian troops invaded Manchuria and the Boer War pursued its course in South Africa.

For the celebration of her Jubilee, the Jagersfontein leaders had presented Queen Victoria with a 239 carat diamond, named 'Jubilee', of

TOP: *Striped black enamel and gold Peking vanity case with rose-cut diamonds and white enamel garlands. Black enamel and gold chain (1920, Cartier collection).* BOTTOM: *Brooch in Louis XV style, which transforms into a belt-buckle. It is made of blue enamel and rose-cut diamonds on platinum mounted in yellow gold. Blue reindeer belt (1906, Cartier collection).*

unusual shape and so perfectly cut it could be balanced on its point. But since Jagersfontein was at war with Britain, the Jubilee was handed back. Many years later it was Cartier who renegotiated the sale of this, one of the most famous diamonds in the world.

The diamond trade was stirred into action by these world events. Founded in 1867, the two groups, de Beers and Jagersfontein, created in 1900 the diamond syndicate and attempted to stave off falling prices by regulating production according to demand.

The so-called '*Belle Epoque*' was, in fact, a troubled and superficial time; entertainment of all kinds animated Paris, the capital of luxury and pleasure. As during the Second Empire, Paris dictated a lifestyle of pleasant permissiveness, and famous courtesans (like Barucci, La Païva, Schneider and Leblanc before them) were sought after by wealthy men.

Anglomania was more fashionable than ever and high society met at Maxim's. Opened in 1895, the then modest establishment was nothing more than a coaching inn until, sold to a certain Benoit – who kept the previous owner's Christian name – it was refurbished in the modern-style décor so popular at the time, and became a highly fashionable restaurant. At a time when unmarried couples were refused access to fashionable establishments, Maxim's welcomed the businessman or the banker in the company of his latest conquest, and the new owner's idea was to invite each evening a few courtesans looking for protectors. The head waiter, Hugo, dealt with the invitations and it was through him that a rich and lonely man could invite a pretty lady to join him at his table. "Everyone went to Maxim's, except legitimate wives: Prince Galitzine, Prince Karageorgévitch, Prince Georges of Greece and, of course, the Grand-Dukes Cyrille, Boris, Michel, Nicolas, Dimitri and Wladimir, whom one was expected to address by their Christian names. It was also frequented by aristocrats like the Prince of Sagan, the Duc de Morny, famous businessmen like Michelin and Dubonnet, celebrities from the stage like Sarah Bernhardt, Caruso, Chaliapine, Mayol, Gaby Deslys (whose price was 1,000 francs for fifteen minutes), or by pioneers of aviation such as Blériot, Gordon Bennett and Santos-Dumont." *

Peking enamel, gold and diamond cigarette case, Panther motif of pavé set diamonds and onyx (Jeanne Toussaint, 1919. Cartier archives).

Louis Cartier was a regular visitor at Maxim's. He was usually to be seen there at about 1.00 p.m., but rarely at night, and three times a week one of the top salesmen attended. The Cartiers had not forgotten what

* John Laver: *Idees et moeurs au siecle de l'optimisme.*

La belle *Otéro, glamorous rival of Liane de Pougy.*

they had learned during the Second Empire: that, although they had been protected by a princess and helped by an empress, it was largely due to the courtesans, favourites of the wealthy, that their fame had spread. Those courtesans, who sent their protectors to Cartier rather than to other jewellers, were therefore naturally allowed certain privileges.

Louis' younger brother, Pierre, whose business qualities and administrative skills were clearly outstanding, never set foot in Maxim's. His moral strictness and conformity – surprising in so young a man – made him frown upon any type of permissiveness. Louis' youngest brother, on the other hand, was invited there on the day of his 18th birthday.

Hugo – the perfect head waiter – was requested by Louis not to make any reference in his famous note-books to their close relationship, and Louis found in him a man whose discretion matched his own and from whom he learnt much. Indeed, Hugo was a man of exemplary reserve. He had a small notebook in which he noted the courtesans' names; each description was followed by 'R.A.F.' – *rien a faire* – 'nothing doing' which meant that she was already accounted for. Those who were still unattached, he would describe as 'Y.M.C.A.', which had nothing to do with the Young Men's Christian Association, but meant *ya moyen coucher avec* – 'available for bed'.

From Belle Otéro to Liane de Pougy and Gaby Deslys, all the royal favourites frequented No. 13 Rue de la Paix. As Hugo recorded in his book, *Vingt Ans chez Maxims*:

> *Madame Otéro came to dine at Maxim's, covered with precious stones, necklaces, bracelets and rings (on fingers and thumbs); wearing a tiara and crests, she looked like a bedizened goddess. Madame Liane de Pougy's table was empty. Then Madame de Pougy appeared, wearing a perfect black velvet dress, but without a single jewel. The first moment of surprise turned into stupefaction when she stepped aside to reveal her chamber-maid : all her diamonds had been sewn onto the girl's clothes. Grand Duke Wladimir was flabbergasted. Madame de Pougy, accompanied by the Count de T., sat down amidst frantic applause; Madame Otéro rose to leave, and as she passed Madame de Pougy's table she could be heard swearing terribly in Spanish.*

The lives and loves of the courtesan-actresses filled the columns of the international as well as the Parisian newspapers. In 1900, little reverence was shown towards the rich who moved in these circles, and much impertinent irony was directed at the moral standards of the famous.

The unreciprocated passion of Léopold, philanderer King of Belgium, for the opéra dancer, Cléo de Mérode, was the talk of Parisian high society: "Will he have her or won't he?" She refused everything: a

*"La belle des belles",
Liane de Pougy, star of the
Folies-Bergère and darling
of the great. She became
Princess Ghika and ended
her days as a Dominican
nun in Lausanne.*

villa in Ostend, a house in Brussels, jewels; and so the world's first
beauty queen was replaced in the King's heart by Emilienne d'Alençon,
a star of the *Cirque d'Eté*, whose ex-protector, the son of the Duchesse
d'Uzès, had spent on her a fortune of three million gold francs.

It was after an unfortunate mistake made at the expense of the
Marquis de P.'s wife (he himself was in love with Emilienne d'Alençon,

who did not restrict her favours to the King of Belgium), that Louis decided to modify completely his organisation and to initiate a system of customer record cards. The Marquis' wife, enquiring about a late delivery, was told that her ring had in fact been delivered the previous week: "Diamonds and sapphires," specified the assistant, in the absence of the salesman. The Marchioness had been expecting a platinum, diamond and ruby necklace and was highly offended. Louis thus lost the husband's custom.

As jeweller to the rich and royal, and to their wives and mistresses, Louis opened a personal file for each customer, recording details, not only about the man, but also about his wife, his mistress, their respective tastes, and their winter and summer residences. The next step was to invent a secret code, known only to a few, which would allow him to make a check-list without disclosing the real value of any jewel. Remembering Hugo's notebook, Louis invented the *'confitures'* code which can now be revealed as it has been out of use for some years. Thus:

$$
\begin{aligned}
C &= 1 \\
O &= 2 \\
N &= 3 \\
F &= 4 \\
I &= 5 \\
T &= 6 \\
U &= 7 \\
R &= 8 \\
E &= 9 \\
S &= 0
\end{aligned}
$$

The letter K indicated a repetition, thus an object worth 2,200 francs was coded: OK SK. Louis, who often appreciated a practical joke, was not averse to a touch of mystery with the precision of business requirements.

A page from the stock book in March 1911 with the prices entered in code.

2

Three generations of Cartiers met together to celebrate Anne-Marie's first birthday. And François, who was 82, recalled the family gatherings which had taken place during his life-time. When asked by Gaston Worth what the feelings of a great grandfather were, he answered: "Weariness, but also some pride." Looking at Alfred, now sixty, he remembered the party organised for his twenty-second birthday. He could recollect almost every detail of the outfit created by Charles-Frédéric. And the jewellery designed for that occasion was now being worn by his daughter-in-law. Alice was relaxed and smiling. There was not that look of apathy in her eyes which had sometimes worried her relatives. The family doctor had recommended Alice to one of his colleagues, a follower of Charcot. François was hoping that the new treatment would be beneficial to Alice and that she would not suffer the same fate as Antoinette, for whom death came as a deliverance. The old man's eyes shone with pride as he contemplated his grand-children one after the other: Louis, twenty-six years old, whose charm and remarkable talent were now becoming evident; Pierre, twenty-three, shrewd, diplomatic, astute, sometimes even cunning, would join the race of international businessmen; Jacques, eighteen, slender and delicate, a dreamer, teased by his brothers for his vulnerability. But the old man knew that he would discipline himself, and that his pride would ensure he measured up to his brothers; then there was Suzanne, sixteen, fast growing up into a young lady whose charm was already having a considerable effect on Gaston's son, Jacques, who had let it be known that he would be very pleased with such a marriage. "Let's hope," François thought, "that if it does take place, it will be happier than that of Louis and Andrée-Caroline." Indeed, there were many symptoms of that couple's discontent.

Andrée often went to stay in Promenthoux, Switzerland, where her father had built a magnificent residence under the snail and cornflower emblem of the dynasty. The young woman loved to go rowing on the lake, stopping sometimes to contemplate the mountains. François had noticed the hard and nervous manner in which his grandson behaved towards his wife, displaying a mixture of suspicion, anger and concern. Knowing Louis was busy with the growing success of the business, François had not asked him any questions. Indeed, François himself – trained in the school of Maître Picard – was delighted with the success, and the previous week had asked to have a brief look at the famous customers' register. The names he read evoked memories of great moments in his past:

> '*Grand-Duke Paul of Russia: a heart-shaped ring in diamonds, mother-of-pearl binoculars, a Saint Georges medal, a tie-pin with an emerald. Grand-Duke Alexis: a shell comb decorated with roses, a round enamelled lighter, a rock-crystal frame, a monocle. Grand-Duke Wladimir: two diamond and ruby trinkets, a hunter-watch.*'

The Grand-Dukes, who had loved Paris under the Second Empire, were positively infatuated with the Paris of the '*Belle Epoque*'. François, going back over four decades, remembered the Tsar's chancellor, Gortschakoff, the Princes Demidoff – their sense of beauty, their enormous love of pleasure – and all those who, from the Café des Anglais to the shop on the Boulevard des Italiens, had contributed to Cartier's fame.

Other prominent names appeared among the customers at the turn of the century: the Rothschilds (James and Henry), Marie Bonaparte,

King Edward VII visits Cartier, Paris, in 1904.

H.R.H. Prince Djemil Toussoum, a pacha fond of giving choker neck-laces, H.H. Mohamed Schal, the Aga Khan, the Duchess of Marl-borough, Her Majesty the Queen of Spain, who had just given her royal husband a cigarette-case decorated with sapphires.

Then there was the Prince of Wales, who became King at the age of sixty, after Queen Victoria's death, at the beginning of the year. His latest orders included a Chinese-style perfume bottle, a cigarette-case and a magnifying glass decorated with diamonds. His wife, Queen Alexandra, had had an Indian chain made with 94 cabochon emeralds and 71 pearls, which had been enormously admired during a recent reception at Buckingham Palace.

Edward VII's Coronation was to take place in a few months' time, and already several royal families had asked Cartier to design – under pledge of secrecy – some convertible tiaras which had become so fashionable during the previous two years. In all, 27 tiaras were created by Cartier for the Coronation.

Queen Victoria's death meant probable changes in Anglo-French relationships. The love of the ex-Prince of Wales, with his beard and roguish looks, for France was reciprocated, and there was not a single fashionable establishment which had not hosted the King. In fact, despite British isolationism, he had regularly paid secret visits to his favourite European capital, where he always received a welcome which delighted him, from the Chabanais, where he had a room, to the Folies-Bergère or the Moulin-Rouge. From the stage where she danced the quadrille, La Goulue would call out familiarly: "Eh, Wales, you buying the drinks?" And he did.

Edward's imminent accession to the throne meant reconsidering plans which had been discussed with the Worths in 1898, to open a Cartier branch in London where the Worths enjoyed a great success, in particular the patronage of the Royal Family. There had been some approaches already. Some contacts had been made and broken off, but now the possibility of a different trend in British politics rekindled interest in the project. The Worths, as well as the Cartiers, could only benefit from winning more custom in London, especially since certain Eastern potentates preferred the Victorian fog and prudery to the naughty reputation of the French capital.

In the spring of 1902, when it became clear that Suzanne Cartier and Jacques Worth would get married within a few years, Gaston Worth sold Alfred his London property in New Burlington Street, which became the responsibility of Pierre Cartier, then twenty-four years old.

The Paris house supplied the London branch; a workshop and a team of designers were to be established later. When the great grandfather expressed his concern that his son was getting too ambitious, Alfred replied that No. 13 Rue de la Paix had become too small for his two sons, to which François retorted that there were three.

Three sons, whose ancestors had known the hell of the Napoléonic wars, 1848, and the Franco-Prussian war; three sons, upon whom depended the success of the family name, and who were to succeed because they enjoyed a challenge, had good financial sense and possessed a great flair for innovation.

The eldest of the three sons had managed to initiate a new and daring trend in the creation of jewels, clocks and precious objects. Another of the sons was to find a future for himself in the United States, where Theodore Roosevelt had replaced the assassinated MacKinley. The New World was very tempting in Alfred's eyes: the Goulds, the Vanderbilts, the Rockefellers and other multi-millionaires frequented Parisian jewellers when they visited France, but how much more convenient to have a New York establishment! Alfred remarked that his younger son would be twenty-one in 1906, and that he could imagine him by then well settled in New York.

3

During the spring of 1903, Edward VII's visit to France was greeted with open hostility; but after presiding over a military parade, honouring with his presence the Comédie-Française and the Opéra, his cordiality overcame the Parisian anglophobia, and, when the King left France, British isolationism was a thing of the past.

A few weeks after the royal visit, a King's envoy confirmed that the New Burlington Street shop would be granted royal patronage the following year after the ratification of the Entente Cordiale, whose foundations had been laid by Edward VII and President Loubet.

After only one year, the success of Cartier-London was well established. While in Paris, Louis, who had just created three ornaments for the King of Portugal, had had the honour of being awarded his first royal warrant. It was with a mixture of pride and irony that he contemplated his first certificate, visible proof of the success he had promised his wife. It was now possible to foresee that Cartier's fame would, one day, be greater even than that of Worth's! But, despite this, Louis had not managed to regain Andrée's affection. Louis realised that the carefree Andrée of yesterday had been an illusion. In fact, she had never learned how to escape the family cocoon, secretly wishing her husband to be a substitute for the protective family.

Thus, Louis' pursuit of power grew more voracious. He brandished his pride like a shield, tempering himself in a desire to dominate; all the more intense because he knew he was on the winning side, secure in the knowledge that many women found him attractive.

It was at the table of Max Lebaudy, the '*petit-sucrier*', the sugar

Alfred Cartier welcoming His Majesty Edward VII to Rue de la Paix (cartoon by Sem).

millionaire, son of Jules, the king of speculators, who had made 53 million francs within days when the General Union had crashed in 1882 and ruined thousands of investors, that Louis first encountered the blue eyes of a young lady accompanying the Marquis de Q. She was superbly elegant, wearing beautiful jewels, and there was an intensity in her gaze which gave character to her face, with its aquiline nose and witty mouth. Louis could not say precisely whether she was beautiful or simply attractive. Noting her reserved manner, he concluded that she was not a *demi-mondaine*.

The next day he approached Hugo who told him that the young woman, who was barely twenty, was indeed the Marquis de Q.'s mistress, and that she had left her parents – Belgian shopkeepers – for him. Officially, the young Jeanne Toussaint was living with her older sister, who had found her prosperous employment, but unofficially, she shared the Marquis de Q.'s pleasant life. The Marquis was a close friend of Etienne Balsan, at whose house Jeanne met Gabrielle Chanel, later to become her devoted friend.

When he returned to Maxim's, Louis was hoping to see the Marquis' lady companion again at Max Lebaudy's table, but only the '*petit-sucrier*' was sitting there, surrounded by women to whom he was merrily recounting the mad venture of his brother Jacques, who had gone to conquer the desert, determined to be declared Emperor of the Sahara.

Gossip nourished the customers at Maxim's. Amidst the bright lights, the background laughter, the popping of champagne corks and the languourous music of the violins (the Tzigane with his red brandenburg jacket and waxed moustache was all the rage in the capital), people at Grand-Duke Wladimir's table were talking about the assassination of King Alexander and Queen Draga of Serbia, who had been stabbed in their bed. The Obrenovitch dynasty was to be succeeded by that of the Karageorgevitchs.

Louis, sitting at the Grand-Duke's table, was listening inattentively to Zoulianov worrying about the political situation in the Far East where Japan was proving a formidable opponent for the Russian navy. Seeing a new customer, the Marquis de Pracomtal, he left the table to inquire further about the Marquis de Q. Pracomtal confirmed that the Marquis travelled for business and for pleasure, that he seldom stayed in Paris, and that his companion always went with him. "Too bad," thought Louis, "she really had beautiful eyes."

The '*petit-sucrier*', completely drunk, was shouting that his brother

Her Majesty Victoria Eugénia, Queen of Spain.

would soon be emperor. Louis, profoundly weary, left the party of revellers.

4

François heard about Princess Mathilde's death with deep emotion. "She was just one year younger than me," he said, "I have a feeling that I shall follow her soon."

He recalled the past, remembering the fascinating personality of the woman whose intellectual eclecticism had ruled Paris for several decades. Maupassant could come to her house drunk as a lord and she would forgive him everything for the sake of his creative talent. François also remembered the masterful way in which she despised trivia and her enthusiasm for creative artists, whether writers, painters, sculptors or jewellers.

François had guessed right – he was to die a short time after his benefactress.

At the end of May, Princess Mathilde's jewel collection was put up for sale. The sale lasted nine days, and the collection of 319 items included jewels, grandfather clocks, small clocks, watches, perfume bottles and various items of jewellery. The Princess' collection also entailed, among other treasures, jewels given by Napoléon III, King Victor-Emmanuel II, pearls presented by the Queen of Westphalia and Queen Sophie of the Netherlands.

Louis would often evoke with exceptional tenderness memories of his grandfather, sadly deploring the fact that the old man had not had the pleasure of attending the celebrations organised for the Entente Cordiale, and of seeing the Rue de la Paix bedecked with French and British flags. Edward VII and his entourage had graced with their presence a reception organised at the Worth salons. Two months after the Entente Cordiale, Edward VII granted Louis the royal warrant and towards the end of 1904 a third warrant was granted by the Spanish Royal Family.

Because of the unrest prevalent at the time in Russia, Louis decided to postpone a visit to Saint Petersburg, where he had hoped to open a branch, although some of his Russian clients had tried to dissuade him. The military failure of the Allies was growing, and the navy and army were both committed against the Japanese forces. As a result, some extremely wealthy Russians were beginning to leave the country, to settle in France for good.

Among the most famous was Princess Lobanoff of Rostoff, fabulously wealthy, beautiful, widowed at twenty. The highly attractive Princess never forgot to remind people that she was a Doldorouky, a descendant of the morganatic marriage between Alexander III and Catherine Michailovna – the same romantic Katia who was later to inspire novelists and film-makers.

The Princess had just bought a town-house in the Avenue Raphaël. She had also had a residence built in Lausanne, and another in Menton, and she had told Louis: "If Russia becomes acceptable again, I shall go back and stay a while in order to shock the Imperial court with my bad manners!" Indeed, Louis knew how terribly boring the Tsarist court had become: Nicolas' German wife, who hated ostentation, had suppressed all pomp, forcing the Tsar to leave the Great Palace (considered too sumptuous) for the Alexander Palace. In contrast, Princess

A diamond choker necklace, mounted in platinum (1905).

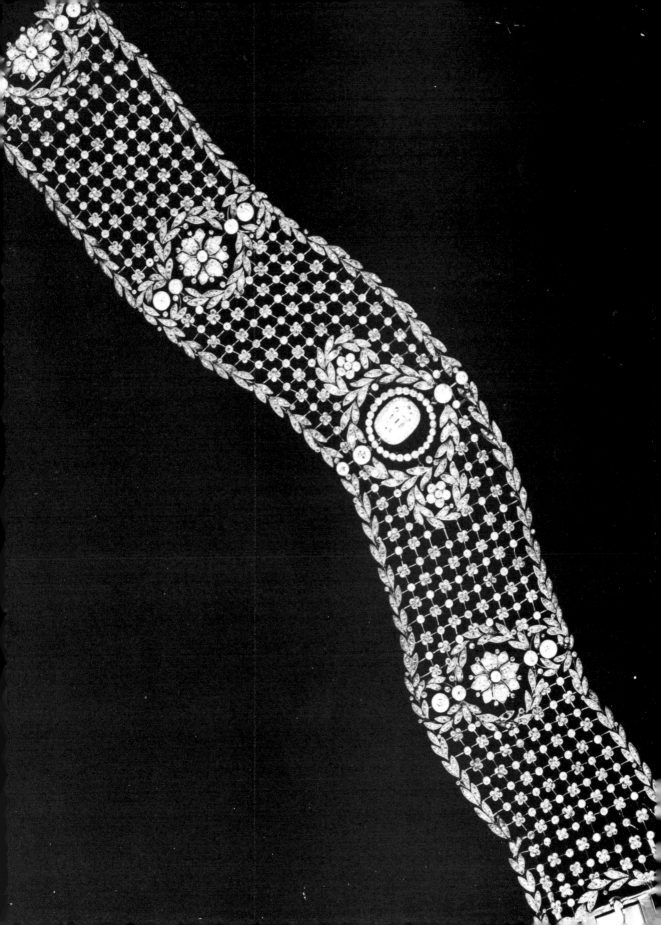

Lobanoff, on her European tours, was always followed by a retinue of twenty people, and by five trunks containing her jewels. Louis was asked to advise the Princess who wanted to have some old jewels modernised – many of them originally owned by Alexander II – and to create for her a collection of modern pieces. "A Russian proverb, my dear friend, land and jewels never betray one."

In her residence in Lausanne, the Princess had a sort of bunker built in the basement. In it, she hid show cases operated by a mechanism which lifted some slats of exotic wood, revealing to the few visitors allowed to comtemplate them, an amazing display of precious stones and real pearls. She would stand there, on her own, admiring her treasures, and, during one of Louis' visits to Switzerland, she told him: "When I die, all these treasures will be dispersed; I should like you to be the valuer for the sale. You must promise me!" Louis promised.

It was through the Princess (nicknamed by him 'The Princess with the jewel') that Louis was introduced to the Count de M., married to one of the prettiest women in Europe. He was a plenipotentiary attached to the Russian court, and wanted to give his wife a tiara embellished with diamonds and other gems which had belonged to his ancestors. The Countess chose a model with 300 diamonds, 37 rose-cut 7.60 carat diamonds and 115 rose-cut 21 carat diamonds. The Count's jewel collection could not provide all the gems, but the Countess remembered she had been given a decoration by the Sultan Abdul-Hamid, normally reserved for diplomats' wives. It was very unlikely that the decoration would contain any diamonds. However, Louis asked the Count to show him the decoration. To their astonishment, they realised that the Sultan had, indeed, given a diamond decoration of exceptional quality and the gems were re-cut and re-set onto a tiara, and delivered to Saint Petersburg in 1905.

In 1906, Alfred Cartier, having just bought a town-house in Rue de Pomereu, decided to give up his administrative functions; the 1898 company was dissolved and the two sons, Louis and Pierre, became associates in a new company called *Cartier Frères*.

Much to his older brother's anger, Pierre went to Saint Petersburg to present an exhibition of recent creations, which was a great success. He was still in favour of setting up branches in Russia, whereas Louis had abandoned the idea, arguing that Fabergé was quite sufficient for the requirements of Tsar and Court. In his opinion it was better to have two exhibitions each year, with the possibility of coming to some agree-

1928 work-shop drawing of ceremonial necklace created for the Maharajah of Patiala. In the centre is the 234 carat De Beers diamond (Cartier archives).
OVERLEAF, LEFT: *Jade screen clock with coral godruns and sphere. Surround of black enamel and gold. Numerals and hands of rose-cut diamonds.*
OVERLEAF, RIGHT: *The reverse side of the same clock showing a black enamel dragon which hides the method of motivating the hands (1925, Cartier collection).*

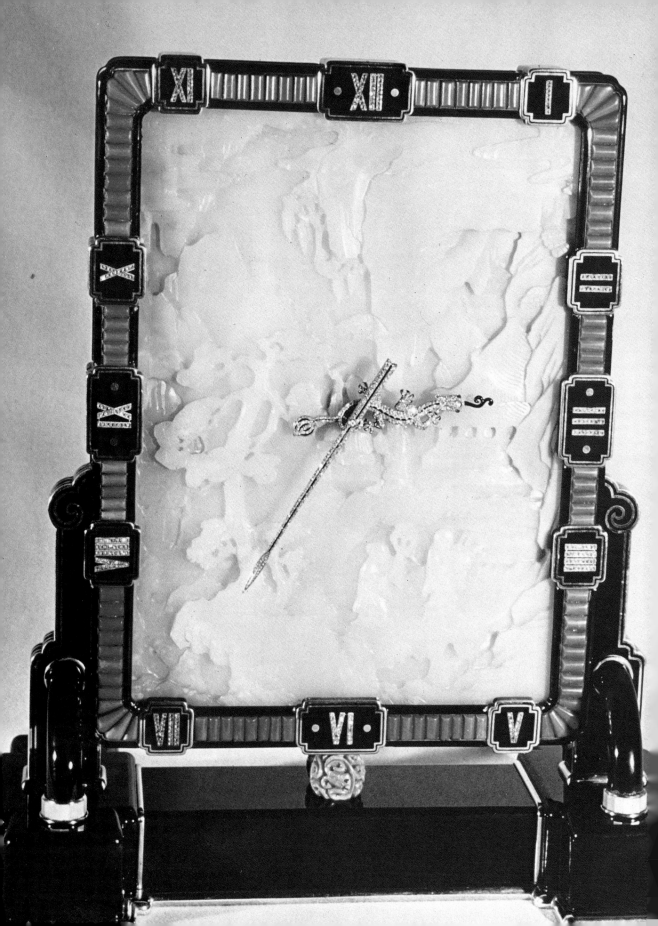

ment with one of the Russian luxury shops. Besides, the gravity of the international situation called for caution: there was unrest in the Balkans, and although Wilhelm II's Moroccan claims had been dismissed at the Algeciras Conference, not only Russia but most of Europe was unsettled. Yet the Parisians of the *Belle Epoque* made it a point of honour not to allow anything to spoil, even slightly, their pleasant way of life.

It was through the Marquis de Montesquiou that Louis met Collette, wife of the writer Willy, and Polaire, the excited and exciting Polaire, of whom Jean Lorrain said that she had "a painfully narrow waist (42 cm), incredibly tiny, so tiny it might snap in her frighteningly narrow bodice, Polaire with her large voracious mouth, with rings under her huge eyes, shadowed and bruised, the incadescent gaze, the wild black hair, the phosphorous and burning red face of a Ghoul and a Salome."

The tender friendship between Colette and Polaire fascinated *Tout-Paris*; the two women could often be seen tenderly intertwined, skating at the *Palais de Glace*. It suited Collette quite well to be the object of so much scandalous gossip.

With her strong Burgundian accent, Colette asked Louis to explain to her the world of precious stones. Like many women, she had a predilection for emeralds, and Louis corroborated the fact that the emerald was indeed a feminine stone, the stone of hope and of lovers; that it was supposed to protect the eyes (hence Caesar and Anthony's engraved emerald monocles). After Anthony, he went on to mention Cleopatra and the mines in Upper Egypt which had once belonged to the seductress, and had been worked in 2500 BC, and which were re-opened in 1818 by order of the Viceroy of Egypt. "But," explained Louis, "Egyptian emeralds are pale, often opaque, and never equal the South American gems of which the most remarkable are to be found in Columbia. Rhodesia and Siberia produced some very fine examples too," he added.

Colette questioned him further, and Louis told her about the aquamarine – a beryl like the emerald – the sailors' stone, the legend maintaining that aquamarines belonged once to the mermaids' treasure and were brought by them from the depths of the sea.

Gold vanity case with black enamel Peking décor, inlay of red enamel with black enamel dragon, with corners of rose-cut pavé diamonds on platinum. Thumb-piece is of baton diamonds (1930).

Polaire explained her distrust of opals, and Louis told how, despite the fear Western women had of its evil influence, in the Orient it was regarded as a talisman because it had been blessed by Vichnu, Brahma and Civa. He recounted the legend: how the three gods, in love with the same woman, saw their beloved one turned into a ghost by the Eternal

One, and each gave her his own colour: Brahma blue, Vichnu gold, Civa red. Transformed into an iredescent cloud, swept along by the winds, the ghost was one day materialised into opal by the clemency of the god of gods.

Louis then described at length the range of the reds, from the violet-red of the almandine – the Crusaders' stone – to the purple-pink of the rhodolite; he expressed his love for the yellow-brown citrine, which, like rock-crystal, belongs to the quartz family, the grey-blue-green colour of the falcon's eye, the blue-brown of the transanite (belonging to the Jade family) and the mica green of the aventurine. Colette jotted down notes, her black vivacious eyes shining behind the thick eyelashes, her small plump hands running nervously through the thick curly hair.

They were to meet often.

Louis was amazed by the young woman's intellectual curiosity. She was two years older than him and he admired her culture, her powers of observation, her love of life and her passion for animals. There was a trace of provincialism in her strong desire to defy convention which he found moving. Colette was very well informed about all the scandalous love affairs. She confirmed the fact that King Léopold had failed to seduce Cléo de Mérode and that he had consoled himself with Emilienne d'Alençon, whose zest for life Colette greatly appreciated. Emilienne d'Alençon was to declare later: "I have known so many kings, including Léopold; the only thing he wanted was to go unnoticed; to fry his own eggs was the height of happiness for him."

Louis saw Colette's stage debut in a pantomime written by Missy de Belboeuf, the Duke de Morny's scandalous sister whom Louis himself had once advised against an over-masculine signet ring. The performance had to be stopped. Colette, with naked thighs, and Missy, dressed as a man on stage as in everyday life, were forced to flee in order to escape the hostility of the audience who showered the stage with opera glasses, shoes and feather-boas.

Colette had a sense of humour but she was obstinate too. For some time she carried on acting in music halls before deciding to devote herself to literature. When *Gigi* was published in 1920, Colette sent Louis a copy with a dedication which paid tribute to the man who had revealed to her the world of precious stones – "those daughters of fire and water" – the man without whom the jewel lesson given by Aunt Léa to Gigi could never have been so accurate, so relevant.

On the 12th July 1906, three chambers of appeal met and announced the annulment of the verdict of the Court of Rennes in 1899, and the rehabilitation of Colonel Dreyfus, declaring that the judgment had been mistaken. "It had taken more than twelve years to obtain justice from that unruly republic when prejudices and passions were rife, but at last it had been achieved," the American writer, William Shirer, was later to comment. But Paris had other concerns, the main one being the Russian art exhibition organised by Serge de Diaghilev, under the patronage of the Countess Greffulhe, one of Louis' good customers. She had invited him and Louis was delighted with the exhibition. "All forms of artistic expression will find a source of inspiration here," he said to Boni de Castellane.

Boni de Castellane, whose American wife had left him at the beginning of the year to go back to her family with their three children, heard in November that his divorce had been granted. The Goulds had eventually become tired of Boni's follies. The insolence, however aristocratic, of a man who says that, before sending invitations, one should first open one's windows and throw away all one's money, was bound in the end to exasperate his puritanical American wife. Boni had ostentatiously erected a palace of pink marble on the Avenue du Bois, had bought a yacht with a crew of 100 men, and two castles, including Madame de Sévigné's in Grignan.

For the house-warming party at No. 50 Avenue du Bois, 250 guests, dressed as flowers, had been invited, but that reception was less sumptuous than the one when Boni had engaged 200 musicians and 600 specially-liveried servants to serve and entertain the cream of the *Tout-Paris*. The gardens were illuminated by 80,000 Chinese lanterns. As forecast by the Baron de Rothschild – cruelly nicknamed 'Haround-al-Rothschild' by Boni – fortune would not smile forever on the same man.

But Boni, fallen from his pedestal, stripped of his dollars, continued to observe Parisian society, delighted by his misfortune, in the same ironical and haughty manner.

Years later, it became clear that the extravagant Boni was also a man of unerring taste. Specialising as an art dealer, he managed to pay back debts he had incurred with antique dealers and art galleries when he had furnished his numerous residences. Boni showed that he had been more than a mere reveller; in fact, he had been a precursor: "In the parties he organised as well as in the furnishing of his houses, he had suggested models in complete opposition to the adulterated aesthetics of the end of the century," stated J. Castenet.

"In the end, I did teach a fair bit to those New World multi-millionaires," Boni said to Louis. But he was not quite correct since he did not know (or pretended not to know) that some Americans, fully aware of artistic changes, had chosen to stay in Paris in order to express themselves freely. Among them, Gertrude Stein who was later to contribute to the success of '*Les Fauves*'; it was Gertrude, leader of the American colony, who introduced the Harjès to the Cartiers.

The Harjès were an unusual family. Their ancestors, of German origin, had gone to seek fortune in America and returned, enormously wealthy, to make their home in Paris, in a sumptuous town-house situated at the corner of the Avenue Henri-Martin and Rue de la Pompe, bequeathed in 1974 to the American Hospital. Brought up as Americans, the Harjès daughters reserved several acres on the western side of the estate for growing maize, indispensable, they said, for their nutritional balances.

Completely by chance, the youngest of the Cartier sons was invited to go to the Avenue Henri-Martin, to discuss the reworking of a family jewel. That meeting was the beginning of a romance which led some years later to the marriage of Jacques Cartier and Nelly Harjès.

The following year, *Boris Godounov* was given a triumphant welcome in Paris. The success enjoyed by Diaghilev's dancers confirmed the wise judgment of the Countess Greffuhle and of the Grand Duchess Maria Pawlowna, wife of Grand Duke Wladimir, a patron of the man known as 'Chinchilla' because of the heavy white streak in his thick dark hair. The aesthetic Grand Duke Wladimir was particularly fond of Louis' creations, and it was through his patronage that Louis was awarded the royal warrant of the Russian court.

The hero of *Boris Godounov*, Chaliapine, the singer with the golden voice, became a close friend of Louis Cartier, and the latter spent several summers at his residence in Saint-Jean-de-Luz. When Chaliapine expressed interest in learning about the various stages involved in the creation of a jewel, Louis was delighted to oblige.

Leading his guest across the floor covered with honeycombed wicker trays, Louis showed the singer round his workshops. The workers, wearing shorts under their white overalls and leather aprons with a large pocket used to gather gold filings, were busy, seated at semi-circular work-benches shaped to accommodate the curve of the body.

Each worker was accountable for the weight of gold he had been given; the wicker trays were regularly removed, the filings collected and sent to be melted down. Infinitesimal particles of gold could stick to the workers' hands, so there were even filters in the washbasins.

How was a jewel created? To begin with, the designer produced a drawing, and then, in 45% of cases, the drawing was subjected to various changes – designers might well be poets but the limitations of technical feasibility had to be considered. The selling price, too, could be a factor. Finally, the drawing, once authorised, was passed to a craftsman whose task it was to create a wax or metal model.

Was a model always necessary? Made either out of ordinary metal (lead or copper) for tiaras, or out of wax for large items, the model was indispensable when the chosen jewel was to include precious stones belonging to the customer. The estimated price of the missing stones was calculated according to the number of empty spaces. If a model was not necessary, the process was as follows: the selection of a drawing, costing, authorisation and then the execution by the worker. The jewel was created in total secrecy once it had been conceived with the help of the customer and his jeweller, the designer and his craftsmen.

Chaliapine told Louis how delighted he had been with his lesson in practical jewellery. Louis then recalled the time when his father had given Léonide Leblanc and other *émigrés* a lecture on mineralogy on the boat bringing them back to France. He was then full of hope, with the commission he had realised from the sale of Giula Beneni's jewels. Giula Beneni, known as La Barruci, had been the favourite of the rich before she died of consumption during the seige of Paris.

The success which had followed the defeat of 1870 had been spectacular enough to turn the heads of those less ambitious than Louis (he had a royal warrant from Her Majesty Queen Alexandra and another from the Court of Siam), but he did feel intoxicated by his early success in being requested by Sultan Abdul-Hamid II to visit Istanbul to value his jewels.

Louis had hesitated before accepting the Sultan's invitation as the Balkans were experiencing deep political unrest, but he had finally agreed a few days after his sister Suzanne's marriage to Jacques Worth. A particularly violent quarrel with his wife had helped him to make up his mind. He thought the journey to Turkey would be beneficial, and that in unfamiliar surroundings, he would be able to take stock of the situation.

He tried to understand his wife's ambiguous words: "I would have liked to have had something to desire!" but without success. In fact, Andrée was still uncommitted to a marriage that she had, nonetheless, desired. He was convinced that, as a young romantic girl, she had loved him in the early years, but that she was still hurt, nine years later, by the haste displayed by both families, rushing into the marriage as though they were concluding a business deal. And rather than trying to soothe her with tender words, Louis had proudly, but mistakenly, quoted figures to underline his prodigious success. From the way she had stared at him at that moment, he knew that she had ceased to love him and realised that they could not go on hurting each other in this way.

Then, there was Anne-Marie, their seven-year-old daughter; the little girl was nearly as disconcerting as her mother. Her behaviour indicated that she had an unusual personality; she was clever but capricious, and incredibly possessive. All through her early childhood, she had suffered from fits which left her exhausted for several hours. There was sometimes a look in the child's eyes similar to that in Alice's eyes (and, in the past, Antoinette Cartier's).

Louis remembered, too, his grandfather's distress when he had once mentioned the word 'curse'.

During that journey to Turkey, only a few close friends knew of the painful moments as he tried to look back on his life – introspection, worries, decisions . . . After his return from Istanbul, Louis became more secretive than ever, and his behaviour was sometimes tinged with an arrogance which surprised even those who thought they knew him well.

Shortly afterwards, in Promenthoux, displaying considerable brilliance, he enthralled the Worths and their guests with a description of his journey to Turkey, mentioning with some self-satisfaction the marks of esteem displayed by Abdul-Hamid II and his retinue, and enthusiastically depicting the fabulous riches accumulated by the Sultan, including the famous Blue Diamond of the Golden Fleece.

Later, Louis would often tell the legend of the '*Bleu de France*' to important customers, but never with such spirit as on this occasion, for he had spotted and attracted the attention of a very pretty woman, one of Jean-Philippe's guests. Was Andrée-Caroline aware of his interest, and was she secretly hurt by it?

Louis continued with his story, explaining how the Blue Diamond had been sold to Louis XIV by the dealer-explorer, Tavernier. The diamond, cut in the Indian fashion, then weighed 110.5 carats; re-cut in a heart shape, the '*Bleu de France*' weighed 44 carats and was presented to Madame de Montespan. Louis XV then ordered that the Blue Diamond be set next to the ruby, *Côte de Bretagne*, on the Golden Fleece.

Then came the Revolution and in 1791, the National Assembly drew up an inventory of the crown jewels and decided to sell them by auction. The Legislative Assembly agreed, but during the nights of the 11th, 12th, 13th and 14th September, a gang of thieves, led by an ex-prisoner, ransacked the royal '*garde-meubles*'. On the 15th September, following a fight among the thieves, a patrol arrested some of them and recovered many jewels and precious objects, but the majority, including the Blue Diamond, had disappeared.

At that point in the story, Louis never failed to stress how the ransacking of the '*garde-meubles*' had had very serious political consequences, the incident being exploited by the Montagnards and the Girondins, who accused each other. Marat claimed that the thieves had been paid by the aristocrats, and in the Memorial de Sainte-Hélène, Las Cases said that Napoléon himself believed that a member of the National Convention, Billaud-Varenne, had financed the Brunswick retreat with the stolen jewels. And the same reason was given to explain Dumouriez's victory at Valmy.

The *Bleu de France* reappeared (after many mysterious deals and unknown journeys) worn by the Queen of Spain, Maria-Luisa, as a pendant, and seen in the painting by Goya. It was later seen in the Netherlands where a lapidary, Wilhelm Fals, gave it its present form. The diamond was stolen by Fals' son, who took it to London to sell. He later committed suicide.

In 1830, the London banker, Hope, bought the Blue Diamond for $90,000, gave it its ultimate name and died suddenly shortly afterwards. His nephew, Henry Thomas, who inherited it, went bankrupt and was abandoned by his wife.

The Hope collection went into liquidation. The jewel's new buyer killed himself, and the Russian, Kamitowski, who bought it afterwards, died some months later as the result of a wound. The dancer who had been given the diamond by her wealthy protector was shot, and the dealer who in turn bought it, was drowned with his family off Gibraltar. Montharides, a broker, who had negotiated the purchase of the diamond on behalf of Abdul-Hamid II, fell from the top of a cliff with his wife and son.

The evil reputation of the Hope Diamond was by now firmly established. It was after buying it from Tavernier that Louis XIV met with his first military defeats, that his favourite grandson, the Duc de Bourgogne died, that Jean-Baptiste Tavernier himself met with a horrible death in Russia, torn to pieces by hungry wolves. Marie-Antoinette and Louis XVI, who had both worn the diamond, were guillotined.

The guests asked many questions: was Abdul-Hamid II not frightened by the evil legend? Louis answered that if the Sultan decided to part with the jewel it would be for financial reasons, and in that case, he himself would be delighted to buy it. When asked whether he felt any apprehension, he retorted that he had decided, once and for all, never to believe in curses, sorcery or witchcraft.

That same evening Andrée-Caroline told him of her decision that they should no longer live together. She was to live with her father either in Promenthoux or in Paris, according to the time of year. She would allow Louis to institute divorce proceedings, and he could see his daughter whenever he wanted. After a discussion with his father-in-law, who advised caution and delay, Louis decided to leave Promenthoux the following day.

That night he was involved in a motor accident on the edge of Lac Léman, from which he was to spend several weeks convalescing. Louis

Cartier, New York (founded in 1908).

was not alone in the wreck which was discovered in the early hours of the morning by nearby residents, who also dragged from the car an unconscious, but extremely pretty young woman. She was the wife of a well-known Parisian personality. The *affaire* created a scandal which was well documented by the press.

The Worth family were disconcerted by the incomprehensible attitude of 'this charming Louis', but immediately upon his return to France, the eldest Cartier brother instructed his lawyers to begin divorce proceedings.

Louis decided to accompany his brother, Pierre, to America, together with Jules Glaezner, nephew of the famous art dealer from the Rue Scribe, who had been living in France for the past three years. Jules had little taste for his uncle's business, but a passion for jewellery which he hoped to convince his parents to allow him to pursue. In fact, Jules, a contemporary of Pierre, had already secretly initiated himself into Cartier both in Paris and London, and Louis was convinced that he would prove a first-class recruit. With Jules' American connections, and his eventual and far-from-negligible financial assistance, there remained only to find premises suitable and worthy of the New York establishment of the great House of Cartier.

5

After a crossing, which lasted ten days, the two brothers first discovered the port of New York, and then the colourful noisy streets, with horse-mounted policemen next to bicycles and tricycles, the ringing of copper bells on red fire-engines, the horns of the cars – mainly Daimlers – the thundering noise of the elevated railway, the clattering of horses' hooves pulling carts and cabs, the bells and the roaring of buses. It was all breath-taking. The foreignness of the surroundings was accentuated by the astonishing variety of architectural styles: a mixture of Georgian brown-stones with external stairs decorated with peristyles and porticos, bay copings with prominent lintels, enormous buildings in Renaissance or Greek style with a profusion of marble columns, the Gothic style of Saint Patrick's Cathedral, the gigantic height of the first sky-scrapers (most of them in the Florentine Renaissance style, ornamented with pilasters and cornices); the visitor's initial astonishment invariably turned to delight.

Jules Glaenzer's family, of Alsatian origin, had become rich doing interior designing for businessmen on Broadway, and now lived in the multi-millionnaires' street, Fifth Avenue. Jules turned out to be a very capable guide, skilfully exploiting the Cartier brothers' visit with an eye to the establishment of an American branch. By word of mouth, the news spread that the men whom Edward VII had called the kings of the jewellers, because they were the jewellers of kings, were not mere shopkeepers, but artistic men with highly cultured minds.

In the year 1908, New York high society, tired of living on Fifth Avenue, had moved to Central Park where some magnificent houses were built in pseudo-Renaissance or in Greek style. The Vanderbilts and the Whitneys had led the way, and were followed by the gentry. This north-bound movement promised to make premises available should the establishment of Cartier in New York prove possible.

The two brothers were invited by the most famous families of that 'society' which, according to the snobs of the time, could not include more than four hundred famous people worthy of the name – the famous '400'. They were surprised at the almost incoherent sumptuousness which ruled the interior design of the houses where all styles co-existed, from the Baroque to the Egyptian.

The famous Morgan himself – Morgan senior – invited Louis to see his unusual library next to his house, situated at the corner of 36th Street and Madison Avenue. (During each of his visits to the United States, Louis returned to the stately XVIth century Renaissance building and admired the pure façade of Tennessee marble.)

Entered through a hall made out of polychrome marble, John Pierpoint Morgan's library contained the treasures accumulated by the old financier in the course of a double life as businessman and expert art collector. He was proud of his Gainsborough, Rembrandt, Poussin, Dürer and Brueghel, as well as of his XIVth and XVth century enamels and jewellery; he was extremely fond of his sculpted marble from the Florentine school, but the library was his greatest pride. It contained over a million rare books; in addition to first editions and autographed manuscripts by Milton, Lamartine, Dickens and Balzac, one could admire incunabula, Greek papyrus, Assyrian tablets, Catherine of Clèves' Book of Hours and a Gutenberg Bible.

It was in John Pierpoint Morgan's library that Louis' vocation for collecting was awakened, and until his death in 1913, the old financier was always very happy to advise him.

Was Louis tempted, during that first visit, to settle in America? He was undeniably attracted and, although he had said on several occasions that he did not want to become an expatriate, he was, for a moment, tempted to leave Paris to Pierre, to establish Jacques in London, and to come to live here, a new and different man. His emotional confusion made him vulnerable to New York, but during a reception he realised he would find it very difficult to adapt to the American way of life. For instance, Louis had been asked about the tragic deaths of the painter Steinheil and his mother, found dead in their town-house, while Meg was discovered tied up and unconscious in another room. With his usual verve, Louis described the background of the Félix Faure affair, and how the President had died the most exquisite of deaths in the arms of the seductive Meg. A slight uneasiness among the audience reminded him of the Anglo-Saxon prudery often mentioned by his grandfather, and which he had then thought somewhat amusing. Pierre skilfully managed to save the situation by evoking the libertine past of a country influence by the permissiveness of the eighteenth century. Louis, somewhat humiliated, suddenly felt homesick.

Premises at 712 Fifth Avenue were expected to be available within a few weeks, and Pierre was to stay to prepare a plan of action. He was especially keen to prolong his stay in New York as there was the prospect of an *affaire* with Elma Rumsey, the daughter of a powerful financier.

On the boat taking him back to France, Louis thought of his impending divorce, at a time when his brothers would soon be getting married: Pierre to Elma, whose family was linked to the powerful Morgans, and the younger to the American girl with the maize field.

Back in the Rue de la Paix, he found that his customers were following very closely the political situation in Central Europe: the overthrow of Abdul-Hamid II by the Young Turks (the Hope's curse, he thought), Austria's annexation of Bosnia-Herzegovina, and Bulgaria's proclamation of independence; political unrest was growing in Russia where the Tsar and Tsarina lived isolated in their palace of Tsarkoie Selo, under the domination of Rasputin, the licentious monk.

In France, the ruling class feared the vote on a motion concerning income tax, a bill similar to the established British income tax: 3% on income, 4% on acquired wealth. Louis realised that the French were less worried by the international situation than the Americans and other cosmopolitan customers.

While in the United States Louis had heard talk of war or revolution and, while still following the family tradition, he tried to become less apolitical and keep a closer watch on the outside world. The question of social demands was not underestimated although the workers employed in the jewellery sector, with their very high salaries, were not likely to go on strike like the miners, wine-workers or railwaymen. It was during this uncertain period that Louis considered the creation of a mutual insurance company to which his workers would have to contribute only a very small share, a project that came into operation after the First World War.

Despite the threatening world situation and social unrest, business had never been so flourishing. The five workshops were overwhelmed with orders, as was Jaeger who had moved into a series of small maids' rooms in the Rue de Reaumur. Louis had managed to convince the Alsatian to work exclusively for him, and all Jaeger's mechanisms for watches, chatelaines and clocks were now finished by jewellers working to sketches drawn by Louis or by designers, most of whom had won the '*Arts Décoratifs*' or '*Ville de Paris*' prizes.

It was in 1909 that Louis engaged Charles Jacqueau, his favourite designer for many years, who came straight from '*Arts Décoratifs*' and

was to accompany him on most of his journeys "in order not to waste any time, and to work together on ideas the moment they come to mind."

Louis always used to carry in the right hand pocket of his jacket a notebook in which he would jot down ideas, record details or draw a sketch with his thick rubber pen; he would then show this to his designer who, from that original, would draw a rough sketch, then another increasingly elaborate piece of work executed in gouache until, once it had been perfected, Louis would give his approval and sign '*Bon à executer*' (Go ahead) in his own hand.

An idea was sometimes inspired by a small detail. For example, in the thirties, while staying in Biarritz, Louis had been watching a joiner work with a plane. Taking out his note-book, he did a very rough sketch, then, turning to his assistant and picking up some woodshavings, he stretched them, dropped them and said, tapping his note-book: "We will design curled necklaces and bracelets like goldshavings." The following year, the workshops produced the first curled bracelet.

From 1910, Louis's awareness that the world of art was witnessing profound changes, spurred him into a frenzy of creative activity. He guided his assistants towards the creation not only of jewels but also of watches, small clocks and other precious objects, made with semi-precious stones in a multitude of colours which he would have found unacceptable five years earlier. It was the influence of the *Ballets Russes*, "that gust of fresh air from the Steppes coming suddenly to cool us, interrupting our sleep with its confused dreams." Throughout the ballet season, Louis went frequently to the Châtelet to watch Pavlova and Nijinsky, but also to immerse himself in the colours of Bakst's costumes and sets, enchanted by the originality of the combination of shapes and colours.

He tried to share his enthusiasm with Jean-Philippe – their friendship had not suffered in any way because of his divorce – but, unlike his ex-associate and friend Paul Poiret, the couturier remained completely unmoved, refusing to adopt the new style where everything became colour and movement.

Pavlova's art would not therefore have attracted Jean-Philippe, who for some time now had been worshipping the Oriental dancer, Greta MacLeod, ex-wife of a Dutch soldier with whom she had lived in India, and who, in the spring of 1905, was introduced to the Parisian public as Mata-Hari. Jean-Philippe had organised several garden parties at

The Rue de la Paix in 1910.

Suresnes where the dancer and her five musicians were the main attraction, but the evocation of the sacred Hindu dances had left Louis completely cold: "She's got a body to seduce a saint, and when she falls naked into her partners' arms, I'd quite like to be in their place; but my admiration stops there. It is nothing more than a mixture of eroticism and a touch of fake Orientalism; that's as far as Mata-Hari's art goes," Louis said in a letter addressed to the Count de M., unaware that his judgement would be endorsed by the famous Antoine, who, after engaging Mata-Hari in 1913, was forced to terminate her contract as she was such a bad dancer. He had to pay her an indemnity of 40,000 francs.

Jean-Philippe Worth wished he had listened to Louis' advice. The following year Paul Poiret decided that legs would be confined and the bust free. He dispensed with corsets, frills and flounces, and used materials with strong colours to create for the Parisian Sheherazade a 'One Thousand and One Nights' fashion, which became highly popular among elegant women, infatuated with Monsieur Poiret's Turkish style. The vogue created by Poiret was at its height when he asked the designer, Iribe, to produce a luxurious catalogue presenting his latest creations, which was sent to leaders and experts the world over – only the Queen of England sent it back.

The hats, ornamented with aigrettes and flowers, had been replaced by tight turbans, which made the face seem small, the new look accentuated by the red cheekbones and by the kohl which enlarged the eyes – quite a revolution when one remembers that until then make-up was only used by courtesans.

Etienne Balsan, an old friend, had allowed Gabrielle Chanel to use his flat in Avenue Malesherbes, to make hats in strikingly restrained style for society women. A new type of woman was emerging, and Jean-Philippe was disappointed not to have foreseen the metamorphosis, especially since Paul Poiret's remarkable success had taken away many of his customers.

However, in London some hats still looked like elaborate cakes, as Louis was able to see for himself when he met Gaby Deslys in the foyer of the Ritz Hotel. Singer, dancer and actress, Gaby Deslys, whose aim was luxury rather than fame, was a well-known *demi-mondaine*, a new type marking the transition between the cocotte of 1900 and the vamp of the thirties; she did not possess any real talent and did not care. Since 1904, she had managed to create a style, which was later to be imitated by Mistinguett, surprising her audiences with the profusion of her

TOP: *Coral and diamond Art Deco bracelet in a platinum mount (1922, Cartier collection).*
BOTTOM: *Bracelet-watch with almond-shaped movement. Case pavé set with diamond (1925).*
OVERLEAF, LEFT: *Work-shop design of emerald, pearl and diamond head-dress created for the Maharajah of Kapurthala (1925, Cartier archives).*
OVERLEAF, RIGHT: *Mystery Clock of rock-crystal, gold and black enamel with faceted coral surround. Base is of onyx, coral and yellow gold. The hands and numerals are rose-cut diamonds in platinum (1927, Cartier collection).*

feathers, aigrettes and furs, and with her shimmering jewels, all of which were genuine. At the end of her performances, spectators queued up to see Gaby Deslys disappear into a Rolls Royce, blowing kisses to the crowd with her chubby diamond-covered hand. As plump as a partridge, she was well aware of her worth (remember Hugo's note-book: 1,000 francs for fifteen minutes); she had just added a royal feather to her lovers' cap in the person of the young King Manoel of Portugal, successor to the throne after the assassination of his father and older brother, some months earlier, in front of Queen Amelia.

The King had asked Louis to come to his suite at the Ritz to discuss the creation of some sets of jewellery – emeralds, of course, since Gaby loved them so much. But what she really wanted, was to have a real pearl necklace as long as herself.

Her insatiable demands were soon to lead to the young King's downfall; his entourage became exasperated by his extravagant expenses. In 1910, the House of Braganza ceased forever to rule Portugal. Gaby repudiated the dethroned king, taking with her 320,000 dollars' worth of jewels to the United States, where she was engaged by Ziegfield for the impressive fee of 18,000 dollars per month.

She had a triumphant arrival in New York, where she was met by a group of journalists to whom she declared, with disarming candour, that, since money was the only protection for a woman in the world, she never gave anything back. To one journalist's question about the value of her jewels, she answered that, wearing all her pearls, diamonds and emeralds, she was worth over 3,000 dollars per pound, adding that this was why she did not want to be any slimmer. It is, however, interesting to see, despite her American triumph, an entry in the Cartier–New York registers for 12th November 1912: "Gaby Deslys – No credit."

TOP: *Cigarette case incorporating a lighter, in Russian style, with* cabochon *sapphire thumb-piece. Fine chain held by gold ring. Made for the King of Serbia in 1926 (Cartier archives).*
BOTTOM: *Pink gold powder compact with a Persian plaque on a blue enamel background, with floral gold and ruby décor. Pavé rose-cut diamond doe and calibre emerald stag (1926, Cartier collection).*

There were two possible explanations for such a refusal: either Pierre had a profound dislike for the courtesans and had not forgotten the actress' sensational declaration, "I never give anything back because money is a woman's only protection against the world"; or, perhaps there had been a message from Paris ordering him not to allow any favours towards the woman who had caused the downfall of the son of the King who had granted Louis his first royal warrant.

Naturally, the managers of a European business established in the United States had to accept subtle conditions in order to succeed. "It is absolutely essential to take great care, especially in the United States where wealth changes very quickly, not to give credit as is done in France; our salesmen do not always remember that they are committing the firm's money; it is therefore imperative to ask Monsieur Pierre or a member of the management for authorization or to inform Paris."

The administrative structure of Cartier-New York was organised along the same lines as in Paris and London, with a few differences imposed by the need to adapt to the American system. This was done with great skill as the three brothers were well aware that, although the Americans still adored anything coming from Paris, there was still much to be learnt from the New World if they were to achieve the highest level of profit world-wide. In retrospect, it could be said that the success of Cartier-New York was the result of carefully planned progress, since in 1908 America was still suffering the effects of the economic crisis of the previous months. And two years after the establishment of Cartier, the powerful trade unions were to forbid the immigration of qualified staff.

One of the first expatriates, transferred from No. 13 Rue de la Paix, was given the daunting responsibility of re-setting the Hope diamond, bought by Louis after the overthrow of the red Sultan Abdul-Hamid II.

The American press had made a great deal of the legend of the *Bleu de France*. However, the curse associated with this historic gem did not frighten Evelyn MacLean, daughter of Thomas Walsh, a mining tycoon, and wife of Ned MacLean, son of the *Washington Post* publisher, who paid 154,000 dollars for the Hope, to which were added 24,000 dollars a year for insurance and security. Although they were not superstitious, the MacLeans wisely took out an insurance policy which stated that, in the case of accidental death befalling a member of their family within eighteen months following the purchase, Cartier would agree to take back the jewel and to pay a large indemnity. The MacLean family had to wait eight years to see the curse come true.

In 1918, their young son, aged 8, escaped the vigilance of the body-guards who were looking after him and was run over by a car. Terribly upset, the father took to drink and became insane, and the eldest girl died a short while afterwards, having taken a massive overdose of barbiturates. Despite the fame and publicity, the sale of the Hope turned out to be a financial loss, as the deal required enormously expensive legal services. The minutes of the Board meeting for the 23rd November 1912 state:

TOP: *His Majesty the King of Sweden, on a royal visit (1913).* BOTTOM: *Her Majesty Victoria Eugénia, Queen of Spain (1925).*

Upon examining our legal expenses which represent a very high sum, we have decided to be more strict. In future, we will have to to think carefully before taking legal advice. We will avoid it as much as possible. We remember with much regret details of the Hope case: it has cost O/S/K/S/K and must be a lesson for us.

O/S/K/S/K equalled 20,000 francs; as in Paris and London, the 'confitures' code was used in New York, together with a system of ciphering which coded the wires so as to make them undecipherable to the uninitiated.

The minutes of the Board meeting for the 30th November 1912 state:

Since our business is likely to become the foremost in the world, given our continuing progress, and if we are to achieve that goal, the Board has lent its support to the application of an administrative system which will allow us to pursue and to bring to a successful conclusion what we have so successfully initiated, and to provide the maximum value for money to our customers so that we shall gain the confidence worthy of our name.

'Worthy of confidence': the key-word of those forerunners who inculcated the concept of perfectionism; 'worthy of confidence': that byword of all three brothers, of whom the youngest, now established in new premises at 175 New Bond Street, was very successful in London, while Pierre consolidated Cartier's high reputation in New York.

Imbued with Verleye's ideas, Pierre knew that the key to success abroad was to take into account American tastes and motives, and to cater to them. He recorded:

I have just designed a rather successful ring which represents a bear and a bull fighting; in France, we would have relied on knowledge of the Roman amphitheatre and used the lion and the bull. But there are no lions in America, and the eagle reminds them more of a condor than of our Roman eagle. Here the bear and the bull represent opposing financial powers: rises and falls in prices; the model can change whether one is Bull or Bear: the bull can win over the bear, or the bear smother the bull.

Not only was it necessary to design according to American values, but also to create, in addition to quality jewellery, a complete range of gold and silver objects, from christening medals to confirmation goblets, and to include magnifying glasses, frames, cigarette-cases, expensive table-services and cut-glass. This new development surprised

Louis, but his brother, encouraged by Jules Glaenzer, was firm: one had to do things the American way, or fail.

In May 1909, Louis was shown the report on the first long journey undertaken by Jules Glaenzer and Prieur, a *'grand vendeur'*. It gave a splendid account of a typical journey undertaken for Cartier at that time. Over a period of seven months, they visited Siam, China and India. The two men's intention was, not only to exhibit their latest creations, but also to buy, at advantageous prices, precious stones, jade and real pearls. After a twenty-eight day crossing, the two men reached Bangkok. The following extracts from their report are verbatim:

November 3rd: arrival in Bangkok at 1.00 p.m., 3% customs duty on all our goods. Firearms had to be declared and were handed to the customs authorities, failure to do so resulting in fines, and they could be recovered only by the Consul. Oriental Hotel could not be worse; one's only hope was to be served by one's own 'boy'. They are terrible thieves; keep everything under lock and key.

November 4th: customs' formalities, unpacking.

November 5th: labelling of goods, visit to the Legation: a very important visit, must not be neglected; one is never completely certain that problems won't arise.

November 6th: J.G. (Jules Glaenzer) visited the Prince Purachatra and received a diploma from the Crown Prince.

November 7th: went to see the Prince with a large selection of jewels. House without style or luxury, but a unique sight; the Prince and Princess chose the items which the Queen might like, surrounded by servants crawling on the floor [sic] and smoking.

November 8th: we were given the list of the chosen jewels.

November 10th: the preparations for the celebrations in honour of His Majesty Edward VII have put a stop to business.

November 11th: unveiling of the statue of the King; splendid celebrations followed by the fireworks lasting several hours. Accidents to be feared and indeed have happened as the fireworks are placed anywhere – it was enough to drive one mad; luckily a torrent of rain has put an end to it.

November 12th: 5.00 p.m.: garden-party, long lines of cars, about sixty of them, with all sorts of decorations (birds, elephants, etc.). The King only appeared in the evening, saying a few pleasant words, in particular to Jules Glaenzer as His Majesty recognized him.

November 15th: visit to pawn-shop, nothing worth mentioning apart from its repellent smell. Not a single pearl, some reconstituted rubies, poor quality. November 16th: no deal, went back to the pawn-shop, nothing worth buying.

November 17th: went to see a Chinese man, owner of a large emporium, who, although very rich, lives in filth in a damp back-street. He examined our jewels, put aside a pair of earrings, but it was obvious that our goods did not correspond to what he wanted; they were not 'showy' enough.

November 18th: visited Mrs. K.S., a Siamese lady, she owns a cock-fighting ring and every Sunday Siamese aristocrats come here to bet. Sometimes there is a fish-fight, the stakes are very high; we did business with her for 120 ticals.

November 19th: visit to a pawn-shop; there are so many of them! Then we watched a big review of Siamese troops: 20,000 men.

November 20, 21, 22: no business.

November 23rd: attempted robbery on our bedroom; it is advisable to get up with one's revolver and keep it to hand all day; these Indians are as sly as snakes and always hide a weapon in their sarongs.

November 27th: appointment made with the Prince; for the 28th with the King. The royal apartment was very showy in style, many marble sculptures and modern objects thrown together. A table was set up to display the jewels. His Majesty appeared, surrounded by the little Princesses; he greeted us, very gracious towards Jules Glaenzer, and made his choice: the velvet necklaces seemed to his liking, as well as the pretty ring and brooch of diamonds, but no pearls: the Siamese consider pearls to be bad luck.

After that visit to the Royal Palace, and while waiting for the Exhibition at Dusit Park, the two men spent a week looking for emeralds and pearls, astonished by the prices asked. On December 6th they had the showcases set up. The King opened the Exhibition at 7.00 p.m.

The stands were very colourful, selling silks, jewels and toys. At 9.00 p.m., visit of the Queen who bought for F.I.S.K. from us. At 3.00 a.m., the Crown Prince stayed in our stand for about one hour and bought for C.S.F.S. The following day, the King arrived with a retinue of small and tall Princesses; the Queen also came, but, although we were always present, only the Prince and the Princesses were allowed to proceed with the sale, and even then, kneeling with elbows touching the floor. From the lowest to the highest, one is always served on all fours, what they call here the 'bye'. In the evening, visit from the Crown Prince, sales worth about C.S.K.S.

On the 8th December, the King, the Queen, the Princes and other dignitaries came back to the Cartier stand, but, as Prieur remarked: "Individuals buy little, the Royal Household is the only major customer, the rose-edged necklace seemed to be the star of the Exhibition. After selling to the Crown Prince some officers' waist-coat chains, we started to pack away the unsold jewels."

On the 11th, the two men, their wicker trunks weighing considerably less, set sail for Saigon where they arrived on the 16th after two days' delay caused by a storm and by mechanical break down. "We had to stop near a penitentiary colony in Poulo Condor, the second officer had been murdered."

The jewels were deposited in the safes of the '*Messageries Maritimes.*' Prieur wrote: "Saigon looks very much like a French provincial town, the climate here is worse than in Bangkok, Europeans often die and the Annamites, who have made their fortune in the rice trade, only like 'showy' jewels."

19th December: aboard the 'Tonkin', *via Hong Kong, two Chinese were drowned during the crossing. Visit to some pearl and jade merchants (exorbitant prices). On the 24th, left by sea for Canton; went by boat to the Island of Schameen, a European concession, checked in at the Victoria Hotel (execrable). Immediately afterwards we hired a guide who took us in a 'chair' to the Chinese city: dirty small street, we went from shop to shop; pearls and jade merchants; extremely tiring to deal with the Chinese, it was a question of who could wear out the other quicker, and it was only on the third or fourth attempt that we reached an agreement. The Chinese are extremely good businessmen.*

The two men eventually managed to buy a few items of jade, and Prieur noted:

Hong Kong is most definitely a very odd city, which has not changed for centuries. Everything here is primitive, there are many brigands; justice is over-simplified, the individual is of no importance.

They also went, in the company of an acquaintance, to the British island of Victoria Town, to meet Sir P.C., owner of an extraordinary collection of ancient vases; but no deal was concluded. Prieur noted:

Europeans stay here just long enough to become rich before returning to Europe, taking with them Chinese jewels.

After they left Hong Kong, aboard the S.S. *Prinz Ethel* bound for Shanghai, Jules met a rich European customer with whom he dealt extensively. After two days of customs formalities, they explored the city which gave them an:

impression of Europe, a very busy city, although not beautiful, it is certainly the most pleasant, the temperature here is low: 0°C.

On the recommendation of famous customers from Paris, London and New York, they went to see some rich European residents, and made a few sales, but their main objective was to pick up some rare items, as baroque pearls were very popular here and used extensively for women's hats. Prieur remarked that, after all, despite their exorbitant requests, the Chinese were always pleasant businessmen:

They do not take offence at any offer, no matter how ridiculous, and at the end of their year, on the 22nd January, which is the date for balancing the accounts, if they are in financial difficulty, they will sell at very low prices.

After ten days devoted to business deals, the two men left Shanghai for Hong Kong in order to finalise some deals initiated during their earlier visit, and where they also bought pearls and jade. Prieur noted:

The very honourable Loon Shing lives in a very old Chinese house built in a most interesting style, of great beauty and abounding in treasures. One can haggle over the price without offending him. Unlike some Japanese, who have in fact been boycotted by them throughout the eastern part of the country, the Chinese always keep to their word.

After Hong Kong came Singapore, where the prices of pearls and emeralds were as exorbitant as everywhere else. Then the two men journeyed on towards India:

We took the train for Madras; one day and one night; parched country, intense heat, inhabitants poor and sad-looking. We hired a guide and went round all the small shopkeepers whose living quarters are strange and dirty. Everything happens in the same room (shop, bedroom, dining-room) with a big white mattress on the floor.

They visited scores of small shopkeepers, in narrow back-streets where business deals were concluded on the doorstep. All they were offered were the same inferior emeralds or baroque pearls.

A coded message urgently recalled Glaenzer to Paris, and Prieur stayed on his own. Three hundred kilometres from Bombay (overnight by train) he tried to negotiate an agreement for the bulk buying of pearls from the Persian Gulf, and for 5,625 francs he had enough for three small choker-necklaces. The next day he inquired about the big buyers. He recorded that:

> *The Nizam of Hyderabad, a near independent state, is the richest; for this kind of customer one would need rather gaudy stones.*

Agra followed Bombay:

> *Horrifying prices, the native district is extremely poor; it is their New Year and they celebrate by splashing themselves with water coloured red by cow dung.*

He wrote of Calcutta:

> *I found Calcutta both extremely ugly and hot; I did not go near the natives because of the small-pox epidemic; 250 victims during the previous week, more than a third of whom were whites. G.L. came to see me at my hotel (all the way from Agra) to offer me pearls at about twenty-three times their normal value, and he showed me two nicely coloured pear emeralds for which he wanted 75,000 francs. I asked him if there was a special lunatic asylum for gem-merchants!*

From Calcutta on to Rangoon:

> *The Shwe Pagoda is a masterpiece of colour and architecture; they have many Siamese customs, business is in the hands of the Burmese, and Europeans find it difficult to compete with these dishonest, thieving people.*

After Rangoon, Prieur stopped at Colombo, where he managed to establish some important connections, and then departed for Europe, arriving there twenty-one days later.

The first exhibition in Siam became a bi-annual event and never failed to be a success, not only with the Royal Family and its entourage, but also with Europeans for whom the arrival of the '*grands vendeurs*', their wicker trunks full of the latest creations from the Rue de la Paix, represented news from France and a breath of Parisian atmosphere.

Whilst the account of this journey appears rather full of adventure, there were, in fact, even more dangerous voyages, in particular one when Jules Glaenzer had to shoot and kill a thief who had robbed his secretary and was about to stab him. Jules Glaenzer revealed this incident many years later to a journalist of the *Washington Post*, much to the anger of Pierre Cartier who was highly shocked by the publicity given to the declarations of the accredited '*vendeur*' to so many famous people, who included Charlie Chaplin, Elsa Maxwell, Irving Berlin and Dupont de Nemours. Jules Glaenzer was the man who had sold, in a single day, two hundred and twenty-two sets of jewellery to the King of Siam – one for each of his favourites.

6

When his divorce was pronounced, Louis' close friends noticed subtle changes in his behaviour, as if he had assumed a role, choosing a mask appropriate to the situation. His acting was so accomplished that he was

Jacques Cartier
(1884–1942).

no longer quite sure of his own identity except that, above all, he had to continue to be the perfect kings' jeweller. In fact, he had recently had the honour of receiving his seventh royal warrant, this time from the Greek Royal Household.

The King of Belgium – and of the '*Belles*' – had just died and was to be succeeded by his nephew, Albert I. Léopold's death had somewhat overshadowed the gossip provoked by Meg Steinheil's scandalous trial, at which she was finally acquitted of the accusation of complicity in the murder of her husband and her mother-in-law. Paris had been very excited by the legal adventure of the 'Sarah Bernhardt of the court-room'; the most famous of names – the ironmaster Borderel and the Grand Duke Wladimir, and even the ex-Prince of Wales – had been mentioned in connection with the crime which had resulted in two victims.

Another subject for gossip was the imminent marriage of Liane de Pougy to Prince Georges Ghika, nephew of Queen Nathalie of Serbia. Liane, star of the Eldorado and the Folies-Bergère, had caused the ruin of many men, some even committed suicide. Liane was unique. She was Queen of the '*Belle Epoque*', the actress whose jewels were said to be worth more than one million francs. Would Liane be lost forever to the stage and to the libertines' pleasure?

Louis Cartier was one of the first to know about the marriage between the courtesan and the Rumanian aristocrat. Stoivesco told him: "A Princess! Wonders will never cease! She is ten years older than him – at least – and only likes women; as for him, he is fragile and ambiguous. All the Ghika are against the marriage, the Prince's mother will stop his allowance, and Liane is far too greedy to keep her Moldo-Slovaque for very long." Louis answered that they could always seek a divorce. Stoivesco, to whom he sometimes confided, knew how sensitive Louis' wound still was, and how he usually tried to appear carefree so that nobody would guess that he was still hurt by his divorce. In any case, if Louis had felt even the slightest desire to confide, he would certainly not have turned for comfort to members of his own family.

His mother, who rarely went out, lived almost as a recluse, and when he went to see her with his daughter, he was aware of Anne-Marie's secret fear, and knew how distressed she was in the presence of the old woman.

Through a chance meeting with an accountant dismissed by Alfred two years previously, Louis heard of his father's liaison with a young widow, and thus realised that for some time his parents had not been living together as man and wife. Being in the mood for confidences, the ex-employee told him how he had met Alfred in a quiet restaurant where he often dined, and how he had exclaimed: "You here, Monsieur Cartier!" The lady companion was most astonished since she had thought her protector was a man of more modest means. To hear that she had been noticed by the famous jeweller when she had thought she was the protégée of a certain Monsieur Duchaussoy was bound to increase her demands on him, hence Alfred's angry reaction. The story typifies the social norm of the times. One should not be surprised at the somewhat unfair dismissal of an employee who became inadvertently involved in his boss' private life. The ex-director of the clock department who told this anecdote explained that relationships between superiors and subordinates were quite different then: the boss was always the boss. "Nice, what did that mean? You could think the boss was hard, irritable, sometimes unfair, but ultimately such feelings were of no consequence."

From then on Louis learned to hide his feelings so well that he acquired his 'often undeserved' reputation for cold disdain. He had few friends. Apart from social connections, which he soon discovered were mainly artificial, he found refuge with the D. family, whom he visited often. Among their children, Louis soon took a special interest in the young G., who was a few years younger than his daughter. The relationship with that little boy, who had become a sort of spiritual son, helped to alleviate the sadness caused by a difficult emotional life, and was a consolation for his own disappointment as a father; Anne-Marie was turning out to be quite a difficult little girl. Louis' solicitude towards G.D., and the latter's admiration for the man who had decided to guide his artistic education and shape his tastes, never diminished over a period of many years. Like a rider training his race-horse for victory, Louis, with unremitting care, guided his protégé towards the learning of a trade in which he was to excel, revealing to him all the secrets of the craft, training him in all departments, from lapidary skills and design, to management, production and sales. G.D. was to become his complete alter ego, and the latter always endeavoured not to disappoint him. After rigorous training, the young man joined Cartier in 1928, and rose to occupy a very important position in the company.

7

For many Europeans, Edward VII's death, only a few months after that of Léopold II, symbolised the end of a particularly privileged era, more especially as the Portuguese revolution, the unrest in Morocco, and Japan's annexation of Korea all pointed to a troubled future.

Determinedly optimistic, Louis Cartier was preparing for the journey which was to take him to Russia, where he had been invited to preside over the Charity Bazaar organised by the nobility. He was to return home in time to attend Pierre's wedding to Elma Rumsey.

In 1928 Louis wrote some particularly important notes on that Russian journey. The Tsar's regime had collapsed eleven years earlier, the First World War had transformed the structure of European society, but Louis remembered, and seventeen years after his adventure recounted:

I was surprised to find that the extreme cold was perfectly bearable. The Neva, full of blackish needles, gave the bath water a rather odd appearance. The muffled silence of the snow gave to Saint Petersburg's avenues and streets, despite the heavy traffic, a singularly mysterious appearance which, because of the absence of noise, was rather magical too. A magnificent city, sumptuous churches, the Empire-style palace; streets full of sledges, the wide river and the canals cutting through the city made winter in Saint Petersburg a truly splendid sight. In answer to Baron Mita de Beckendorff's invitation, I put on my silk jacket, my Russian medal, and left by sledge in quest of that beautiful Petersburg. Through the snow which had just begun to fall, I could see the yellow carricks of the court coachmen and footmen, decorated with a tightly composed design of the crowned double-headed eagle. When I arrived at Baron Mita's palace, I found he had had the kindness to send his valet Claude, a Frenchman from the Jura, who took me to his master. Reaching the palace, the antechamber door partly opened, Grand Duke Boris' head appeared and he said: "Well, well, Louis Cartier is here; and what have you come to Russia for?" The antechamber was full of grand dukes and noblemen from the Court; gathered around the Grand Duchess were some Russian princes, Dolgorouki and many others whose names I have forgotten. The Baron called me over to speak to the Grand Duchess, who led me to the drawing-room next to the antechamber. I felt so intimidated at finding myself alone inside the vast drawing-room while the rest of the Court had stayed respectfully in the antechamber. I confirmed to the Grand Duchess that I would attend the Charity Bazaar; she acknowledged it with her usual kindness and promised to give me two Court ladies to help with the sales: Princess Demidoff and Princess Belosesski.

The Club where the Bazaar was to take place was an enormous palace belonging to the nobility. One had to go down fifteen or so steps to enter, and from the entrance the spectator's gaze immediately encountered the vast room flanked on three sides by enormous pillars, and then, behind the pillars were smaller rooms which formed the side-aisle of the imposing cathedral.

All the stalls were run by the cream of the aristocracy selling on behalf of the city's poor; the enormous horseshoe-shaped table was presided over by the Grand Duchess to whom I went to pay my respects (and who introduced me to the Duchess of Leuchtenberg).

Maria Pawlowna asked me, somewhat mischievously: "You, for whom historic jewels have no secrets, can you guess who once owned the Rivière Diamond worn by the Duchess?" It was none other than the Rivière Diamond given to Joséphine by Napoléon (negotiated on two occasions by Cartier).

I returned to the stall I shared with Princess Demidoff and Princess Belosesski, and carried on with business. We were visited by the Dowager Empress, and by H.H. the Grand Duke Mikailovitch, and other Grand Dukes who never came to Paris.

On that day, the whole of Saint Petersburg's nobility was anxious to acknowledge my presence at that magnificent charity fête.

The Guards' band was playing inside the vast palace, and I was struck by the pleasant and reserved attitude of the crowd. I remember an old peasant woman, wearing her best clothes and her old Russian kakoschnick, standing in her colourful garments at the top of the stairs. I still recall the dignified way she walked downstairs to go to the stall of Grand Duchess Wladimir to whom she gracefully paid her respects. I can still see the smile and the great kindness with which that very grand lady, Maria Pawlowna, responded when the peasant woman kissed her hands.

I was also struck by the extremely free and tranquil way in which the crowd moved. The most perfect order and friendliness reigned everywhere; nothing seemed to be guarded, and if the police were present, no one was aware of them.

At the end of the sale, we had the pleasure of handing over 26,000 roubles to the Grand Duchess, which was the profit of the sale organised for the benefit of the destitute of Saint Petersburg.

There were very many historic jewels in Russia, and Baron Mita invited me to go and see Prince Lwoff, who opened an enormous box and revealed to my astonished eyes a huge object which I identified as a cuirassier's helmet. When allowed to touch it, I was surprised to find that the helmet was made of gold. The Prince told me that it was none other than King Murat's helmet, the very helmet he wore during all the battles of the Russian campaign, mentioned by Marbot in his Memoirs.

By way of historical anecdote, Baron Mita told me that, in Saint Petersburg, there was a monument guarded by Grenadiers. I listened incredulously as he explained how Napoléon, at the time of his great friendship with the Emperor Alexander, had sent him one hundred men of his own personal guard who were to provide the same service for the Russian Emperor. Successive emperors had had the courtesy to retain these men of the Imperial Guard, who were replaced, after their deaths, by Russians wearing the uniform, weapons and the bearskin of the French Emperor's guard.

Many years later, Prince Youssoupoff explained to Louis that the warm welcome he had received in Saint Petersburg should be seen within the context of a new turn in Franco–Russian relationships. For some time, the alliance had been weakening – Russian indifference during the Agadir crisis, French neutrality in the case of the Bosnia crisis – and a strengthening of the relationships was necessary. Louis Cartier, the ambassador of wealth, was the jeweller whose exhibitions attracted, twice a year, all Europe's royal families.

Louis wrote in his note-books:

In the course of my professional life, I frequently had the honour of meeting royal families; and many monarchs or members of their families came to the Rue de la Paix to see our new creations. They loved to see the new ideas which would gradually spread throughout the world.

One day, the Grand Duke Paul and his wife were sitting in my office, examining a large diadem with sapphires which was going to be presented to their daughter and step-daughter (then Princess Wilhem of Sweden, now Grand Duchess Marie); suddenly I saw the Grand Duke, who was sitting on my left, near the glass door, lean forward and call "Arthur!" The other customer, astounded, turned round and came towards us, it was H.R.H. the Prince of Connaught, brother of His Majesty Edward VII, and the two princes expressed their delight at meeting here.

From time to time, we were visited by His Majesty Edward VII, in particular during his spring visit to France. With the start of the new season, customers the world over were attracted to our show-rooms. I can now recount how one day the Grand Duchess Maria Pawlowna told me: "Louis, I have been enthralled with your exhibition, and I'll be coming back tomorrow with the prettiest princess of Europe who really must come and see your magnificent jewels." And indeed she came back with the Crown Princess of Rumania who was a magnificent blonde beauty.

The Balkans war. Salonika under Turkish rule. The occupation of Rhodes and the Dodecanese by Italian troops. Constantinople threatened by Bulgaria after the Seige of Andrinople. Austrian mobilisation against Serbia. The proclamation of the Republic of China after the young Emperor's abdication. The world was in turmoil and yet Louis refused to be worried. Nothing must be allowed to become an obstacle in the way of his aim, obstinately pursued – "our business is likely to become the foremost in the world, given our continuing success."

The large increase in the number of staff was a visible sign of success: 13 designers, 13 accountants, 13 secretaries, 13 storemen; 13 was his number. He scorned superstition but believed in signs, which amused some of his assistants who nicknamed him 'H.M. the Sun-King, or Louis-the-Great, or Louis the 14th'.

He was not slow to hear about it. Louis always managed to discover what was being said behind the scenes; he did not concern himself with the opinions of those living in his shadow. In that establishment, where, like a theatre, he was director, author, stage-manager and leading actor, those who surrounded him only existed because of his splendour. He was, in a sense, almost royal; sometimes generous (though never lavish), and yet extremely careful (though thrifty rather than mean); these changes in his behaviour were part of his role, intended to puzzle his competitors.

At the end of April, on hearing that, among the 1,390 victims of the *Titanic* sunk by an iceberg, there had been five important Cartier customers, he sent the following wire: "Send flowers for each funeral – if there is to be a funeral."

On the 8th May 1912, the Cartier-New York correspondence file mentioned under TITANIC: body of Mr. Y. not recovered. The body had supposedly been sent in the Postal Telegraph Company's ship, *Lackay Benett*, and thrown back into the sea. Some papers claim that the

Blue reindeer evening bag, with yellow gold frame. Pavé diamond bar with carved emerald and ruby motif. Button clasp is of carved ruby and set in platinum (1929, Cartier collection).

body had been thrown back because it was unrecognisable, but they never gave any further details. Unable to disprove the story, his family did not start any action aginst the White Star Line. Rumour had it that, according to a survivor, Mr. Y. had climbed aboard a life-boat and, as he refused to give up his place to a woman, the officer in charge had shot him. It is apparently for that reason that the body was thrown into the sea, and that his family forbade the publication of any article, wishing to protect the dead man's reputation.

The sinking of the *Titanic* was one of a series of disasters at that time, but Louis attached much more importance to the departure of his head designer who took with him a great many drawings, than to the London Conference which met to study the serious political situation in Central Europe, and the possibility (according to the diplomats) of imminent war.

There was feverish unrest, as the world faced a period of intense rearmament. President Raymond Poincare re-established three years of national service, but Louis, in his stubborn quest for fame and material success, was becoming self-centred, all the more so as he was aware of the surprising changes affecting Andrée-Caroline's life.

Andrée had joined a group linked with the new movements which was causing some excitement in Paris; it consisted of intellectuals, artists and creative people. Mention was made, in the Rue Lamarck, where Caryathis was giving dancing lessons, of a young woman with huge blue eyes, who answered to the name of Andrée Paulet or Pawley.

Andrée-Caroline also often visited Isadora Duncan, the friend of the emaciated-looking Van Dongen, who became infatuated with 'the stranger hiding in the dark' and wanted her to become his model. Andrée declined, but he produced some sketches where Andrée's features, as photographed by Nadar, are recognisable.

Andrée met Cocteau and Picasso, and all those who contributed to Europe's spiritual and artistic regeneration and who had chosen Paris as the international centre of creative ideas. Apparently she had no emotional involvements and wanted only to feel, understand and participate, freed at last from suffocating middle-class conventionality.

Once, Louis thought he recognised her – she was so different though, that he did not dare to approach her – at the Théâtre des Champs Elysées, one evening in June 1913 during a performance of *La Tragédie de Salomé*. So, Andrée lived, thought and moved in avant-garde circles, content, sure of herself and living life to the full. He wondered what her

Gold cigarette case, engine turned, with black lacquer and diamonds (1930).

reaction would have been to the scandalous performance of the 'Rites of Spring', to have been faced with Nijinski's indecency and immodesty. Had she felt concerned by Schmitt's command to the angry audience: "Silence! Whores of the XVIth *arrondissement!*"

Louis explained Andrée's behaviour as a renunciation and (was it just pride or the last traces of tenderness?) he chose, for a while, to believe that his ex-wife's behaviour was a complex and subtle game, cleverly played by a woman still in love, trying to re-kindle her partner's interest by her unpredictable behaviour. The illusion comforted him for a while. But some time later Andrée met the man she would later marry.

Louis' mysogyny was such that when he heard that his brother Pierre had had a daughter, Marion, Louis sighed sadly: "Another woman in the family! Have you ever heard of a talented woman-jeweller?"

The first big exhibition of jewellery in Canada took place at the end of 1913. In February 1914, Louis was shown the report on a three months' journey undertaken by Prieur, from Quebec to Montreal and New York.

Arrival in Quebec. At the docks we went through buildings crowded with immigrants, some poor Russians, Bulgarians, Italians, looking for work. The buildings stretched for 200 metres, divided into departments; immigrants are sieved, sifted and submitted to a strict medical examination; for the smallest flaw, these unfortunate people are refused entry and the shipping company has to repatriate them at its own expense. After the medical, the immigrants are given a badge to wear, and are guided to the states they have chosen. There are even some agents hiring them on the spot. There are posters announcing that a certain company needs 200 men and that another is willing to take on labourers. How many among those passing through these ugly buildings today, will later have multi-millionaire children?

Prieur concluded a major deal with M.B. who was fabulously wealthy and extremely fond of beautiful jewels. He then sailed to Montreal. After landing, he hired a landau, and perched high on enormous wheels, he wrote:

I found myself shut up in a black box without being able to see the bends and the small streets; after being bumped and jolted about, I arrived at the Saint Regis Hotel. In the restaurant, women wear their day-clothes, as indeed they do at the theatre, which explains why the Canadians and

Her Majesty the Queen of Roumania, wearing a Cartier tiara with seed pearls and sapphires. (The central sapphire is 411 carats).

Americans wear caps when they visit our Opéra in Paris. How I understand those wealthy enough to afford to visit us in Europe where they are served politely and stylishly, and where the 'dollar god' is not always invoked.

In the Rue Sainte Catherine, bar follows upon bar; you have to eat if you want to drink (even if it is only a sandwich), in order to keep up appearances. Some fiddling goes on here; the Jesuits preach abstinence, but their cellars are packed with whisky. When they conceived their laws they were careful to protect themselves. Looking at the shop-windows, one can understand what pleasure it must be for an American or a Canadian to come and buy beautiful things in Europe. They have a practical sense here, but as for artistic sense . . . they have no idea! It must cost a lot of dollars, beauty is relative to price, so you can imagine how awful!

After the Rue Sainte Catherine, I came to a district where shops were packed together, the bar windows darkened – as if seeing people drink were a crime. Worst of all, however, was the undertaker's shop: in the window there was a coffin and beneath it a sofa covered with dark laces and silks, intended for the laying out, at home, of the dead in their finest clothes. This is going too far, even for the theatre, certainly not Anglo-Saxon in tone, nor yet quite Greek either.

The exhibition lasted three days – with four showcases – and was an astounding success. There were many sales, and also some important contacts made for the purchase of gems. Prieur recorded his delight, and left by the night train for New York where he visited Cartier:

A real hive of activity – a miniature Paris – I am longing to see Manhattan, this city is beyond description, Singer and Woolworth forty-storey buildings overlooking the port, a magnificent view, the fifteen-storey houses seem tiny; an indescribable impression given by all this intense activity, tubes with express lines, trams, elevated railways, I am fascinated.

After reading the report, Louis sent a wire to Prieur (who was abroad organising another exhibition), which said: "Are you a reporter or a *'grand vendeur'* Cartier? Irrelevant personal remarks. Best regards, however."

Louis' acrimony could be explained by the revival of persistent rumours concerning income tax. The debate was in the news because of a dramatic incident, provoked by the publication in *Le Figaro* of a letter written in 1911 by the Minister of Finance to his first wife: "I have defeated this income tax idea, while seeming to defend it; I am acclaimed by the Centre and the Right, I have not displeased the Left; I have managed to move towards the Right, which was absolutely necessary." The publication of that letter, three years later, had an explosive effect. Caillaux's second wife took the law into her own hands, killing the director of *Le Figaro*, Paul Calmette, in his office.

A feverish spring season; high society was preparing for its annual exodus to Deauville, Biarritz and Monte-Carlo. Imitating the Cartier jewel exhibition, Paul Poiret had organised a triumphant tour. After their European success, his models were all the more humiliated by the way they had been received by the Baroness de Rothschild during a private showing at her residence. Poiret vowed to avenge his dear models, and two weeks after the snub, the Baroness was turned away from his salons. Madame de Rothschild swore to try to destroy him and persuaded many of her acquaintances to deal from now on with the 'up and coming' Gabrielle Chanel.

In December 1910, Chanel had left Balsan's bachelor flat and had established herself at 21 Rue Cambon, thanks to the financial support of her new protector, Arthur Capel, who financed her first shop in Deauville in 1913.

Arthur Capel, Chanel's great love, had appeared in Parisian society around 1910. Owner of Newcastle's collieries, attractive, a sportsman, a hard-working playboy, anxious to make his interests profitable, he forged ahead enthusiastically. Capel, 'Boy' to the ladies, juggled with love, business and politics with a detached disdain for gossip; many said that he was the illegitimate son of one of the Péreires.

It was through Jean-Philippe Worth – secretly delighted by Poiret's misfortunes and not afraid of Chanel's recent success – that Louis heard of the gossip going round the world about *haute-couture*, high society and *demi-monde*. Later, Louis was to get to know Boy Capel and Coco Chanel very well. He could not imagine, listening to Jean-Philippe describe how the 'Sultan' Poiret had expelled the Baroness from his salons, that the mysterious blue-eyed woman from Maxim's moved in this same circle.

In the spring of 1914 the new British monarchs, King George V and his wife, were given a warm welcome in Paris.

On June 28th, during a military parade in Sarajevo, capital of Bosnia, the Archduke Franz-Ferdinand, heir to the Austro-Hungarian empire, was assassinated by a student.

International unrest was followed by a lull; at the beginning of July Raymond Poincaré left for Russia, where the number of strikes and demonstrations was growing alarmingly.

July 20th: the first hearing of Madame Caillaux's trial began. July

23rd: Austria demanded an enquiry headed by a Viennese commission
on the Sarajevo incident. Confronted with an answer judged unacceptable, Austria, five days later, declared war on Serbia. July 28th (that
same day): Madame Caillaux was acquitted. July 29th: Austrian armies
bombed Belgrade. July 31st: Italy's proclamation of independence;
Russian mobilisation; France received the ultimatum from Germany.
Jean Jaurès was assassinated in the Café du Croissant at 9.30 p.m.
August 1st: Germany declared war on Russia. August 3rd: Germany
declared war on France and invaded Belgium. August 5th: Japan, the
United Kingdom and its dominions joined in the conflict, while the
United States proclaimed her neutrality.

. . . Since that afternoon in June when Countess Sophia had
embraced her dying husband, clutching in her hands the green feathers
of his helmet blackened by the Archduke's blood, thirty-nine days had
gone by. During the convulsive movements of those thirty-nine days,
the *'Belle Epoque'* was expiring.

Against the background of cries – "To Berlin!" – and the echoes of
the German guns, could be heard the sobbing of the women. The *Gare
de l'Est* swarmed with red and black uniforms, gun barrels decked with
flowers.

It was the end of an era.

CHAPTER FOUR

The War

1

After many months of mental depression, Alice Cartier died predicting an awesome future. Her last words were addressed to God, to whom she entrusted her three sons.

While Jacques, the youngest, had been posted to the Aisne, Pierre found himself with the Third Territorial Unit in Cherbourg. Louis – invalided out of the army because of his car accident – could then supervise the affairs of the three branches when business started again. It was obvious that only the New York branch (which had lost nine of its French staff, called upon to serve their country) seemed to have reasonable prospects. Louis was convinced of this after reading a letter from New York headed: 'American Opinion'. It was the copy of an article published in a trade journal:

> *The fact that there is a war in Europe does not mean we have to get excited. Business is thriving so well that we cannot afford to lose our self-control. We hope the conflict will be a short one; our harvest is predicted to be better in quality than any other before, business is excellent, and the best thing for us to do is to go on working quietly. The savings which have been realised for some months have put the United States in a very strong position and enabled us to face the European political crisis, which would not have been the case had this crisis occurred at a time of great uncertainty. The jewellery trade will probably come to a halt because of the Transatlantic crossing, but luckily our stock of precious stones is sufficient, and it is believed that the Anglo-French fleets will be strong enough to secure the continuation of trade with the United States.*
>
> *With the huge crop to be harvested this year in this country, we will have a surplus of 140,000 bushels of wheat compared to previous years. The high prices fetched by that harvest, due to the excessive demand created by the European situation, indicate that American farmers are likely to*

become very wealthy, which will largely balance the decrease that we will have to suffer in the export of manufactured goods and in the jewellery trade.

Faced with this gigantic problem, the Mexican question is of secondary importance. It is not the time for business to lose confidence, but, on the contrary, for us to keep calm and collected.

Neither Theodore Roosevelt, nor his successor, President Wilson, had wanted to recognise Victoriano Huerta as President of Mexico. Because of the civil war between Huerta and his opponent, Carranza, the U.S. fleet and army intervened in 1914. War was avoided following agreements with Argentina, Brazil and Cuba. The U.S. government recognised Carranza in 1915.

However, in New York the stock-exchange was demoralised; the exchange rate was $10 for £1 sterling. From Cherbourg, Pierre sent a wire with instructions to purchase the maximum quantity of gold, and to divide it between three banks. The two brothers met in Paris, then in Cherbourg, in order to establish the basis of a commercial policy founded on the 'logistic evidence' (sic Louis Cartier); American neutrality was still an important asset for the immediate future. Instructions were wired from Paris to Cherbourg to stop the manufacture of fancy jewels and the small group of jewellers and setters dealing only with the production of large items ordered by American multi-millionnaires since February 1914.

Further instructions were given that the new stock of clocks was to be sealed and deposited in a bank; no pieces were to be shown to anyone. (Since May 1914 Cartier had been informed of some imitations of their watches and small clocks).

It was also agreed to proceed in the most diplomatic way possible with the settlement of the invoices of American customers who had ordered items and collected them in Paris.

At the beginning of October, Alfred's nephew, General Roques, was killed in action, and Gaston Worth's eldest son, Jean-Charles, was seriously wounded.

After their strikingly fast advance, the German armies then settled down to trench warfare, and Europe prepared for a long conflict.

As predicted by Louis, business took off again in New York; the multi-millionaires, caught by the war in Europe, had come back "delighted to have escaped the horrors; they had had to suffer many

TOP: *Bracelet with calibre rubies, round-cut diamonds and baguette diamonds, in platinum setting (Cartier, 1930).* BOTTOM: *Diamond brooch created by Cartier, London, for Her Majesty Queen Elizabeth II. In the centre is the first pink diamond (approximately 25 carats) extracted from the Tanganyika mines, and offered as a present by Dr Williamson, a Canadian gemmologist, to the Princess Elizabeth on her marriage in 1947.* OVERLEAF: *Hexagonal clock in mother-of-pearl, carved coral, pink and black enamel pivotted on two rock-crystal Foc dogs; columns in rock-crystal with flower motif in coral and carved emeralds, rubies and sapphires on a lapis base; serpent hands decorated in black and white enamel (1926, Cartier collection).*

unforeseen losses such as motorcars, luggage, etc. . . . they had had to pay astronomical sums to secure their passage back to the United States, and, despite their very conservative attitude towards luxury expenses, we still predict good business this year, to judge from the increase in the number of visits and the interest displayed by the customers in admiring our jewels. In spite of everything, American women will have to get their Christmas presents, and already many of them have chosen their gifts.''

American high society frequented the French jeweller's show-rooms with an eagerness in proportion to the anti-German feelings of the time, and the turnover of Cartier-New York was stable, despite the fact that some multi-millionaires, out of respect for the Allied struggle, were opposed to any ostentatious display of wealth. Mrs W.K. Vanderbilt, for example, reproached her husband sharply for his gift of two rings ornamented with two 45 grain pearls.

On the 7th May, 1915, the sinking of the *Lusitania* (1,198 dead including 128 American citizens) by the Germans shocked and angered the United States and, despite the danger of crossing the Atlantic, many Americans went to France.

More than in any other European capital during the war, Paris was the centre of elegance and a sort of frivolity. The city was described as ''a privileged place where one can only tread with pride and respect, like a prince in his gardens.'' Paris, which witnessed the triumphant success of Mistinguett (with her necklace of four rows of pearls, her ostrich feathers, aigrettes and boas); Paris, where every night Maxim's was packed; Paris, where soldiers on leave tried to forget the horrors of war.

In 1915 in Paris, luxury trade experienced a new phase of expansion: people bought and sold, trying to make the most of those fleeting moments, a sort of cocooned existence with a huge question-mark at the end; officers and pilots gambling their leave away. Time enough to think about the fighting tomorrow! Men like Audemar, Garros, Morane, Helly d'Oissel, Paul-Louis Weiller (heir to the extremely wealthy Lazare) lived then as if they were to die the next day, with an extraordinary hunger for pleasure. Laughter, orgies, suffering, these were exceptional times, when people relaxed, argued and concluded deals. And in Biarritz, the capital of speculation, Gabrielle Chanel had opened her first fashion house with fashion shows and dresses at 3,000 francs. It was an enormous success.

It was common knowledge that Boy Capel — appointed to the

'Hindou' parure. Gold rose diamonds and coloured stones (1950).

Franco-English commission by his friend, Clémenceau – had financed
Chanel who, operating from 21 Rue Cambon, Deauville and Biarritz,
was building her successful empire, partly because she had undoubtedly
a great flair for dress design, but mainly because she was virtually the
only one left in the couture trade. Poiret had been commandeered to
produce coats for the army, while Jean-Charles Worth was convalescing. "It is always the same old thing," said Alfred to Louis, "on one side,
heroes and victims, on the other, cowards, traffickers and shirkers."

'Shirker' was a term which offended Louis' sense of pride. After

*Pierre Cartier
(1878–1964).*

many requests, Louis was appointed N.C.O. in charge of administration with the Red Cross. It was an especially satisfactory position, since
it allowed him to work for the future with a clear conscience and to
supervise the business at No. 13 Rue de la Paix which was now run by
women workers.

Anne-Marie was living in Switzerland. If Louis sometimes missed his
daughter's presence, he did not tell anybody close to him. It was at this
time that his love for dogs began. Somewhere in the Aisne he adopted a
stray ratter who became his mascot. The ratter was to be followed by a
Pekinese and by a Maltese dog.

At the end of 1915, he decided to go and live at The Ritz where, defying convention, many Parisian women of high society dared to be seen at tea-time; some of them even lived there – an answer to the problems of servants, heating and food supply. Alfred occasionally met his son at the hotel bar. "This wretched war is changing all our values; in my day, only the *'pétroleuses'* wanted to appear emancipated. If high society women start aping the lower classes or the *demi-monde*, there's going to be confusion."

If there was to be confusion, then Louis was determined to make something out of it. He told his father how the impulsive Caryathis had recently sacrificed her luxuriant hair, ferociously cutting it, and leaving it, tied with a ribbon, on the coat-rack of an imperfect lover. It was likely that her example would be followed, and Louis could foresee that many eccentrics would have their hair cut short, and this foresight had already led him to sketch some hair slides intended to supersede the heavy shell combs.

Moral values and attitudes were being profoundly changed by the war, and in 1916, when France counted one million dead or wounded, Louis Cartier was already preparing for the future. In tomorrow's Europe, where very few kings would reign, he would still be the King of clock jewellery, even if he could no longer be the Kings' jeweller. He engaged the Couet sons, who had inherited exceptional skills from their father, worthy of eighteenth century craftsmen, and he gave them the task of researching into the creation of mysterious small clocks – the famous Mystery Clocks. These mysterious small clocks were – and still are – one of Cartier's great successes. They indicate the time seemingly by magic (they have no axis and the movement of the hands is apparently unexplained). In fact – and here lies the creative touch – the hands were linked to a crystal disc by a worm-screw mechanism or by a chain housed in the frame. Each of these discs was covered with another crystal, either clear or coloured, and cut like a diamond.

This deliberate determination to eliminate the realities of life in order to devote himself to success, was one of many paradoxes in the man who was often a prey to doubts, and who would sometimes sink into deep pessimism from which he would later recover, abruptly pulling himself together.

An artist and innovator, with touches of genius, he was well aware of his gifts, but he also wanted to be seen as a man of wealth and set himself above ordinary human values. This was one of the Cartiers' characteris-

Louis Cartier's 'Tank L.C.' watch, inspired by the First World War tanks.

tics, and was also evident in Pierre who, until his demobilisation, tried to combine his military and business interests. Contrary to what might be thought, this demanding behaviour, instead of annoying his assistants during those dark hours of war, did in fact inspire them, and many on short leave or while convalescing came to 13 Rue de la Paix 'to lend a hand'.

Louis explained the fascination for jewellery by the mystery of precious stones:

Light received, reflected, 300,000 km per second, something to do with a stone's water property. Unless it could be explained by the geographical location of our premises. Grandfather always used to say that Madame de Pompadour had been buried somewhere in Rue de la Paix, perhaps even under No. 13, who knows . . .

As the war raged on, Europe grew weaker by the day. British soldiers were being supported by the first tanks, and in December 1916, Louis, sketching and crossing out, created the definitive design of the famous tank watch L.C., based on previous work, but now highly simplified, "like a tank," he said to his assistant, Verjoly. While Louis was perfecting the design of a watch which would bear his initials, General Pershing was fighting somewhere in New Mexico, pursuing Pancho Villa and his gang. Some twenty-two months later, Pershing, Colonel William Hayward and a few other officers were presented with the first tank watch L.C. as a tribute to the American Expeditionary Corps.

In January 1917, Louis heard from Princess Murat that Rasputin had been assassinated, and that the instigators of the plot were two of his best customers, Prince Youssoupoff and Grand Duke Dimitri. The assassination took place on the 30th December 1916 in well-known and extraordinary circumstances. In his book, *How I Killed Rasputin*, the Prince evoked his adventures and mentioned on several occasions the role played by his jewels – and by Cartier – during his life before and after the First World War. "We will see him again," Louis told the Princess, "he is under a lucky star." The safes in No. 13 contained jewels from the collection of Prince Youssoupoff, now under house-arrest by Imperial decree.

With the cold weather, starvation, riots, mutinies, strikes and looting during the winter of 1916–1917, soldiers and civilians were thoroughly demoralised after three years of war. Under the revolutionary pressure which was soon to expand throughout Europe, the Russian armies collapsed, the Tsar abdicated on March 15th and Prince Lwoff, who had so courteously welcomed Louis to his palace in 1911, became head of the government beside the scheming Kerenski.

On April 2nd, with the overwhelming enthusiasm of the civilian population, the United States joined in the conflict. But the troops' cry was still: "Peace – down with the war! End the slaughter!" The Somme, Verdun, the Chemin des Dames; 61,000 men were sacrificed in May and 21,000 deserters counted by the end of June. The military authorities were forced to pass 150 sentences and to carry out 23 executions. Pétain took over from Nivelle as head of the French forces.

On February 13th, Mata-Hari had been imprisoned in padded cell No. 12 of St. Lazare prison. (The same cell that had been previously occupied by Madames Steinheil and Caillaux.) France was alert to the menace of spies ("be careful, be quiet, enemy ears are listening"), suspecting the Kaiser's agents as much as the revolutionary propagandists.

Like all businessmen, Louis was forced to increase his employees' wages, a circumstance which, with the payment of income tax, established after years of procrastination and based on the American tax system (2% on income since 1915!), made him remarkably irritable.

Pierre, having been demobilised, was once again in New York at the head of his business. Despite the prevailing austerity, trade was stable and the stock of precious stones had significantly increased contrary to the predictions of certain pessimists.

Multi-millionaires were tending to move nearer to Central Park, and the undisputed Queen of High Society, Grace Vanderbilt III, had chosen to live at 86th Street, where she could admire the greenery. Jules Glaenzer told Pierre that Grace Vanderbilt's best friend, Maisie Plant, the dazzling wife of the extremely wealthy commodore, also wanted to come and live near Central Park and was trying to sell her splendid four-storey town-house, built in 1904 by the famous architect, Gibson, at the corner of 53rd Street and Fifth Avenue. Now, Maisie Plant was extremely fond of jewels, and Glaenzer had noticed her fascination with a real pearl necklace which she came to contemplate almost every day.

How was the deal concluded? There are several versions but no witnesses. Here, first, is Nancy Randolph's account. As gossip columnist of the *New York Tribune*, she wrote:

> *Mrs. Plant and Mr. Cartier were dining at the same table and she told him of her admiration for the wonderful necklace.*
> *"Why don't you buy it?"*
> *"I cannot afford to pay $1,500,000 for a necklace."*
> *"Give me your town-house and I'll let you have the necklace."*

A second version, written by Brooke Hayward, author of *Haywires*, says:

> *There was, however, no doubt that old Morton Plant was terribly in love with her; as a wedding present he gave her $5 million, adopted her son, who was later to marry the actresses, Constance Bennett, Edna Dunham and Marjorie Kling (Maisie's son cost the commodore a fortune), but more than that, he also sold his town-house on Fifth Avenue to Cartier in exchange for a row of pearls that they had at last discovered after much searching, and which matched perfectly a row of pearls he had already given her.*

A few months after the conclusion of that deal, in true American style, all Cartier departments were transferred to Morton Plant's ex-town-house, to which Pierre, wisely, made only a few changes. The Cartier building on Fifth Avenue had been declared a classified building by the City of New York.

The double-row necklace whose value was estimated at one and a half million dollars in 1916, was sold for $170,000 in January 1957. The cultured pearls industry had caused the price to fall by 89%.

2

On the 18th May 1917, the excitement in Place du Châtelet reminded one of the elegant atmosphere of pre-war receptions: high society attended a performance of *Parade* with décor by Picasso, choreography by Massine, music by Erik Satie, libretto by Jean Cocteau. (Cocteau, then aged 27, was a medical orderly with the Red Cross and had recently made Louis' acquaintance.) The event, under the Comtesse de Chabran's patronage, was organised for the benefit of refugees from the Ardennes, and Louis was very sceptical about the success of this first cubist ballet. But, despite not liking *Parade*, he was greatly amused by the uproar provoked by the performance. Whereas the Futurists were talking of genius, the *Tout-Paris* was indignant; the uproar lasted several weeks and, in the end, Erik Satie was condemned to one week's imprisonment, a fine of 100 francs, and 1,000 francs damages. The future leader of the *Groupe des Six* had sent to the particularly scathing critic, Poueigh, a post-card with the words: "Sir, you are an ass, but an unmusical ass." Poueigh, feeling deeply offended, had sued him and won. The judgment irritated Louis who greatly appreciated Satie, Debussy and Ravel.

The performance of *Parade* left Louis more puzzled than indifferent, but was, nevertheless, a source of inspiration. He had been fascinated by the audience, and his note-books of that period are full of projects confirming both his remarkable powers of observation and his foresight. Indeed, he had contemplated and analysed at length the already-emancipated women with short hair and long tunics, who foreshadowed the 'liana-girls' of the future. Freed from constraints, with bare arms and short dresses, they wore wide flat bracelets, strands of pearls – more and more pearls. Tall and shameless, he realised they would have to be adorned differently. Chanel had permitted them to show their ankles, and she would end up by changing them completely, and – who knows – perhaps even flattening their bust! Chanel even cut her own hair short, three years after her friend Caryathis, and was promptly followed by Charlotte Lysée (whose husband, Sacha Guitry, had left her for the very young Yvonne Printemps), Misia Sert (explaining to all and sundry how the Russian revolution was like a vast ballet), and Gabrielle Dorziat and Cecile Sorel, both with short hair, made up like idols, white eyelids, black eyes, red lips, dressed in silver lamé, brown, beige, mauve and black. They had temporarily banned the more brilliant colours ("We are at war, aren't we?"), which were soon to return in even greater and more startling profusion. Louis could hardly have imagined that the colour he had been the first to introduce into jewellery in 1910, was to be mentioned forty years later by Cecil Beaton: "Monsieur Cartier was the first to mix colours, saying: 'I predict a great future for blue and green'." Indeed he had dared to contrast emeralds and sapphires, and was planning now to add rubies and the whole range of coral in juxtaposition to sombre onyx and the milky pink of pearls.

At that performance of *Parade*, he realised how he would adorn these women of the future whose voracious appetites for life made them eager to please in a new way.

The summer of 1917 was a time of trouble, with political intrigue following scandal. Between visits to the trenches, Clémenceau, wearing his battered hat and his loose army coat, launched his attacks. In his editorials in the *Canard Enchaîné*, in his speeches at the *Senat*, he spared no one: from Malvy to Almereyda he denounced the frightful effects of anti-militarist propaganda and governmental blindness; he even dared to criticize the fabulously rich newspaper magnate, William Randolph Hearst, whose pro-German sympathies he hated; his motto still was: "War, war to the end." Using every argument to strengthen his position, 'The Tiger' even managed to win his opponents' confidence and, by a vote of 418 to 65, the fierce Republican became *Président du Conseil* on the 19th November 1917.

Thirty-four days earlier, Mata-Hari had bravely faced death at Vincennes where she fell, struck by eleven bullets. Among those who condemned her execution, Jean-Philippe Worth was one of the most ardent supporters of 'the woman spy'. Years later, Judge Mornet was to admit to Paul Guimard: "Between you and me, there was no need to

Small, eight-sided clock, made of nephrite with double-faced gold dial. The numerals and hands are made of gold and black enamel (1929).

make all that fuss!'' And the novelist concluded: ''Mata-Hari's death may have been useful, but Mornet's ironic remark makes me wonder whether it was just.''

Late in 1917, 200,000 British soldiers were preparing to go up to the front line and the United States granted the Allies a loan of $21 billion in gold. Gaby Deslys, back with Harry Pilcer from her triumphant tour in the United States, was once again delighting audiences at the *Casino de Paris*, and the gossip columnists announced the appearance of a new-comer, Maud Loty, to the world of show business and *demi-mondaines*. A future 'Maxim's lady', she had almost spent her first fortune and had ordered from Cartier a necklace with four rows of real pearls.

The dramatic defeats of the first months of 1918 forced the Allies to re-group under the single leadership of Foch, and Parisians, terrified by German bombs ('Big Bertha' was only 100 kms away from Paris), were leaving the city.

On June 11th Mangin's offensive stopped the German advance. On July 17th occurred the massacre at Ekaterinnbourg of the Tsar, his family and entourage. The next day the military situation changed in favour of the Allies and the Germans began to retreat. On the eve of the great offensive of August 9th, Foch was promoted to General. His baton of office was ordered from Cartier by the Minister of War a few days after the Armistice, and was formally presented to him in 1920.

3

For the French, living on a ration of 300 grams of bread, the last months of the war were very difficult; the epidemic, Spanish influenza, had been spreading since August; despite this, famous courtesans managed to organise luxury dinners serving champagne, lobster, foie gras . . . the price of the supper being more expensive than at Maxim's which closed at 9.30 p.m.

To please one of his friends who was staying in Paris, Louis had agreed to go and see the ex-protégée of Count de M., who had sent out paying invitations for the evening of the 10th October. Arriving late (he was well-known for his lack of punctuality), Louis hastily gave his stick, hat and coat to the servant, walked towards the hostess, and suddenly stopped; intuitively he sensed great happiness to come. And, indeed, the door opened and a young woman entered, wearing a

Parure by Nina Dyer, consisting of a bracelet, a brooch and a hat-pin. Set in diamonds and sapphires.

striking hat that closely fitted her small head. In the space of but a few years, how her beauty had grown. He looked at her perfect profile for some time, but she had not seen him. She carefully examined a shrub with white flowers in a porcelain *jardinière*, and murmured: "Just what I love," her slender hands fluttered round the plant as if to caress it for an instant. When at last she turned round, with a faint smile on her lips, he noticed a vague sadness in her blue eyes.

Whether by chance, or not, they found themselves sitting next to each other at dinner. They talked of the war, of life and death; there was something in her reserved manner which he felt forbade him to flirt. He was dying to ask questions, to mention that evening at Maxim's when her blue eyes had intrigued him. She powdered her face, and revived the shine on her lips with her mini-tube of lipstick; she showed him her make-up set, bejewelled with onyx and diamonds: "Your sets are really beautiful," she said; then, stroking her platinum and diamond bracelet with her finger, she added: "And I am crazy about your bracelets." The fact that he had not recognised any of his own creations was an accurate measure of his emotional state!

She told him that she had been a Cartier customer since 1915, having spent a fortune in the Rue de la Paix, and he wondered why he had never met her there. The next day he bought at Lachaume's a shrub exactly like the one she had admired the previous evening. The first thing he did was to look up the record cards: indeed, Jeanne Toussaint had been a valuable customer for the last three years.

It was some consolation for having missed her at the Rue de la Paix when he discovered that she had always come accompanied. She had left Count de Q. in 1913, and had been with Count V., an air force officer killed in 1916. Looking up Count de Q.'s record card, he noticed that Jeanne's replacement had been Yvonne Printemps, for whom he had ordered in 1914 a slim bracelet with the words: *"Lilas pour bien longtemps, mon joli Printemps*" (Lilacs forever, my pretty Springtime). Recently married, the Count had ordered a diadem for his wife. Inconstant in love, but faithful to his jeweller, Louis noted wryly – the kind of man he appreciated!

Jeanne was now living on her own, filling her moments of leisure by making tapestry evening bags for her friends, who were also friends of Chanel.

The following week, Louis sent her another shrub, and she wrote back: "It is splendid, but the other one is as strong as ever."

It was at this time, when Louis sensed that his life was about to change course, that a curious incident occurred which he mentioned in his notes. The evidence suggests that it was Arthur Capel, 'Boy' to Chanel and many others, to whom Louis was referring when he wrote:

Towards the end of the war, an Englishman leaving for Finland came to see me at my office, Rue de la Paix, asking if he could be of any help during his journey. I asked him to go and see, in my name, the Grand Duchess of

The Cartier 'glasshouse', the offices in 1917.

Russia who was living in exile near Oslo. I can imagine the Grand Duchess's astonishment when she saw this Englishman who offered her his services and was successful in helping her to cross to Sweden on a British torpedo-ship.

Back from his expedition, this gentleman came to tell me about his mission; he showed me a necklace that I had previously seen in Saint Petersburg. It is the most extraordinary sapphire necklace I have ever seen; it obviously came from the English court because, between each sapphire, there was in turn shamrock, thistle and rose.

On the 10th November 1918, in the wake of the Hapsburgs, the Hohenzollern dynasty collapsed, the Republic was proclaimed in Berlin, and the German plenipotentiaries were summoned to Rethondes by Foch.

On the 11th November, in the capital decorated with Allied flags, Parisians were shouting their joy, acclaiming the man whom they had once hated. 'The Old Man', 'The Tiger' was now called 'Father Victory'. Meanwhile, Jeanne and Louis were living the first moments of their passion.

Fifty-two months of war and nine million dead; the bloody years were to be followed by the post-war period, and then by the Roaring Twenties. At forty-three, the eldest Cartier son discovered that he was totally happy for the first time in his life.

CHAPTER FIVE
The Post-War Years

1

The year of peace treaties, the year of disenchantment and fear, and the revolutionary tidal wave that swept through Europe, even though the Red Armies with the allied troops' support were momentarily dominated by the Whites. In Moscow, the Soviets had founded the Third International and Fabergé, who had been the Tsars' jeweller, had been jailed, freed, put into prison again, and finally freed yet again, to catalogue the Imperial jewels. After three years devoted to repairs and to compiling the inventory, Trotski allowed him to leave Russia for Lausanne.

In Bavaria, where those with a nostalgia for the past were plotting for the reinstallation of the Wittelsbach family, there was a 1st Class Iron Cross corporal registered as No. 7 with the Socialist Workers' Party. Like his friends, Röhm, Goering and Rudolf Hess, Adolf Hitler, 30 years old and sickened by the injustice of the Versailles Treaty – sang the praises of a pure Germany, free from Jews and Marxists whom he hated with equal violence. A similar revulsion of Bolshevism was to prompt the former red agitator, Benito Mussolini, who had been thrown out of the Socialist Party in 1914, to found the first fascist group in Italy.

In Paris, where a new 10% luxury tax had been imposed in 1917, Louis and his brothers decided to set up separate financial structures for their businesses, so that possible difficulties of the one business should not affect the financial situation of the others; a separate watch-making department had already been founded by Edmond after his retirement from the business.

Despite the inflationary situation, Louis was splendidly optimistic, reflecting the joy in his life with Jeanne. At every possible opportunity, they drove through France in his white drop-head motor: Normandy, Ardèche, Burgundy, Basque, Jura, "as if his mission had been to teach me beauty!" Jeanne was to say fifty years later.

Frequently, they stayed in the sixth century castle of Count M., and Louis, as Pygmalion, was amazed to notice a little more each day how much the young woman's perception was growing beyond his wildest dreams. During one of their stays, the eldest Cartier was told about the auction for the 'bejewelled princess' according to the wishes of Madame de Lobanof de Rostoff (née Dolgorouki); Louis was appointed as the expert. There were 280 items, the sale lasted 7 days and raised 7 million francs and it drew the world's jewellers and collectors to the Lausanne-Palace.

It was through an item in the *Gazette de Lauzanne* that they learned of the death of Arthur Capel at the wheel of his car: he was on his way to Cannes for the New Year celebrations while his young wife, in England, was expecting the birth of their second child. Jeanne, who knew Chanel's passion for Boy, was tempted to go and join her, but Louis persuaded her that Coco would be easily consoled. Arthur Capel behaved like a gentleman and did not forget her in his will. He left her £40,000. However, Jeanne was furious and, in a rage, tried to explain Chanel and her ambiguities to Louis, who was observing her cat-like behaviour. He had not yet nick-named her 'the panther'.

However, she was soon to become a 'panther' in more ways than one: she was the first of the Mad Years' elegant ladies to sport a tigerskin coat made by Révillon from skins brought back from Kenya; she could see in the crouching big cat the forerunner of some extraordinary jewels – onyx, diamonds, an emerald drop depicting the implacable gaze; the name 'panther' suited her, too, because of her redoubtable outbursts.

In their travels, in their work, Jeanne was emerging as one of an instinctive class. Louis, who was a remarkable discoverer of gifts, could see this and his role consisted in teaching her everything about his own craft; Western and Egyptian art, as well as Persian, Hindu, Chinese or Byzantine. It was exciting to use Jeanne as a messenger of ancient traditions, and he found great joy in doing so which enabled him to forget many problems of the day; the flight of the former Russian Imperial Army, the splitting apart of society, the triumph of trade unionism (the workers had at last obtained an 8-hour day!). One of Foch's close friends recalled the marshal's disillusioned remark: "What if we had fought for nothing?" This was a particularly defeatist comment at a time when the Senate was in the process of trying Caillot for spying for the enemy; but France was far more excited by the trial of Landru than by the legal difficulties of the former minister. Besides

Maitre Moro-Gaffiéri, the lawyer of the famous murderer (who had been engaged 93 times and whose 10 victims had been burned in his retreat at Gambais), had found an unexpected supporter in Cocteau, whose witty remark was soon heard everywhere: "A mediocre lover burns memories, locks, letters, gloves and flowers; is it not simpler to burn the whole lady?"

Cocteau-Rimbaud had become Radiguet's Verlaine; he wanted, after having launched the fashion for ankle-bracelets, to own a ring both sober and original. One can imagine his long magician's hands waving in the air, explaining the contrast between a jewel ring and the signet ring (which was a symbol of high culture, the first jewel not to be a jewel but exclusively a sign of identity). In 1923, Louis Cartier submitted to the author of *Potomak* one of the first models of the triple-ring; Cocteau ordered two at once, the second one being for his darling Radiguet.

The sister of the famous Moyses, remembering an evening spent at the Boeuf sur le Toit, evoked a moody Radiguet looking, now absently, now cruelly, at his left ring finger, turning the 'triply saturnian' ring – Cocteau's own definition – between his thumb and index, taking it off and throwing it towards another table. One of the guests recovered it from the bottom of his glass, wiped it on the satin collar of his jacket, and returned it ceremoniously. Radiguet, with a thin smile on his fat lips, put the ring back on. "The terrible lovers must have had another tiff," observed Clicquet-Pleyel, and Radiguet lightly kissed his ring finger and smiled to the assembled friends.

At the age of 20, he had just had an extraordinary success with *Le Diable au Corps*, was working on his corrections of *Le Bal du Comte d'Orgel*. He did not know that he was to die a few months later.

2

America had five million unemployed and 20,000 bankruptcies, caused by excessive production, a drop in exports, and the catastrophic fall in prices. England was feeling the economic effect of the Irish war. In Paris, society was surviving, and parties given by certain 'great people' – among others Poiret and le Comte de Beaumont – delighted the gossip columnists, whose main concern was to show the world a picture of the capital where pleasure and luxury still reigned supreme, and where, for the first time, maharajahs were beginning to flock.

Contemporary witnesses still remember the amazing vision of the One Thousand and One Nights, evoking the arrival of Oriental potentates at the Rue de la Paix, Place Vendôme, followed by their factotums who carried heavy chamois leather or jute bags, tied to their wrists with plaited leather thongs, and opened them to pour onto the table thousand-year old gems, diamonds, rubies sapphires and emeralds, all there for 're-facetting'. It was not only England that was worried by Mahatma Gandhi and his obsession with non-violence (which had attracted millions of followers since 1908). Many Indians had settled in Europe, and it was in London that Louis, during a working session devoted to the modernisation of Indian jewellery, talked about his financial worries.

Which, of the two brothers and the father, was it who suggested, seriously or in jest, that the best way to avoid the heavy tax on celibacy would be to re-marry? Our information is contradictory, but the main point remains. Louis, facing his family clan, realised that what was worrying them far more than inflation, social problems and the isolationist policies of America, was Jeanne, and Jeanne only.

He told them so, deeply upset at realising how things stood. There they were, all four of them; Louis played the game of light-hearted complexities all the better to intrigue them, to alarm or overwhelm them, to dominate and let them know that the 'outsider' was closer to him than anyone had ever been, and saying that they knew nothing of the tough and authentic Flemish girl whose motto 'Keep going or die' they did not understand. Why should he not marry her?

During the row – re-constructed through the eyes of several witnesses – we can imagine the cunning Alfred, observing his three sons. The lined face of the father looking at his eldest son, knowing that Louis was thinking: "I can defy them, they have succeeded in their love life and know it, and they are terrified lest I should marry a former tart; they can see a huge reaction among the wealthy Harjès and Rumseys, uproar in American society and shocked society people in London." Louis, sure of himself, was smiling with an ironical glint in his blue eyes.

However, Alfred knew how to win over his son, if Louis had indeed wanted to do battle. He did not talk about scandal, disrepute, but merely asked (his eldest son) whether he would marry *before* or *after* his own daughter, Anne-Marie's, marriage to a descendant of Comte Louis Victor d'Apreval.

He wanted to remind Louis that, under the Terror, Comte d'Apreval had exchanged his title for the common name of Révillon, and founded a dynasty which would revolutionise the furrier's craft . . . Révillon had been given a grant of 1,000 louis by Louis XVIII, and his factories ranged from Europe to the United States and Asia. Louis Victor d'Apreval's great grand-nephew, Rene Révillon, had recently become engaged to Anne-Marie Cartier. Why not follow the marriage between fashion and jewellery with an association between furs, fashion and jewellery?

During the last few years, Louis had not worried about his daughter very much. He talked about "the right to happiness", about his satisfaction at slapping the face of a pre-war society which was ever more snobbish. But nonetheless there were problems. Was it because all Paris knew of his affair with Jeanne, that his application to join the Golf Club at Saint Cloud had been refused yet again? Would he have to beg the sponsorship of a Pracomtal or a Guiches, who claimed to be his friends, but only saw the shopkeeper in him? He was the jeweller of the Kings, and yet just a shopkeeper. Nothing had changed since Louis-Philippe.

Alfred told his son that his reaction was one of spite. As Louis listened to his father, he could see the face of his old grandfather, François, whipping his pride when he had told him the secret of his origins. And so eventually Louis agreed not to marry; only for Anne-Marie was he prepared to sacrifice himself, but he would do so with one reservation: he would keep Jeanne as a friend and collaborator. He had decided to be her Boy Capel; he would do for Jeanne what the captain had done for Chanel, defying society and subsidising her to help her realise to the full her exceptional gifts.

Thus the matter was settled and Louis turned briefly to business. He reminded them that war had interrupted the realisation of a project which he had wanted to set up – a department devoted to the sale of various objects inspired by the New York designs, which he would christen 'S' as in '*soir*'; he wanted Jeanne's exceptional gifts to be recognised in the importance of her role there, and did not want her hemmed in to her role as 'the lady of the evening bags'.

Nobody objected. They breathed a sigh of relief, delighted to find Louis again, bright-eyed, speaking fast, expressing his aims clearly; 'they' had had a narrow escape – and yet they were annoyed not to be able to work out whether the previous sparring had been aimed at testing them or not.

The week following this gathering – which the eldest Cartier was later on to refer to as "the exceptional Cartier family council" – Louis asked Mr. V., a genealogist who lived at Port-Marly, to begin research into the origins of his family.

On 8th April 1921, in the Church of Saint-Honore d'Eylau, Anne-Marie Cartier married Rene Révillon; on 21st June of the same year, Pierre Cartier, elected president of the French Chamber of Commerce of New York, was awarded the *Légion d'Honneur*, which was also to be awarded to Louis three months later.

And when a friend congratulated him about the extraordinary success of his three sons, saying "London, Paris and New York – Cartier's rays are shining on both continents," Alfred answered, the mischievous look in his eye softening the bitterness of the remark: "I had to separate them – they were three enemy brothers."

CHAPTER SIX

The Wild Years

1

Florence, Cairo, Marrakech – Louis and Jeanne continued their search, invited by the Glaoui for whom the eldest Cartier designed his first waterproof watch: "I should like to be able to swim in my swimming-pool while knowing how time is flying." The Pasha's demands reminded him of Santos-Dumont and his first wrist-watch, and he remembered tenderly the pilot who, forgotten by all, had returned to his native Brazil suffering from loss of memory and speech difficulties. Louis promised himself one day to go to Santa Lucia and see Alberto whom Paris had once adulated and now totally forgotten.

Travelling close to Jeanne enabled him to discover the many facets of her personality: her positive intelligence was allied to instinctive artistic perception. Jeanne had inherited from her Flemish and Lorraine fore-bears notions of balance and harmony, of severity too; she loved the Romanesque and Gothic periods, she was enchanted by their simplic-ity. But he firmly opposed her wish to take drawing lessons: "You would spoil your gifts."

After each escapade, gay Paris awaited them; there was work to be done, but here again, they felt the need for escape: The Ritz, the *dansants*, night-clubs, where Louis studied – without taking part – the revellers' behaviour: black bottom, bear dance, crab dance, and, naturally, the ubiquitous tango; the American liberators had brought the French a taste for whisky, cocktails, frenetic living and jazz. One night in The Ritz, three Americans sat down at Louis and Jeanne's table; they were an attractive couple and a huge man; the young woman, fairly tipsy, told Jeanne she wanted an evening bag like hers, and also a brooch, and a two-row necklace. Jeanne offered her the bag. Louis made an arrange-ment to meet Fitzgerald, found Zelda delightful, if a bit crazy, and Hemingway amazing.

The announcement of the discovery made by the Japanese

Mikomoto hit the jewellery world like a bombshell. Going back to attempts made in the fifteenth century, he announced the massive distribution of cultured pearls which were to transform the market totally (although, curiously, seed pearls kept their afficionados; but the opposite happened in the Thirties, when the utmost chic was to own huge strings of cultured pearls "by the yard, darling, by the yard it's simply divine!").

The shockwaves of Mikomoto's discovery were soon dampened by the Branicki sapphire scandal, which made headlines. In 1840, one of the world's most celebrated sapphires (weighing 300 carats) came into the possession of le Comte de Branicki; the gem was set in a circle of diamonds, and the piece was worth 3,250,000 francs, the sapphire alone being valued at 3 million gold francs. In the spring of 1918, Comte de Branicki (who had inherited the gem in 1884 and was returning home) had to stop in Kiev to surrender his visa to the German authorities who were occupying the town. The sapphire, his one precious possession, was hidden in a tobacco pouch concealed in his revolver pocket. As the train drew out of Kiev, he noticed the stone's disappearance, but considered it useless – and dangerous – to tell the German authorities.

During a visit to Paris in 1919, he told Louis about the misadventure (he knew from his family that one of the Cartier forebears had had the jewel "in his hands"). From then on, both the police and the jewellery world embarked on searches and were finally successful because a seamstress entrusted the secret to the wife of a seed pearl engraver: the sapphire, denuded of its diamonds, was with a lapidary who had just acquired it and was arrested the very next day. As Louis tells us in his journal:

> *As soon as I heard of his arrest, I wrote to the judge to explain that I was convinced that the lapidary was incapable of a dishonest act. I was called in as witness and appointed as expert by the judge who pronounced that if the lapidary had started to re-cut the stone, it must be in order to facilitate its sale, as he could not have ignored its origins, and to reduce its size would make it a unique piece. I merely answered that the Branicki sapphire was not the only one in the world, and took from my pocket a 411 carat sapphire which I was later to sell to the Queen of Rumania. I can still see the judge's face when he looked at this amazing stone, and I had no difficulty in convincing him that my attitude towards the lapidary was merely one of esteem and human kindness. A few days later, the man was freed, and*

presented me with one of the pieces from the historical sapphire as a sign of gratitude.

Cartier hit the headlines once again; they were the victims of a swindle in Athens. One of their craftsmen had been sent there to repair a highly valuable necklace, together with a salesman who was to show the latest jewellery to Princess Anastasia of Greece (former wife of the British tin king, Leeds).

The season was in full swing in the Greek capital; among the idle clients of the Grande-Bretagne Hotel was André de Farmas, who claimed to be the nephew of Ambassador Quinos de Léon, and who drew attention to himself by the gifts and passion he lavished on a beautiful young widow.

While the craftsman repaired the necklace belonging to Princess Anastasia, the latest Cartier creations were shown to the entourage of Christopher of Greece, whose wife decided not to embark on another purchase, having just ordered a jewellery set worth 120 million francs for Xenia, soon to marry Leeds Jnr. The salesman decided to try his luck with the clients of the Grande-Bretagne Hotel; André de Farmas was enchanted by an evening watch and acquired it for a widow lady friend, who also seemed tempted by two other pieces in the collection.

The following day, the lover expressed the wish to purchase a necklace and a bracelet worth one million francs; he said he was awaiting his uncle's agreement for a loan of 500,000 francs, and suggested settling the rest by drafts. In the following hours, a cabled reply ordered the salesman to do his utmost to be helpful to the ambassador's nephew, who asked to see the whole collection again. During the interview, André de Farmas telephoned His Excellency Quinos de Léon, who confirmed that he would be sending 500,000 francs the following day. The delighted lover told the young widow, who asked him to join her in Suite 105 where she was staying; both men went up to the first floor, and the salesman discreetly waited in the parlour, having entrusted the lover with the whole collection. After the delighted exclamations of the widow, there was a long silence. The salesman, at first worried, then in a state of panic, dashed through the door to discover that Count Quinos de Léon's 'nephew' and his beautiful accomplice had fled through the adjacent suite, which had been reserved by another accomplice. André de Farmas was to be arrested two months later in Hamburg, but the merry widow was never found.

Around the same time, Louis was the victim of such an amazing fraud that he only told a few close friends, as he found it most humiliating to have been so superbly deceived. A client bought a Persian Gulf pearl weighing 56 grains from him and returned a few days later, expressing the desire to buy another pearl, exactly similar. Louis replied that finding an identical pearl was impossible for Cartier and only possible for God, but the man insisted that he wanted another pearl at any price.

New York, Calcutta, London and Hong Kong all received orders, and miracles sometimes do happen. Or so Louis believed when he learned that another pearl was indeed offered for sale by an anonymous seller; the price was exorbitant: two and a half times that of the first pearl. Louis nonetheless acquired it and cabled the client, who confirmed that he wanted to buy, that the money was arriving the next day and he would collect the pearl at the end of the week. He never turned up, having achieved the amazing feat of reselling, for $2\frac{1}{2}$ times its value, a pearl which Louis always refused to part with (although he offered it in 1925 to Countess Almassy).

When telling this tale and, after explaining to the uninitiated that, in the jewellery business, one's word is as good as one's bond (whatever the sum involved), Louis would always conclude by saying: "Why on earth did I not smell a fish? I did know that the pearl was *unique*."

More thefts in jewellers' shops; in 1922, the press devoted many articles to the latest protection measures, alarm systems, bullet-proof windows; all these protections merely stimulated the imagination of crooks, and 13 Rue de la Paix became the first victim of a theft using putty which was later used in many other jewellers' thefts. This type of theft inspired the producer of *L'Honorable Catherine*, in which Edwige Feuillère was the outstanding thief in skirts!

An elegant fifty-year-old man was looking at rings on a tray; he didn't like any of them, and asked to see other jewellery. During the temporary absence of the shop assistant, one of the errand boys watched the client through a series of mirrors, unobserved, until the assistant's return. The client seemed interested by the contents of the second tray, so the assistant took the first tray back to the stock-room. The client hesitated between emeralds and rubies, and then announced that he would return the next day with his young lady friend. As the assistant was seeing the client to the door, suddenly, to the client's great annoyance, one of the directors politely asked him to follow him into his office: one of the rings had disappeared. Grumbling and offended,

Alice Haynes, wife of His Highness Prince Albert of Monaco.

the client allowed himself to be searched. Nothing was found but there was no doubt that a ring had disappeared. The director and the assistant apologised for the inconvenience and the irate client left.

One hour later, a gorgeous young woman entered the main hall, seeming very nervous and continuously removing and replacing her gloves. She said that she wished to buy a tie pin for her husband "at a reasonable price." She chose, paid and left.

Three days later at 7.00 a.m., a cleaning woman was energetically rubbing the edge of a light oak table in the main hall, thinking absent-mindedly that nothing was more depressing than a jeweller's without jewellery and that she never got a chance to look at the shining gems. As she continued to rub, scratching away at a light stain on the beige chamois leather in the centre of the table, she suddenly noticed that, without realising, she had collected a curious lump in her duster, presumably from under the hard edge of the table. "I thought it was hardened wax, but it was simply a lump of putty, bearing a pretty pattern – a pretty pattern indeed!" . . . The impression was that of the sapphire and diamond ring, cleverly lifted by the fifty-year-old man and collected by his accomplice an hour later.

They were both arrested in Rome the following year.

2

Thirteen royal warrants decorated the walls of Louis' office – thirteen was his lucky number. Since 1918 the King and Queen of the Belgians, His Majesty Victor Emmanuel, Prince Albert of Monaco and the Prince of Wales had all added their names to the Cartier list: "You symbolise the utmost in French taste and quality."

Soon there were to be no kings left, and the Russian nobles who had managed to escape by selling their gems had become gigolos, chauffeurs, butlers and taxi drivers. The world seemed to be upside down. Archduke Dimitri had become Chanel's lover (she was now recruiting her sales ladies among the exiled gentry), and Louis became more than ever confirmed in his scepticism at the sight of the royal testimonies. He could not shed this pessimism, and grew increasingly touchy with his staff, including Jeanne.

There seemed no point in trying to cheer him up. What could they know of his fears and bitterness of mind; of his vision of a sombre world

Vanity case of jade plaque openwork, scattered cabochon sapphires and set with rose-cut diamonds on platinum. Mother-of-pearl sides with baton diamond push piece (1930).

where French Divisions were likely to be sent to Germany; where famine and bankruptcy reined in Austria; where Spain was being torn apart by the Moroccan problem; and where the Greeks had abandoned Smyrna to Mustapha Kamal and Victor-Emmanuel had given Italy to Mussolini. He often used to think aloud and his colleagues became used to and understood his volatile temperament. He was accustomed to relaxing in the design studio and would whistle quietly while observing his designers. Then, if they became noisy, he would say to the dogs "Let's leave them, it's their mad hour!"

On one occasion the master clock-maker himself nearly said 'no' to him, when Louis brought him a lump of amethyst and some drawings, and told him to "get on and shove a clock in there." For many years, Couet had collaborated harmoniously with Louis, but really this was too much and he could see no future for the amethyst clock. He knew never to say that things were impossible, that time was needed, knowing in advance that the familiar reply from Louis would be: "There is plenty of time, patrons are never in a hurry; I have the money and the patience to await results."

The 'patience' of impatient people was well known to Couet; he would say that two or three years would be required, and the boss would reply as usual: "No hurry, patrons are never in a hurry . . ." but would always add the usual rider: "We ought to hurry before the taxman ties me up altogether."

Everyone on the staff was on tenterhooks up to the eve of the December exhibition, and at 5.00 a.m., dressed in his tails, a carnation in his buttonhole, Louis arrived in the main hall where the designers and staff were busy putting the last touches to the windows. He was looking tense, and was followed by the dogs. His lack of any comment was a sign of pleasure. He stepped out into the dark towards the Ritz, where Jeanne collected him at noon the following day. "When he lost count of time and I had to go and get news, he would emerge from the bathroom in a haze of steam, preceded by his yapping dogs, looking surprised and grumbling 'I have forgotten the time yet again'; he would dress in barely ten minutes, his buttons askew, in a dream," said Jeanne.

On December 30th Jeanne came to wake him at midday. She already understood that they would not be spending New Year's Eve together as he would be engaged elsewhere.

Jeanne was soon to know the someone else, who effectively sealed her fate; the beautiful face, the astonishing grey eyes and the elusive

TOP: *Panther bracelet and pavé set diamonds, onyx, facetted emerald eyes mounted in platinum (Cartier, 1980).* BOTTOM: *Perfume bottle of coral, black enamel, diamonds and pearls (1926).*

Countess Jacqueline Almassy, the second wife of Louis Cartier.

Hungarian charm of Jacqueline Almassy had just entered Louis' life; a 28-year-old widow, scion of the palatine princes.

Countess Almassy had left her native Hungary shortly before the Revolution. She refused to return to Budapest after the hundred days of Bela Kun, and finally settled in Paris after travelling through England and Portugal. She met Louis at the house of Vertès, the painter.

At first, Jeanne had found them ill-assorted; 'she' was slightly taller than Louis, whose girth revealed his capitalist middle age. When he told Jeanne of his doubts, she encouraged him, saying in a serene and confident manner, "You must live your life as you wish."

Louis the charmer, Louis the unpredictable, had decided to avoid embarrassing questions, wondering whether all this was very serious. Here he was, preparing to leave for Budapest with Jacqueline, who had told him that the most splendid palace in the city was up for sale, feeling a need for enthusiasm and a change of air at a time when he had just been presented with a grandson.

In May 1923, Louis received an anonymous letter which told him that, before he met the Countess Almassy, she had been a guest at a reception given by a Spanish *grandee*, to which His Majesty King Alfonso XIII, visiting the capital incognito, had also been invited. The letter said: "They arrived separately, they left together, and the King seemed very much in love." However, this did not alter Louis' feelings. He was well aware of certain aspects of the private life of the Spanish King, his ardent love of actresses, particularly music-hall stars. It was Alphonso's tenderness towards Mistinguett which had moved him to approach the military authorities in 1916 to obtain the release of Maurice Chevalier whom 'the Miss' had been sorely missing.

Mistinguett had been succeeded by Gaby Deslys, an Amazonian woman, who took royal revenge on her rival for having lured Harry Pilcer from her. The King's present favourite lady was Maud Loty, to whom he had recently made a gift of two magnificent emeralds in a box concealed in a basket of flowers.

Louis and Alfonso XIII both disregarded the subsequent fate of these royal emeralds, revealed in the following story.

In 1928 Maud Loty was on her way to Brazil to meet a very wealthy lover. On the second day of the voyage, she was appalled by the treatment meted out to the migrants on the boat, and demanded that the Captain should provide better food for them, since "my own greyhounds are better fed than these people." She was told that, to feed the migrant passengers in the same manner as the first class passengers would be extremely expensive; Maud then handed over her emeralds as security saying, "In Copacabana, my friend will foot the bill." He did, but with such bad grace that the following week, after selling her emeralds, Maud was to return to France, alone.

This anecdote was related to the author by Maud Loty herself. In 1950, the author met the former queen of gay Paris, who was scratching a living by reading the future in the palms of revellers between Pigalle and Montmartre. Maud was living in an attic amidst rubbish and empty bottles. A gala was organised to enable the former actress to enter a home; she was dressed by a designer and a furrier provided her with a beautiful fox cape. Maud, beaming with joy, presided from the main box. But two months later, she ran away from the home to return to her shadows.

3

Louis had observed Hungary distantly during his travels on the Orient Express. Now he was to be introduced to it by Jacqueline Almassy. Hungary was a kingless kingdom, eternal, strange and mysterious; a mixture of plains, forests and herds of animals, mountains and lakes, and many artistic remains bearing witness to 150 years of Turkish occupation. Louis was delighted by it all.

The palace was like a ship, high up on the hill with magnificent views over the city with its eight bridges spanning the Danube. It reminded Louis of certain Provençal villages, and he immediately fell in love with 5 Tarnock Utca, a huge gothic palace with ogival windows and an imposing internal courtyard. It had housed the American Embassy, and Louis bought it, at the same time as two private houses in the Verbocki street. "Whether Jacqueline marries me or not," he wrote to Jeanne, "the purchase of Tarnock and the Verbocki properties is a remarkable deal in these inflationary times."

During these leisurely months, did Louis anticipate a difficult future ahead? Presumably not, since he was much in love with Jacqueline, twenty years younger than himself, and conscious only of living through a vital period of change in his life. All the evidence gathered in Budapest suggests that he deliberately entered a new world, delighted to discover in himself a different person. His greatest weakness, a taste for honour, should not be forgotten. The wound was still sore from his not having been fully admitted into 'society', and there was still a desire to seek revenge on a humiliating family whom Louis had never forgiven for supposedly dominating him during the Family Council.

As the husband of a scion of the Palatine Princes, he would belong to the elite and could be integrated into a way of life in which he would command the interplay of disappearing doors, two-way mirrors and masques; this points to an element of childishness in the behaviour of an anxious man whose duality of temperament was to emerge even more later in life. Among the princely friends of Countess Almassy, none had

Jeanne Toussaint, responsible for the 'S' Department in 1923, and placed in charge of high jewellery by Louis Cartier in 1933.

any idea that even while in Hungary, Louis continued to supervise the activities at No. 13, nor that he continued to work, in the quiet of his study, on future creations. The sketches would reach the Rue de la Paix regularly every week.

In Paris, London and New York, Louis remained all-powerful, whereas in Hungary, Monsieur Cartier was a colossally wealthy man, a lover of art, well-known through his forebears who had, in former times, dealt in jewels throughout the world. Thus Dr. D., related the following significant anecdote:

> *Prince Esterhazy owned a Cartier lighter, and Louis said that his grand-father had sold his first lighter during the Second Empire; the Countess' reproving look told him unequivocally there was no question of Louis Cartier ever making the least mention of any trade, and so he never referred again to the shop-keeping past of his ancestors.*

When the necklace of the Austrian Empress was sold to André Citroën, no names were mentioned either in Budapest or in Paris, where only a few people – a diamond dealer who had worked in the old days for Alfred and Hugues, André's brother, who was now travelling the world as intermediary for the three brothers – knew the Dutch origins of the car magnate's father. "When I am in Hungary, I have to be available, erudite, charming, but I am never to be working!" he wrote to Jeanne.

Louis' travels enabled him to re-enter his former skin to expend his energies; he travelled from London to New York, but especially to Paris, and Jeanne's Louis was totally different from Jacqueline's; he was warm-hearted and kind when he was with Jeanne; authoritarian and despotic when with the Countess, who had never forgiven the Hungarian moujiks for their total adhesion to Bela Kun's communism. Jacqueline Almassy was taking revenge on her staff for the Hundred Days, and directed inflexibly: "She used her whip freely, and counted the sugar lumps; she required her maid to sleep at the foot of her bed when she was ill," says Dr. Krayoli.

Thus, the two Louis's, though totally different, integrated admirably; they perfectly and unswervingly assimilated their contradictory roles. The Hungarian period enabled Louis not only to design superb jewels, but also to prepare new statutes for companies which were to be attached to No. 13. Varying formulae were elaborated for modern times, and everyone, from errand boy to director, had to follow him (they were all referred to as grognards, the term used for Napoleon's army); and all staff realised that the master was keen to maintain the firm's prestige. In a Europe where kings were becoming rarer, the kings' jeweller had to surround himself with the best: graduate administrators, prize-winners and art school graduate creators. Whether in Budapest or in Paris, he showed himself to be more daring than ever.

The Hungarian periods of contemplation enabled him to sort out the internal difficulties of an empire which had become enormous; he knew all about vendettas, about occasional jealousy and hatred between some of his collaborators, about 'banana skin' – sic – policies; he knew that when he promoted one man, he created one ungrateful man and seventy unhappy ones; it was, therefore, important to reorganise the wheels of the huge machine so that: "Once you, Pierre, you, Jacques and I have gone, everything must go on and Cartier must survive, and the torch must be handed on through us."

At that time, nothing was that easy; people stole his ideas, and his staff (such as D., who had won first prize in the Ville de Paris competition, and went on to Janesich to make a sword for an Oriental potentate, the working drawings for which had been executed in Louis' own workshop. But Louis was to have D. back, just as he would re-employ many others who had left slamming the door behind them). Sometimes he did not forget, and pursued with tenacious rancour those who had taken him in, betrayed or robbed him as some of them did; but he also had, at his side, staff whose devotion reached fanatical proportions.

And, indeed, it is hard to see how they would not have followed this extraordinary master of creation, who dreamed up the most sumptuous objects, and used the resources offered by jade, lacquer, mother of pearl and coral, earlier sold by Prieur, Glaenzer and others. Through the magic of creative transposition, age-old mother of pearl, coral and jade acquired a new life in which sapphires, pearls or rubies mingled, such as the tiny Annamite with his conical hat, who was the central character on a mother of pearl plaque dating from the fifteenth century and became a Provençal shepherd asleep at dusk (thereby symbolising the red Venus; the shepherd's star; the milky pearl, the full moon, and the Great Bear diamonds).

In homage to Lord Carnarvon, Louis used his influence on his designers to create objects and jewels inspired by Egyptian High Art, some of the pieces unusual, but always strangely beautiful, such as a lady's sewing box, made out of ivory and solid gold, encrusted with diamonds and onyx, each face of the mini sarcophagus being enriched with sphynx heads of carved emerald. The legend of the curse on the archaeologists worried Louis, who only made two copies of the '*sarcophagi*'.

Was it the necklace offered by Lord Carnarvon to Liane de Pougy that Princess Georges Ghika tried to buy, offering a sum so out of proportion that it was impossible for Louis not to please the beautiful Liane? Many contradictory rumours circulated about the couple: although the Prince received only a small allowance from his family, Liane led a life of luxury in her house at Noailles, where she sumptuously received the best of the Paris intelligentsia: Max Jacob, Jean Cocteau, Rouveyre, Gabrielle Dorziat, Cécile Sorel. The ex-courtesan queen devoted part of her free time to literature and mysticism, continuing, however, to make free with girls for her own pleasure, to her decadent husband's intense satisfaction.

The courtesans of the Naughty Nineties, having become the elder princesses of the Roaring Twenties, were reduced to selling their jewellery. Louis was all the more delighted with the success of his new 'S' department which offered his clients the opportunity of acquiring, apart from Jeanne's evening bags, various objects made of silver, sumptuous travelling cases and – the latest innovation – pastel-edged writing paper which could feature, at the letter-writer's request, his arms and portrait in the water mark.

During a fitting for a tiara, the Countess of Noailles said: "Are you not worried about spreading your talents a little thinly?" to which Louis replied that he simply desired to foresee the wishes of his clients. "If the King of Spain chooses his writing paper here, and the Maharajah of Kapurthala his greeting cards, I will have no sense of failure whatsoever!" The Countess approved, but said that she was still rather worried about her tiara, which she found too classical. Louis told her that, within two years of the Decorative Arts Exhibition, creators were in a state of disarray similar to that which had haunted Modern Style artists twenty years earlier; they had hesitated between luxury and austerity and some people had referred to a form of 'spiritual asceticism' . . . 1925 jewellery must obey certain geometrical requirements: relief, sobriety, moderation were the key words, and 1925 would star diamonds, the cubic crystal *'par excellence'*, set in platinum, which was the most austere and least shiny of precious metals, but allowed the gem to stand out all the better; platinum was a metal which Louis had imposed almost 25 years earlier.

His plans also included contrasting onyx, corals and emeralds, and the inclusion of red and green lacquer, but he decided to banish totally all allusions to flora and fauna. Madame de Noailles listened, fascinated, as he went on to explain that the current artistic explosion, which was to be recorded in 1925, had its roots in the Art Nouveau: in 1909, realism, fauvism, cubism, African art; and Paul Iribe's rose, which ridiculed flowery evanescences with translucent enamels, was closer to Lalique's work than it seemed at first sight; Louis reminded Madame de Noailles that, if Lalique had worked for Cartier in earlier days, Iribe, who was a genius and attempted all things, had also collaborated in the creation of certain of his jewels.

To Louis' gratification the Countess of Noailles declared that she would be delighted with the tiara made of onyx, diamonds and emeralds since the king of jewellers considered its style to be at the spearhead of Art Deco.

Here was geometry, movement, colour, and Louis, when he signed the workshop chits, knew that his concept of modern jewellery was obeying laws defined by Massin under the First Empire period. He was to discuss this with the art critic, Robert de Cizeranne, who wrote in September 1925:

As Cartier foresaw it, pendants shaped like regular or irregular hexagons, swastika shapes, extremely simple combs with pears and faceted coral which were designed in 1820, are in no way dissimilar from the 1925 style of jewellery.

There was, however, innovation in the opposition between onyx, diamonds and the milky green jades allied to pink corals. The emphasis on movement was symbolised in pendants, so softly articulated that they looked almost alive, following the rhythm of the elegant women who wore them like a second skin, clinging to crêpes, jerseys and satins.

4

In September 1923, Louis was shown a document from the manuscript department of the *Bibliotheque Nationale* which had been passed on by Mr. de V., a genealogist; according to this document Louis Cartier was the descendant of Louis Babriel Cartier de la Boutière, who had been granted a baronetcy by His Gracious Majesty Louis the Fourteenth in 1698. After serving Count Bussy-Rabutin, then Maréchal Turenne, Gabriel Cartier de la Boutière had entered the service of the Duke of Orleans as Gentleman of the Chamber; the Cartier coat of arms was: "Azure escucheon with three gold diamonds, two placed at the head and one at the side, the blazon stamped with a helmet crossed with a demi-coronet dressed with gold azure ramplings."

Louis was at first proudly surprised, and then uncomfortably dubious. He read the document repeatedly, and finally called in the best graphologist in Paris. His ambition could have been satisfied by such a document, attesting as it did to his noble origin, but he was not a man of compromise, and there were three areas of suspicion: scribblings, additions, and two illegible names; moreover, he felt that for 100,000 francs in 1922, he was entitled to demand authenticity – having only put down a quarter of the money on account.

Following searches in Albi, Lille and Toulouse and several months of research, as well as the graphologist's confirmation, Louis knew that his redoubtable flair had not deceived him: the genealogist was a fraud. When de V. threatened to sue him for defaulting on his initial financial agreement, claiming that another expert's report would prove that his documents were authentic, he received the following reply from Louis:

> *I may be a baronet in your mind, but Louis-Joseph Cartier, never satisfied with approximations, requests you to be contented with the amount received, and orders that you stop all research concerning his ancestry.*

Jeanne used to tease him sometimes, mischievously transforming him from magnate into baronet. "Let's not talk about it, let's think about it," he would reply. He didn't care about the baronetcy any longer since, on the 10th January 1924, the Mayor of Budapest had sanctioned his union with Countess Almassy. None of the Cartier family attended the wedding; the only one who had been invited, Alfred, apologised for not being able to undertake such a long journey.

Alfred was now 83 and following, although in a different way, the same road that his ageing father had followed. Though disenchanted, he was nevertheless contemptuous of modern times and anxious for the future. He had kept up with his acquaintances in financial circles, and was able to measure, with a mixture of perplexity and worry, the consequences that the systematic destruction of the German mark exchange rate (4 million to the dollar) was having on the monetary world. It was clear to the French that the enemy would not pay; the defeated Germany would never be able to pay its war debts in spite of the economic recovery which had succeeded American loans.

The franc's delicate state resulted, in France, in the voting of a new 20% tax on income. In parliament, the Left had united – they had 26 communist deputies; the socialist-communist press denounced the carelessness of moderate politicians, who had enabled capital to vanish abroad. In the Elysée Palace, Doumergue, who was a friend of Edouard Herriot, was replacing Millerand, the 'protector of the wealthy and the bourgeois'; Alfred had been badly affected by the recent death of his friend, Gaston Worth, and refused amidst all this chaos to speculate on the future of the luxury trade.

His only joy consisted in gathering together every Sunday his Worth and Révillon great grand-children, who were to take on the mantle of inheriting the custom of the cream of European aristocracy from Paris, London, Rome and Madrid, and whatever else remained. But what was to be his children's future? Another kingdom had recently collapsed: George II of Greece had been forced to abdicate to the republic in the person of Venizelos. Yet, what was to be the future of these children? Alfred and Jean-Philippe Worth often asked themselves this question, only to conclude that they were too old by then, belonging as they did to the past, and Jean-Philippe, recalling to mind a party in the Tuileries gardens, guaranteed that he could still design crinolines as worn by the Empress and by Madame de Metternich as well as their hook-bonnets and their little parasols . . . Alfred remembered with nostalgia the elegant grace of ladies of former days, a grace which contemporary women seemed to have lost the secret of – "all tomboys" – and Jean-Philippe would acquiesce and criticise the severe outfit of his daughter, Andrée-Caroline, who was dressed by Chanel. At 40, Louis' former wife seemed only a few years older than her daughter, Anne-Marie. The two women only had a distant relationship. In spite of having two children, Anne-Marie always resented her parents' remarriage, sometimes blaming them for the collapse of her own world. "Her claims stem from greed," the old Cartier grandfather would say. To which Jean-Philippe Worth would comment that little Anne belonged to the bruised and unhappy breed of people who always longed for perfection.

Jean-Philippe Worth had for many years relinquished the administration of his fashion empire to his nephews, and was living his last years in serenity, oblivious of family quarrels, resolutely ignorant of political and social squabbles, and disinterested in the world of luxury. He was not worried that women dressed by Chanel looked like underfed telegraph operators; he found it faintly comical that the insatiable Coco should follow her slave period with a Greek phase, and design not only Antigone's costume, but also her first jewellery.

Jean-Philippe, with bushy eyebrows above his tortoise-shell glasses and his brightly coloured face sporting a short grizzly grey beard, was spending the twilight of his life in a different world, one that was not inhabited by royalty and elegant ladies, although occasionally he would visit the odd former client or certain great actresses. He now devoted his life to disabled servicemen, a guarded secret respected by his close friends.

After his death on the 10th December 1926, the veil was lifted and Paris society learned, through Maurice de Waleffe, how the great Jean-Philippe Worth had devoted the last years of his life to "his blind friends" – and what "blindness" they suffered: black men without faces, one without arms, another with no legs and yet another who had no mouth and could only feed through a straw; he would care for each one of them and call them "my darlings, my children – they have no family; what they need most is moral comfort and tenderness."

Alfred Cartier once went to a meal given in the huge dining room of the Worth house on the Champ de Mars and told how, after lunch, a pianist came to play and:

Those who had legs danced, and a man who was but a blind trunk, but still had ears, listened; later, supported by the host and his staff, he was taken together with the others back to their apartments, as Monsieur Worth used to house them as well as feeding them.

"I will found a magnificent home for blind and disabled servicemen," Philippe would sometimes tell his friend Alfred. However, his untimely death prevented this earthly dream from being fulfilled.

5

Prince Felix Youssoupoff and his wife managed to cross the Crimean border, paying dearly for their freedom with some items from the treasure which had been accumulated by one of the richest families of ancient Russia. Among the jewels, two statuettes – one of which was attributed to Benvenuto Cellini – had been set into a rotating gold base by Cartier during the Second Empire; there was also a black pearl which had belonged to Catherine the Great, and subsequently to Louis-Philippe, the Blue Venus and several necklaces, bracelets and tiaras; altogether some thirty exceptional items. The remainder of the collection was still in Russia, Youssoupoff remarked to the three brothers when they were all in London together:

The Maharajah of Patiala. Head-dress and ceremonial necklace are Cartier creations.

*It is so well hidden that I defy the cleverest Bolshevist to discover it. When
I return to my country, I will find my marvels again.*

Such optimism seemed remarkable – all the more so since France had
just recognised the Soviet government, but it was understandable,
knowing that exiles received bulletins printed in Moscow which
informed them of all the difficulties that had sprung up since Lenin's
death. From February 1924 there was violent dissension between Stalin-
ists and Trotskyists, and Prince Youssoupoff said "so a conflagration
will happen, the regime cannot last, and we will go back – I am
impatient to look at my beautiful possessions again!"

Sadly, the police discovered the treasure while carefully searching the
Prince's house; a People's Commisar, intrigued by an unevenness in
some hanging brocade, ripped it apart, took out a piece of wall and
discovered a steel safe containing a fortune in diamonds, emeralds,
sapphires and rubies, all set in gold or platinum.

The American market offered opportunities for the negotiation of
the sale of the jewels which had been brought out by Rasputin's
murderer. After the 1921 depression, the U.S.A. was experiencing a
level of economic expansion without precedent: in 1923 alone, 500
billion francs' worth of jewels were sold, representing more than 50%
of the world trade. Certain prize pieces from the Tsars' treasure had
reached New York in the coffin of James Jones, a seaman who had died
in the Black Sea; they were bought through the intermediary of banks
dependent on the Federal Reserve Bank. From the Romanoff jewels
Pierre acquired The Imperial Crown and a 120 carat emerald which had
belonged to Catherine the Great.

It was decided to spread the sale of the Youssoupoff jewels over a
period of nine years, following various agreements between the Prince,
the three Cartier brothers, international banks and various insurance
companies. The sale of jewels belonging to Russian emigrés had to be
treated extremely discreetly, whereas an enormous amount of publicity
surrounded the sale of the Thiers jewellery collection, organised in 1924
by the Louvre Museum. The first lot number in the catalogue was the
famous triple pink pearl necklace.

All the world's jewellers wanted to acquire this historical necklace,
which had been put together pearl by pearl. It was sold, row by row,
and acquired by the three brothers for a total of 12,746 francs, each
brother putting a third of the total sum. The three brothers also clubbed

The Royal Elephant with solid gold palanquin (Kapurthala festivities).

together to buy Queen Marie-Antoinette's necklace which, according to romantic legend, was bespattered with blood from the Revolution!

It was Jacques Cartier who was to sell the Queen's necklace to the Duchess of Sutherland. Pierre sold the solid silver dinner service which had belonged to Napoléon I, and Louis sold the world's biggest sapphire to the Queen of Rumania. Pierre, who had become the Pope's secret chamberlain, was also involved in selling some jewels which had belonged to H.H. Benoît XV, as well as the ruby from the Golden Fleece which had been given by Francois II to Charles V as a pledge during his captivity in Madrid.

One can imagine the amazement of the Queen of Spain when, after the death of her godmother, the ex-Empress Eugénie, she received a parcel from France containing about twenty fans, amongst which she discovered a jewellery box which revealed the sparkling light of the favourite necklace of the wife of Napoléon III. Fifty-nine years after the fall of the Second Empire, this historic necklace was exhibited in Barcelona at a show organised by Pierre Cartier and presided over by the Queen of Spain.

A few months later, thousands of miles away from Spain, another Imperial set of jewellery was displayed at a feast in Kapurthala, to which Jacques Cartier had been invited by the Viceroy. Louis was a friend of Francis de Croisset who underlined the following passage in '*Nous avons fait un beau voyage*':

> *The doorway seemed ablaze; people gasped as the Maharajah of Patiala, accompanied by François I, entered looking like the King of Spades; on his neck, amidst the diamond rivers bedecking his shoulders, shone the neck-lace of Empress Eugénie; his skin was dark, his eyes like those of an imperious idol's and his mouth carmine; across his turban, which resembled Charlemagne's crown, he wore diamond drops, sparkling like fireworks, which bedewed his eyes. The chandeliers focussed upon him. He held the spotlight and diffused it. He was immense and, as he held the stage, he epitomised the India of the maharajah. I looked for his officers but could not see them. I could not see anything for I was totally blinded by the magnificence.*

In the margin of the underlined passage, Louis wrote:

> *This turban had been created for Patiala, and was splendid; and the sword which had been designed for the feast at Kapurthala, was an Imperial piece, even more delicate than the ruby walking stick of the maharajah of Jam Nagar. It was for the festivities at Kapurthala that we designed and created medallions for wearing on turbans and on the shoulders, and these were also worn by maharajahs in Kashmir and Bikaner, and by the rajah of Mandi, Alwar, etc.; as you can see, Jeanne, this is the Indian Empire; I would like you to discover it. There are panthers in India as in Africa.*

However, it was at the Vesinet, and not in India, that Jeanne first confronted a panther; it was the famous panther which stood in the hall of the pink palace of Marchioness Casati. The panther was animated through a mechanism which enabled it to jump, with its claws extended, its eyes spewing out flames, to "discourage the thieves," the Marchioness said to Jeanne, who had arrived before the other guests to advise the hostess on her choice of jewels. Outrageously made up, with huge kohl lines emphasising her dark eyes and accentuating the purple

Lapis clock made for King Farouk. Engraved Imperial jade. Hour markings of rubies in gold setting. Hands of rose-diamonds (1946).

dye of her hair (which had been bright green when she had visited the Rue de la Paix the previous week), Casati was choosing and commenting on her choice of jewellery; and Jeanne could see that the Marchioness' taste was as refined as it was eccentric, and that her artistic taste was excellent. All Paris society was gossiping about the Marchioness' perverted tastes, saying that she was the mistress of her black chauffeur, with whom she frequently went on decadent outings – naked under her sable coat – picking up young men and women, preferably from modest backgrounds, and indulging in strange saturnalia either in her midnight-blue Rolls Royce or in the marvellous temple of Apollo at the bottom of her country park.

Louis, while reading Jeanne's letter telling him all about the reception at the Casati palace, recalled that three generations of Cartiers had supplied the various owners of the pink palace with jewellery: François, the ancestor, who was jeweller to the Persian millionnaire, Tata (who had bought the pink palace from the ship dealer, Schweiter, for three seed pearls and an emerald); his own father, who had been purveyor to Comte Robert de Montesquiou; and now the third generation were jewellers to the extravagant Casati, who had been installed at Le Vesinet since Montesquiou's death. It was easy to see that the Marchioness, who was gleefully frittering away the allowance given to her by the King of Italy – of whom it was not known whether he was her natural father or a former lover – would not keep the pink palace for very long. Louis read again the end of Jeanne's letter:

> *The sight of the stuffed panther has confirmed me in my desire to create a panther-jewel; if we manage, it will be something quite different from the one we designed in 1922, and which I now refuse to wear.*

Many years were to pass before Jeanne was able to create the marvellous panther worthy of her African vision; the first was acquired by the Duchess of Windsor.

There were brooches, hat-pins, bracelets – and for Commanding Officer Paul-Louis Weiller, a mother-of-pearl clock topped with a tiny jumping beast. The panther was to become the mascot jewel of the jewellers of kings, thereby consecrating the naturalist style of Jeanne Toussaint.

The 'Louis Cartier' Diamond, 107 carats 07, shown for the first time in New York in 1975 during the Louis Cartier centenary celebrations.

6

Alfred's body was now resting by those of François and Alice in the family vault in the Gonnards cemetery at Versailles, which Louis had designed in a style as simple as a Greek temple. He had told his younger brother, that one day they would all be here, having forgotten all notions of hierarchy and false pride. Pierre had been unable to come to his father's funeral as he was in Miami. Louis wondered what his reaction would be when he learned that the Countess was expecting a child. Jeanne had said:

> You know, boss, there is a Lorraine saying which claims that a child born within three months of the death of a close relative will be of the same sex as the dead person; I hope you will have a boy.

Jeanne was the first to hear the news, in a telegram which said:

> Hurray for the Lorraine saying, he is called Claude and weighs eight pounds.

That very night, to celebrate the birth of Louis' child, she invited Gabrielle Chanel, Misia Sert, Sanchez Elia and Christian Bérard to Maxim's. Jeanne was totally happy, which irritated Chanel who did not understand her meekness. Jeanne recorded:

> We had a violent row; her constant jibes had exasperated me, and in any case we liked to have a row in order to be able to make up again. Coco Chanel rather liked to show off before the right sort of audience.

The audience was indeed remarkable that evening: Misia Sert, former muse of the White Revue, friend of Diaghilev and Stravinsky, favourite model of Renoir, Bonnard and Vuillard; the amazing, refined and intellectual Misia, who had decided to cultivate Chanel; Bérard, too, who loved Jeanne Toussaint as a brother loves a sister, and who had just finished a portrait of her but did not yet know that his art would act as a catalyst on the styles and various artistic genres of his time. Coco Chanel had great regard for Bérard, especially as he now designed stage sets – which had presumably been submitted to Jeanne Toussaint beforehand: he would say to her that if she did not like it, she must say so and he would chuck the whole lot out (there is not one of Bérard's sets which was not previously approved by Jeanne). Like Louis Cartier, 'Bébé' (Bérard) was also aware of her gifts as a colourist.

Did Bérard's admiring friendship for Jeanne annoy Chanel in the same way as Misia's sudden affection for Coco irritated Jeanne? Fifty years later Jeanne was to recall:

I knew all about Misia's legend. She was, at that time, stage queen of 'the intelligentsia', but some of her affectations exasperated me and I remember that, during the evening, Misia said to Gabrielle that she had a divine way of playing with pearls – she was wearing a necklace which had been a gift from the Duke of Westminster, whose mistress Coco had recently become. Coco adored jewellery; she had increased her collection since buying her first item – a tiara ordered from Louis by Boy Capel. I said to Misia, 'She plays with her pearls just like Lanthelme used to do in the old days – and Lanthelme was inimitable.'

Lanthelme, who had been one of the most beautiful courtesans of the 'Naughty Nineties', had been the friend of the wealthy owner of Le Matin, the banker Edwards who subsequently fell in love with Misia. Edwards had organised a cruise on the Rhine on which both Lanthelme and Misia had been invited, and Lanthelme fell overboard; nobody was ever to know whether it was a crime, an accident or a suicide. Soon after this drama, Edwards married Misia who eventually divorced him to marry the Catalan painter, José-Maria Sert.

The exchange over, the evening which had been organised to celebrate Claude Cartier's birth went on at Coco Chanel's in Faubourg Saint-Honoré. Champagne and vodka were flowing – Chanel liked vodka since her affair with Prince Dimitri – and Bérard drank rather a lot; he was not yet smoking opium. Cocteau came to join them, and it was a real party, with masses of people dancing, laughing and singing, most of them totally ignoring the reason why they were at Chanel's. Then another disagreement arose between Chanel and Jeanne. She continued her memories:

She was saying: 'We are not the marrying kind.' I had never considered marriage as an end in itself; my love life with the man I had nearly left for Louis was harmonious, he was aristocratic, rich and had a private house in Biarritz, but I had above all 'married' Cartier's. I loved the job which 'he' had taught me, which I was still learning and always would. I loved it madly! The job gave me a dignity I was proud to assume, and I was all the more disarmed by Chanel's comparison of our destinies: 'We have both been tarts, I am the world's greatest fashion designer, you will become an

internationally renowned jeweller; we have had our crutches, I 'Boy' Capel, you Louis Cartier, but we will always remain the women they abandon, the unmarrying kind, the sterile ones!'

At that stage, Chanel was obsessed with giving the Duke of Westminster a son; she was forty-two and the party organised for the birth of Louis' son was bringing to the surface very old feelings of bitterness.

The relationships between Louis Cartier, Chanel and Toussaint were indeed ambiguous, and they also had much in common: Gabrielle and Louis were both in turn extraordinarily mean or generous; both came from the Auvergne; the interlaced 'CC' designed by Cartier preceded by several years the interlaced 'CC' of Chanel 'No. 5' (which is very similar); when a friend of Louis' commented on this, the elder Cartier made this disconcerting reply: "In this trade, everybody copies everybody else" – when there are no particular similarities between Chanel and Cartier's activities. It is important to remember Coco Chanel's sudden frenetic activity in the design of jewellery – fake jewellery, inspired by original pieces – and that her first designer was Iribe, who had started with Cartier; we must not forget, either, the famous diamond exhibition which took place in 1932 at Chanel's, with the help of the Diamond Consortium, and had international success which prodigiously annoyed Louis and inspired him to react in consequence. Despite the depression, he bought a stock of precious stones which was considerably larger than what he knew he would need (generally decided a year in advance). As he remained *the* leader, other jewellers followed. And it can be said that it was not so much the De Beers Exhibition at Chanel's, but Louis' daring which marked an important upturn in the market, which had been stagnating.

Two hypotheses can be put forward to explain the ambiguity of the Chanel-Cartier relationship: either there was, on Louis' part, a tender complicity towards Chanel in memory of a brief romance, or else Chanel felt an old bitterness based on the knowledge that Jeanne, of whom she was inordinately fond, had been at some stage the mistress of Boy Capel.

Cartier watches from the 'Roaring Twenties'.

7

Louis wrote to Count M. in 1929, that twenty-eight years later he was rediscovering fatherhood.

This was truly a revelation. Whereas he had been rather indifferent to Anne-Marie, four-year-old Claude was a source of constant delight and Louis gave him maximum attention. However, he had to pursue his roving destiny, going from San Sebastian – which was his official residence and where he spent a few weeks each year – to London, Paris and New York. The main port of call remained Budapest, where the young Hungarian prince lived.

In the palace at 5 Tarnok Utca, a suite was reserved for the child, two nannies appointed for his education, together with a French tutor, until he was ready to go to the College du Rosey.

Since 1923, Louis had kept away, not so much from Hungary, as from the Hungarians; he did not like Jacqueline's friends, and refused to accompany his wife to certain parties. He did not like hunting with Prince Esterhazy (who owned 50,000 hectares), whereas the Countess was there constantly; she also spent a lot of time with close friends of Prince Regent Horthy.

Louis' sailing boat was moored in Geneva in the private harbour of '*l'Elma*', a property recently acquired by his brother Pierre, and he would go sailing on Lake Balaton with his only Hungarian friend, Count Stefan, who hated Horthy and his crowd.

In a letter to Count M. dated 28th March 1929, Louis says:

The beauty of Lake Balaton, surrounded by the Bakony mountains, is quite different from that of Lake Geneva. I once told you that what defined me was my love of my job, my collections, my ambition and sailing my boat. If one day they ask about me, I authorise you to say that, after 50, what I loved above all were my son, my job, my collections, my dogs and my boat. Sailing on the lake is good for forgetting the Budapest atmosphere, full of political intrigues and monarchist aristocrats who do not approve of Horthy's policies; the Countess is welcome to take sides; I want to be above such things; luckily, Stefan is a precious friend in my dull gilded exile, all the more precious since we meet in secret while Jacqueline goes about her social engagements or her hunting.

Six years after falling in love with Jacqueline, Louis was accepting the failure of a marriage which was no more a success than his first. Without

*A 'tortoise' clock of enamel
marble. The tortoise shows
the hour and the minutes.*

his son and without Stefan, life in Budapest would have been barely
tolerable, and Louis confessed his fascination for Stefan, who was 54,
educated, cynical, blasé – and yet curious about everything. The Count,
who had recklessly spent a chunk of the colossal family fortune, was
then living with an uncle, whose sole heir he was.

When he was introduced to Louis by Doctor Dubrocki, Stefan had
exclaimed: "Cartier? So you are Cartier the jeweller?" And Louis was
told how, in Vienna in 1913, Count Stefan, who was on the jury of a
military tribunal, had, for the first time, heard the name of the jewellers
at the Rue de la Paix. It had been mentioned by the judge in his
accusation of Lieutenant W., who was a homosexual involved in a spy
scandal. The main exhibit in the evidence had been a solid gold cigarette
case with a cabochon lock, which had been given by W. to his lover,

Lieutenant D. And the prosecutor, showing the cigarette case, had concluded that:

> *You were being blackmailed, your pay could never have enabled you to pay for, or offer this valuable object to your friend; admit it, you must have turned traitor.*

Stefan concluded:

> *That a beautiful homosexual lieutenant should sell state secrets in order to offer a Cartier cigarette case to his current lover must indeed be a glorious title!*

John Osborne was inspired by this authentic episode to write a play, *The Good Patriot*, which was translated by Pol Quentin, and was broadcast in April 1974.

Jewellery played a vital role in matters of death, politics, corruption and love, and the friendship between Louis and Stefan was established from the start; Stefan became Louis' talking gossip column: "In Budapest," said Louis to Count M., "I am certainly as well up as you are on all the Paris gossip."

In 1914, Stefan's brother-in-law had fallen madly in love with Frehel, a young singer at the Eldorado, and had abducted her to his Rumanian estate.

After several months of perfect bliss, the beautiful singer had got bored and had run off back to Paris: the desperate lover despatched Stefan to her, bearing a 20 carat diamond, but she told Stefan:

> *I would rather sing 'Sur les bords de la Riviera' to my Parisian public; tell your baronet brother-in-law that Rumania . . . me off, and take back this bloody stone!*

Stefan, himself, had been madly in love with Gaby Deslys. He was in despair after her death in 1920, and had come to the auction of the courtesan's jewels, wanting to buy back the main item amongst her possessions, which was a necklace with seven pearls – one of them black – weighing 695.96 grains. The auction reached 2,400,000 francs. Stefan gave up the necklace, realising that his intention was morbid, since Gaby had died as a result of refusing the operation which would have saved her, but which would have left a scar on her beautiful neck. In her will, Gaby left all her fortune to the poor of Marseilles, and an annuity to her former lover, Harry Pilcer, who certainly did not need it, supported as he was by a huge, very old and very rich Greek who smothered him in gifts.

It was through Stefan that Louis learned of the marriage difficulties of Liane de Pougy, whose princely spouse had run off with the diva's girlfriend, only to return, repentant, a few months later. Liane was gradually becoming detached from social life, taking refuge in literature and the church. She ended her days in Lausanne, as a Dominican nun, and was buried on the 27th December 1950. Another *demi-mondaine*, Eve Lavaillière, had entered the Order of St. Francis and preceded her in the religious orders.

Stefan, who could no longer take part in the social life which had been his *raison d'être*, existed vicariously through anecdotes, and cursed the financial problems which prevented him from living as sumptuously as he had. Soon, no man would be able to ruin himself for a woman – where were the ladies of yesteryear?

The ladies of yesteryear?

Polaire had died. Emilienne d'Alençon, her hair cropped, wearing a dinner jacket, smoked cigars and chased after young girls. La Goulue was ending her days in a caravan, displaying a mangy menagerie to passers-by, who could not have imagined what her houses, her carriages, her outfits and her jewels might have been like. *La Belle* Otero was now living in a small flat in Nice, having gone through a capital of 50 million francs in Monte-Carlo, and was surviving on an alimony from the *Société des Bains de Mer*. Louis mused:

What became of the black jacket encrusted with diamonds which Jean-Philippe Worth and I designed for you, and which suited you so well?

The lionesses of former days were an endangered species. A few lion cubs remained, threatened by inflation, drugs or drink. Cabanel smoked opium, Maud Loty got drunk, a few pale imitations attempted to break through, and Louis came to the conclusion that new actors were trying to interpret, without conviction, a different role on an old stage set in a play hastily rewritten by an unimaginative author.

Defunct dynasties were being succeeded by new ones: monarchs of the world of corned beef, chewing-gum, shoe polish, oil, cinema, drugs and tobacco. Hill, who owned Lucky Strike, could not conceive of life without a multitude of Cartier accessories, ordered a pair of braces at the Rue de la Paix.

Café-concert singers were replaced by talking picture stars; the world

Created in 1932 for His Majesty the King of Yugoslavia, a small pocket watch in pink guilloché enamel, gold and diamonds, attached to a match case by a dress chain of seed pearls and enamel.

was changing, but Louis was quietly living through this transition period. The jewellery trade was going through a period of incomparable prosperity, and all art lovers and collectors were wanting clocks and jewelled watches. Not wanting to be hemmed in by the 1925 style, Louis had directed his designers towards Oriental styles, using Imperial jades, rubies, emeralds, sapphires and diamonds for decoration (for less sumptuous designs they used red jasper, mother-of-pearl, coral, turquoise and lapis-lazuli). When one of his collaborators told him that his style could seem rather too ornamental, too fussy and heavy, Louis answered that the range of creations designed between 1923 and 1930 would mark the wealth of an exceptional era.

Every royal family, every international museum either possessed, or was awaiting delivery of, a clock or carriage clock, and the latest design was destined for King Alexander of Yugoslavia: it was a pink enamel fob-watch, joined to a round match-box by links of gold, sticks of mother-of-pearl and seed pearls. The workshops were finishing the smallest watch in the world, which would be hidden under a tiny diamond which could be lifted by the pressure of a finger, and Louis had just patented for the whole world a brooch in the shape of a rose, whose moving petals were made of diamond sticks and the stones arranged in such a way that the flower-like brooch would unfold under finger pressure, and keep its shape at all stages of opening.

Louis was continuously creating. It was essential always to do better, and increasingly he found that his art contained more and more powers of invention. In his fever of creation, he was able to forget the financial and political scandals which were shaking France and menacing the régime.

The first scandal had been the arrest of Klotz, who was Clemenceau's Minister of Justice, an inveterate gambler who was compromised by dud cheques and other crooked deals. This was followed by the Hanau scandal and, most recently, some people had started to worry about the behaviour of Serge-Alexandre Stavisky, who had recently been freed after 18 months in prison. Like Marthe Hanau, Stavisky was a friend of ministers, deputies and stars – he had just bought the Empire Theatre and, like her, he owned two newspapers, *Volonté* on the left and *Rampart* on the right. Since his first imprisonment in 1913 (for forgery and corruption), the attractive Sacha, a former pimp and drug trafficker, had gone up in the world, entertaining, at home or at the Restaurant Coty on the Avenue de Wagram, politicians or journalists who were usually delighted to discover that their napkin contained a present, in most cases some sort of Cartier nick-nack.

Like Paris, London and New York were also in the middle of a period of extraordinary prosperity; the wedding of the beautiful Princess Astrid of Sweden and Leopold, Crown Prince of Belgium, was the cause of sumptuous new creations. Even more than the Europeans, high society Americans were living in a world of frenzied luxury: jewellery purchases of $400,000 to $600,000 were frequent occurrences, and Louis was rather worried; he had enough experience of money markets to realise that this euphoria was dangerous: "He who eats too much will get sick." In a letter to Count M., Louis came to the conclusion that his brother, Pierre, had become an isolationist in the same way as had the country in which he was living. The isolationism was explained by the bitterness of the Americans, as defined in a quip by Verger, a journalist on the New York *Herald Tribune*:

All we have got from our intervention in the world conflict has been to be despised by the English and exploited by the French; the war has also given us 'flu and prohibition.

Discussions concerning the settlement of war debts were increasing, a feeling of francophobia was being carefully orchestrated by the American press, and the United States, impregnated by the Republican slogan – 'a chicken in every pot, two cars in every garage', existed in a state of exasperated nationalism.

On becoming president, Edgar Hoover had assured the people that his programme would be devoted to eradicating poverty, but neither he nor the rest of the American population realised immediately what the consequence would be of the huge financial crash which was to become known as 'Wall Street's Black Thursday'.

On the 24th October 1929, 12,894,650 shares were to change hands, causing a suicide epidemic in New York; a man who requested a room at midnight in the Waldorf Astoria Hotel was asked: "A room on the 50th floor? Is it for sleeping in or for jumping out of?"

Millions of people out of work, riots, hunger, despair: Wall Street's Black Thursday was ringing the knell of the previous decade full of illusions, and yet in Paris, Cartier was preparing the December exhibition devoted to India, which the whole press applauded. *L'Illustration* wrote:

This is a dream world, the incarnation of a fugitive Oriental dream; we admired the incomparable gems of Patiala's crown, reset by Cartier at the Maharajah's request. At Cartier's, dreams take shape, we are in the world of the One Thousand and One Nights, and the beauty and extent of his collection surpass the imagination.

CHAPTER SEVEN

The Difficult Years

1

At the beginning of 1931, America had seen its production diminish by a third, the Gross National Product fall from 104 to 56 billion dollars, and the average individual income had fallen from $678 to $360. There were 12 million unemployed in 1933 on the eve of the election of F.D. Roosevelt, and by then no country was being spared from the rising tide of economic difficulties.

Payment of war debts to American allies had been suspended, and this was putting pressure on Franco-American friendship; both Pierre Cartier and his close friend, Paul Claudel, who was French ambassador in New York, each played the role of mediator wanting, to be "a Frenchman bringing to everything a French passion."

Claudel, author of *Tete d'Or, Partage de Midi* and *l'Otage*, had been a close friend of the Cartiers since 1928; his daughter was at the same school as Marion; so when the poet's son fell madly in love with the jeweller's daughter, Elma Cartier agreed that this was a logical development in view of the parents' own mutual background. In April 1933, when Paul Claudel was preparing to leave the embassy, and was working on the proofs of *Jean Charlot*, the elite of New York were invited to the wedding of Marion Cartier and Pierre Claudel. Neither Louis nor Jacques attended the wedding.

Jacques, who had been gassed in 1917, had had to abandon his post as President of Cartier-London and was living in St. Moritz where he had founded, together with his life, the Jacnel company (Jacques-Nelly), which was responsible for the distribution of the 'S' products in Switzerland. The youngest brother in the trilogy was to collaborate closely with Jeanne Toussaint, and their relationship, having been purely professional, became of a friendly nature.

Louis, who had had cardiac trouble in February 1933, had to take a complete rest for a few months, and was constantly reminded of his

The Duke and Duchess of Kent (1934).

vulnerability by the box containing the minute pills which he always had to have by him. He wrote to Count M.:

> *I remain condemned to avoiding outbursts, rages and cares; I have to swallow one or two pills at the slightest warning: what is the point of glory and riches under these conditions, when medicine more than age makes you humble?*

Only his wife, a few Hungarian friends of hers, Stefan, Count M. and Jeanne knew of the seriousness of his condition. Intrigues were to multiply at the jeweller's court, and Louis was fully aware that No. 13 remained the centre of this art and industry. On the surface, everything was working as he wished. It was a perfectly regulated machine but, as he was to write to Jeanne:

*Knowledge of my condition could be the grain of sand, do not tell anyone
about my state; keep an eye on the puppy which Stefan will give you; he is
still a little young to be really clean, call him Nouck, I have kept his sister;
Nouck will be the witness of an even closer tenderness.*

Jeanne, always formidable, was proving indispensable, looking after
not only new creations and stock, but also keeping an eye on a world of
setters, enamellers, lapidaries and watch-makers. Faithful to the training she had received, she had digested perfectly the lesson of the past
and, to cope with the economic crisis, was now able to direct those
heading towards a new style – finding bold solutions in difficult times.
For example, in 1933 Jeanne used gold (platinum was exhorbitant).
That year, Jeanne stood for simplicity, sobriety and a deliberate break
from the luxury of previous creations to impose a simple style, and she
also managed to harmonise, especially on the watch-making side, fifteenth and sixteenth century Japanese influences, with their riot of
colours and creations within which modern settings matched ancient
statuettes and Egyptian ceramics.

2

The principality of Monaco was in fashion again, thanks to the gossip
columnist, Elsa Maxwell, who was a friend of the Prince, and in
Monte-Carlo, Louis chartered a yacht, the *Cyprius*. After several
months of inactivity, Louis was busy and intent on reconquering his
wife. Their first important guests on the *Cyprius* were Grace Moore,
Winston Churchill and Gloria Swanson, who was wearing two stretching platinum bracelets enriched with diamonds – "a marvellous feat of
technicality," remarked Charlie Chaplin, who was an afficionado of the
jeweller of kings.

Jacqueline Cartier was the magnet and star of all parties, where her
elegance and sumptuous jewels sparkled. Louis was in his element. He
wanted to be happy, to forget the annoying existence of the life-giving
pills; to be happy, despite the rise of Nazism in Germany and the
paralysis of its economy. Louis believed in Roosevelt's 'New Deal', and
he had decided to set up a branch in Cannes. "All economic crises are
bound to be overcome, and soon millionnaires and stars will flock to the
Cote d'Azur," he said. Nothing could stop the discussions, neither the

*'Rosace' parure. Rubies
and diamonds mounted in
yellow gold (Cartier,
1982).*

riots nor Stavisky's 'suicide', nor political upheaval – "whatever happens, Cannes will open in 1935."

He wrote to Count M. that optimism is the antidote to physical weakness, adding that Stavisky's death had reminded him of the birth of his idea for the clip brooch (the handsome Sasha had offered hundreds of them to his guests).

I thought of the clip brooch when Jeanne, who was playing with her mother-of-pearl plaque, was placing it now on her shoulder, now on her waist, now on her breast, complaining, 'What in the world could we do with this thing, one would have to pinch the material, it's too heavy for a brooch which would ruin the material, but it is so pretty, so beautifully decorative.' I put the mother-of-pearl plaque away, intending to think about it, but didn't until the time when I was staying on your estate in the Morvan and I saw a woman hanging out the washing with wooden clothes pegs; the principle of the clip brooch was born. Nobody took it up at first; now it is a triumph, and the new hair-clips confirm the fascination. Please say thank you to your washerwoman.

The year 1934, which had started with bloody riots on the 6th February, ended with the wedding of the Duke of Kent and Princess Marina of Greece. The description of the young couple's jewels delighted ordinary people, who for a while forgot the drama of that year as they heard of the luxury surrounding the royal wedding; in France, King Alexander of Yugoslavia had been assassinated, also Louis Barthou; in Germany, there were terrible Nazi repressions and over one thousand killings during the night of the long knives.

1935 began in a disturbing manner: in the Sarre, 90% of the inhabitants voted for the attachment of their region to Nazi Germany; the Italian invasion of Abyssinia unsettled many people in France, who had sung the praises of Mussolini; the whole of Europe was wondering about the Stresa conference and the Franco-Soviet pact; in Paris, one government followed another without managing to thwart the catastrophic financial collapse.

André Citroën was filing for bankruptcy, Paul Poiret was slowly sinking into oblivion and poverty; he was soon to share his sandwiches with the pigeons on the Promenade des Anglais; Jeanne, whom Louis had placed in charge of the top range of jewellery, was achieving miracles to satisfy customers who were worried (for the first time since the discovery of the Transvaal mines, diamonds had dropped in value), and sumptuous jewellery sets were difficult to sell.

Chimera bracelet, with crossed heads, Diamonds and rubies on yellow gold (1980, Cartier).

However, the clock and watch-making department was doing tremendously well, and Jeanne was encouraging the designers to create a new range of objects incorporating watches: paper-knives, ink-wells, desk-top clocks and carriage clocks, pens, etc.; the keenest customer was the Maharajah of Kapurthala, whose record collection of clock pieces reached 348 items (a specialist spent all his time looking after them all and winding them up).

1934–1935 was to be Jeanne's 'Qajar' period and, as she wrote to Jacques Cartier:

Enamelled gold, hanging ear-rings, seed pearls, we are creating quality jewellery to delight our patrons, we are keeping the flag flying, and, if you consider the number of craftsmen who have gone under – more than 20 jewellers have given up since the beginning of the crisis – we can only congratulate ourselves that we did right to design jewellery in a less exalted context.

Jeanne was keeping an eye on No. 13's prestigious position with all the more care since her boss had returned very tired from the inaugural sailing of the *Normandie*. Before returning to Budapest, he had told her that he had serious decisions to take very soon, "which may concern you as well." She had answered, "When you made me your principal collaborator, you took the only important decision for me."

There was no bitterness left in Jeanne, who had known for a long time, through Jacques, how much the family regretted the coalition of former times. Nelly Cartier had then told her, "You were the only one who could have made Louis happy, we are convinced of it."

It was too late. If Louis had remained the beacon of her life, Jeanne's road would have been lit up by the tenderness of the man who had loved her for many years, and whom she would eventually marry. They met either in the private house he had given her in 1920, or in her flat on Place d'Iena, where she entertained the international elite – the Prince of Wales and Wallis Simpson were among her closest friends, as was Cecil Beaton; he wrote:

Madame Toussaint's flat, where a few select friends are invited, is another side of her sensitive but rigorous femininity. We must trust her taste, and gradually we notice details in this harmonious whole; her flat is like a secret which few people are privileged to share with her. The nearly empty panelled rooms are arranged in a modern way, and yet the furniture consists of rare and marvellous sixteenth century pieces. On the parquet floor,

The Qajar period of Jeanne Toussaint (1950). Necklace of seed pearls, coral beads, coloured stones and diamonds, pendant of seed pearls and coral, mounted in gold and enamel.

polished like a mirror, stands an antique vase filled with white lilac; an exquisite table sports a Greek sculpture and, on a shelf, a robust lily bursts out of a piece of Chinese pottery; elsewhere the head of Buddha, sitting on top of a column, projects its shadow on a sculpted screen. A pale fur rug lies on a huge sofa covered in white satin and scattered with champagne-coloured cushions. Madame Toussaint's fabulous four-poster bed is draped with a heavy satin which is neither white nor grey nor blue, but all of these together; this flat is purity itself, the luxurious equivalent of utter simplicity. The extreme intellectual beauty of the flat is the result of the combination of the sensitivity of an artist and the passion of a collector. In her jewellery creations as much as in the quality of the wine and the food she gives her guests, Madame Toussaint shows voluptuous sensuality, which reveals a creator who knows man does not live by mind alone. Jeanne Toussaint is the typical example of the kind of French taste which colours the whole of life; a jeweller by calling, she also displays a talent for living.

The Jeanne of 1935 expressed, in the jewels she made, her gifts as an architect and as a sculptor, and Princess Bibesco said of her that her influence would extend throughout the world. Her liking for unusual settings and the juxtaposition of different stones confirmed her style, at once classical and original, as well as her concern for proportion and balance.

"Have I learned my lesson right?" asked Jeanne when showing Louis a jewellery set in Indian style, and he approved the contrasts between aquamarine, coral, amethysts and tourmaline, turquoise and onyx; the combined colours inspired from the Orient, defined an inimitable style which was copied throughout the world.

3

In May 1936, the Popular Front reigned in France, which was paralysed by unprecedented strikes. Louis called his Hungarian lawyer to organise the safeguarding of Madame Cartier's interests in case – he insisted that this was only a hypothesis – he should envisage divorce proceedings: he had decided to retire to his Spanish estate and assumed that the Countess would refuse to follow him there.

Mr. Kestlei said that since February Spain had been in the grip of the *Popular Front*, and that anarchy was reigning, whereas the Hungarian

Cartier, Cannes.

territory's integrity was guaranteed by the international convention of The Hague. Louis' face coloured when he replied that he had no brief for international conventions, and added that Hitler's ambition would soon know no bounds, that the occupation of the Rhine region had entailed no reprisals, that nothing was happening except talk, talk, talk; 'they' had talked on ad nauseam about German guns aimed on Strasburg. His decision was taken, he had thought about it carefully: from September, all his collections, his pictures and antique furniture would leave Hungary and be shared between his San Sebastian house and the house at the Rue Saint Guillaume, he would leave the palaces in Verbocki Utca to the Countess.

On the 14th July 1936, after the murder of Calvo Sotelo, Spain entered into Civil War.

In France, confusion reigned and the luxury trade was in a state of total paralysis; all Coco Chanel's seamstresses were occupying the workshops, to her utter indignation, and she swore that she would get her revenge.

During the summer of 1936, Louis, who was in Biarritz, realised the absurdity of his future as an official resident in Spain, about to be dispossessed by the Civil War, and the owner of three Hungarian palaces which a world conflict would soon dispossess him of. He was convinced, like many of his peers, that the victory of the Popular Front in Spain would bring about the rise of bolchevism in France, and believed that a revolution was due to happen, but that a military coup would sort it all out.

He talked to Jeanne about the ridiculous nature of his situation: "From Budapest to San Sebastian, I shall soon have nowhere, all I need is for a revolution to take place in France and I shall lose my house in the Rue Saint-Guillaume!" And yet, despite this pessimism and the growing economic difficulties, he went down to Monte-Carlo to discuss the setting up of a Cartier shop in Monaco; there was soon to be an ideal setting alongside the Hôtel de Paris, which was the hotel where he had in former days met Diaghilev, Stravinski and Chaliapine.

As he had reckoned, the Cote d'Azur was now attracting the international elite all the year round; royal families, exiled princes and millionnaires rubbed shoulders in the Hôtel de Paris, where Edward VIII was staying incognito. Wallis Simpson, who was staying with American friends at Le Canet, came every afternoon to meet the former Prince of Wales.

The three of them dined together, and when, at the end of the meal, Louis announced that he was planning to open a Cartier branch in 1938, the English King answered that, from Monte-Carlo to Miami, London to Paris, Wallis and he would remain faithful patrons.

And so it was that Louis learned of the coming royal decision that Edward VIII preferred love to power. He envied the King his courage, remembering his own abdication before his Family Council; his regrets were increased by a remark from the King, who was admiring Jeanne's many gifts: she was, at the time, creating a set of jewellery for Wallis composed of sapphires, pearls and diamonds.

Edward VIII had had a chance to see, in the Rue de la Paix showrooms, the Academician's sword made for George Duhamel out of rock crystal, with a decoration of flowers and leaves and a lotus flower, the sacred flower of India, on the handle; the head of a snake was

Cartier, Monte-Carlo.

emerging from the flower, the snake symbolising medicine; Louis recognised that Jeanne's naturalistic style was growing and that she would continue to amaze them all.

On the 6th December 1936, Edward VIII told the world that he was abdicating in favour of his brother, George. Louis was in New York, where Pierre Cartier had just been appointed official French representative for the Art and Technology Exhibition which was to open its doors in May 1937. The younger brother's responsibilities in the social and diplomatic world were acquiring more importance than his activities as a jeweller; he was now merely supervising Cartier-New York, which Jules Glaenzer and his son-in-law were managing.

The illustrious father-in-law of Pierre Cartier's daughter had fallen in love with gems, and was preparing a 'mystique of precious stones'; Louis and his brother were privileged to read the first manuscript written by Paul Claudel, and devoted to diamonds. The elder Cartier brother was moved, and acknowledged that an authentic poet was the only person who could express the symbolism of the diamond.

With pick-axes, with miner's bar, through patience, man has questioned the most compact and most concentrated substance concealed in rock, and he has found it in quartz and basalt; he found the chestnut in its shell, the fine crystal at the heart of the bomb, an eternity which is the product of effort, a quintessence, an internal fruit obtained through the compression of a world.

There are two types of geological creation: one is obtained through a process of disintegration, such as with granite which becomes clay. The other – just as the philosopher who, sifting through a multitude of facts, reaches a concept, an abstract gem of a perfect definition – is a kind of creation or parturition, an end in itself which escapes rot through simplicity. The earth's entrails have given birth to this bezoar. It is through cosmic pressure, through an action like that of a world revolting against its own inertia, the telluric crushing, the vomiting of an internal fire, matter buried in the deepest earth and yet brought out by the inexorable search of one hand, the thousand years old crushing of interpenetrating layers, all the mystery, all the metamorphic activity finally produce such a diamond, a sacred crystal, a perfect and translucent walnut which has escaped the rotting husk. And yet, it is not yet perfect! Man's hand has to caress the inviting stone. A slow polishing action must remove the inherent darkness, increase the cleaving, obliterate the defect, awaken the secret eye, complete the sketched rose. The facet must multiply the prism. Daring must go beyond refusal. The solid number, the mineral miracle, must happen; in the hand of the craftsman, the minuscule sun must appear, whose rays are the result of geometry. No longer a mere mirror, but a source.

"I can forgive him Tete d'Or," observed Louis.

CHAPTER EIGHT

The Dark Years

1

Revolution was rife in Spain, China and Russia where executions followed trials. France was in a disastrous financial state, and Leon Blum was forced to let Chautemps take his place.

In March 1938, German troops entered Vienna.

At the end of March, one of the top Cartier salesmen and his secretary took a plane for Tirana to present to King Zog I the jewellery sets which had been made for his wedding to Geraldine, the Hungarian daughter of Count Jules Apponyi. The Cartier representatives were also bringing the tiaras which had been ordered by the Princess.

On the way back, their mission accomplished, the two men registered the trunk containing the remainder of the collection, and then went through customs. They were about to embark when an Italian officer, with his aide-de-camp, told them to give up their seats. The salesman tried to argue, and the officer, his gun at the ready, shouted an order. The plane took off and shortly after a formidable explosion shook the airport building; no survivors were to be found. "We have just had a miraculous escape," said the white-faced secretary. "Certainly," replied the salesman, "but the collection has disappeared."

During the Second World War, English officers patrolling Albanian mountains were surprised to find peasant women wearing splendid jewellery, and told the authorities. A minute part of the collection was thus recovered.

King Zog I awarded a Certificate of Royal Appointment to Louis Cartier, and at the time could not have foreseen that he would only rule for one further year, after which he was forced into exile by the presence of Mussolini's troops.

For millions of French people, the summer of 1939 revealed the pleasure of relaxation. The last fling before *l'affaire des Sudètes*. On their return from their first paid holidays, most of them received their mobilisation orders.

The engine turning shop (1935).

At the end of September, after the Munich agreements, Daladier and his British counterpart were welcomed at le Bourget as messengers of peace by a delirious crowd; the spectre of war was receding at the price of the partition of Poland.

Louis had prolonged his holiday in Biarritz, and every day he met his old friend, Enrique de Meneses, who was the *New York Herald* correspondent and had founded *Cosmopolis*, a magazine of which the eldest Cartier was the main shareholder.

After the fall of the monarchy in Spain, Meneses had been disappointed by the Republic; he hated all forms of dictatorship and had chosen exile in 1936 for himself and his family; he had been working on a novel for a year, and discussed it at great length with Louis. Louis encouraged him: "*Condemned to Death in Both Camps* will be worthy of your talent. Denounce communism as you denounce Franco, and I am convinced that your book will be the greatest testimonial on the Spanish Civil War."

OPPOSITE PAGE, TOP LEFT: *An engraver at work in the design shop.* RIGHT: *Model-making.* BOTTOM LEFT: *A diamond mounter at his bench.* RIGHT: *The final stage of the specialist: the finishing touches to a brooch.*

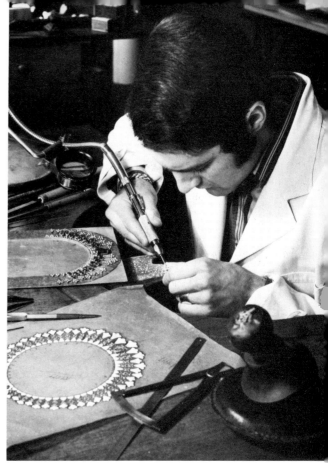

Meneses and he shared so many mutual memories: the extraordinary meal they had in the palace of Count Cimera (the most elegant man in Madrid), a reception given by the Duke of Alba in his palace of Liria, yet another reception given by the Duke and Duchess of Medinaceli where Louis had been received like an ambassador, and the shattering discovery of Granada which had been for Louis the source of inspiration for a whole line of creations!

All this was now of the past, as much for Meneses in his exile as for Louis, who had sworn that he would not live in war-ridden France under German occupation. They both searched for truth whilst playing golf, "This may be our last game, who knows whether the summer of 1939 will see us together! Whatever happens, you must continue your work!" *Condemned to Death in Both Camps* was to appear in France in 1946 under the title *Frappe Mais Ecoute*. In the meantime, Louis Cartier's friend had been put in prison at Franco's orders for 27 months for writing *Le Cheval d'Attila*.

On the 3rd September 1939, the whole family, who had gathered in Biarritz, split up and left in different directions: Pierre and his wife went to Geneva, their daughter, Marion, and her husband left Bordeaux on the first sailing for the United States; Jacques refused to return to Saint Moritz, saying, "If I must die, I want to do so on French soil," and so Louis put the estate at his disposal; he insisted that Anne-Marie should accompany him to America with her children, but she refused. There was an expression in her eyes and in her voice which deeply worried Louis, and he therefore resigned himself to leaving her in France; in any case, her nervous condition was likely to get worse when she met Claude, whom she called "this other child of yours." He could hardly blame her for her attitude; her husband's death from a brain haemorrhage during a stay in New York had made an already delicate condition worse.

Louis dashed to Paris where he had to take important decisions because of the mobilisation of many of his staff; he gave Mademoiselle Decharbogne power of attorney, and confirmed Jeanne's responsibility for de luxe jewellery. The three of them dined together and Louis remarked, "I, who was such a mysogenist, now leave my empire to two women, you must admit it's funny!" During the meal, Jeanne told him that, on mobilisation day, Chanel, who was increasingly sour about the triumph of Schiaparelli, her rival, had closed down her business, sacking all her workers without warning, and had thereby taken her revenge on them for the 1936 strikes. Louis commented that this was typical of Chanel. The three friends parted with some emotion.

"I thought of getting a divorce four years ago," he said to Jeanne. "I knew it," she answered. "You can go, if not in peace, at least in the knowledge that we will do our best to preserve and maintain the prestige of Cartier's name."

This was a strange war. The fighting took place only between the Maginot and Sigfried lines. Since September, Europe had been living in a state of expectation, but a few Parisian salons continued to be the scene of sumptuous parties.

In the Rue de la Paix, Jeanne sought inspiration in designs created during the difficult years, and the workshops concentrated on those created between 1933 and 1937; among others, she loved the caged bird, and asked the advice of Etienne Bellanger, director of Cartier-London, and John F. Hasey, who had spent some time in Paris: they both approved.

In April, Hitler's armies occupied Denmark, invaded Belgium and Holland on May 10th and reached Abbeville on the 20th. A number of changes took place within the Allied Forces: Marshall Pétain was appointed Minister of State, Charles de Gaulle became Under-Secretary of War and General Weygand became Commander-in-Chief. In England, Churchill replaced Chamberlain.

After Belgium's surrender and the battle of Dunkirk, Italy declared war on France and Great Britain, and, on the 14th June, Paris saw the arrival of the German soldiers. On the 17th June, Pétain asked for a truce; in London, General de Gaulle was preparing the statement he was to pronounce on the BBC the following day in the office of Jacques Cartier.

For seven days, until the 25th June when the armistice took effect, General de Gaulle's headquarters were installed in Cartier's office, and Jacques' Rolls-Royce was placed at his disposal.

The Resistance badges were all to be made in London.

In *Le Général*, written in collaboration with Geneviève de Gaulle, Pierre Galante says:

At the beginning of July 1940, the General met his first American at Monsieur Etienne Bellanger's, who was the Director of Cartier in London. This was John F. Hasey who had just arrived from Cartier, Paris. John Hasey said, 'One evening, my friends Mr. and Mrs. Bellanger, invited me to dinner at their Putney house, and the guests of honour were

General and Madame de Gaulle. After dinner, the General questioned me about conditions in occupied France, and on my plans – I had nothing special in mind at that time. When the guests had gone, the Bellangers asked me for my impression of the evening and of the General. I replied that he seemed fantastic and could not lose. The next day, I joined the Free French forces in the Foreign Legion. In August, I took part in the expedition to Dakar. Of course, the General was serious, reserved, even cold, and yet there was in him a sensitive streak which he did not hesitate to show: when he learned that I had been seriously wounded in Damascus in June 1941, he immediately ordered my transfer to the United States so that I should be in hospital there. When Colonel Pierre de Chevigne, Charge d'Affaires for the Free French in Washington, asked who would pay for all the expenses, General de Gaulle said, 'We will.' Then, one day when I was still in hospital, I received a letter from him in which he wanted to tell me personally that, as I had been the first American to shed blood for the Free French, I would be the first American to be awarded the Medal of the Liberation.

In December 1940, the windows in Rue de la Paix displayed a number of brooches and pendants in the shape of caged birds. The German secret service, who knew that Cartier-London had helped de Gaulle and that one of the senior Cartier-New York associates had joined the Free French Forces, summoned Jeanne Toussaint to the Hotel Majestic; the reason for this was that the caged birds were considered to be a case of unacceptable provocation.

"The caged bird symbolises the Occupation – please explain."
"The first caged bird was a trinket designed for a bracelet for Yvonne Printemps in 1933."

"And the other trinkets?"
"A dog, probably a rac, they were the vogue at the time, an Eiffel Tower, other designs, I can't remember."

"So why choose the bird, and the CAGED bird specifically?"
"Because I like birds."

"But what do you know about Etienne Bellanger and John F. Hasey?"
"They are London and New York colleagues who were working in Paris, and they left as they had come. Since 1908, it has been the general custom for important associates from the United States or Britain to come for a stay at the Rue de la Paix."

Louis Cartier in the autumn of his life.

"We will see you again," said the officer.
"I remain at your disposal," said Jeanne.

Curiously, the German authorities never bothered Jeanne again, apart from a visit to the shop during which they had a detailed look at the documents concerning Yvonne Printemps' bracelet. There are two hypotheses: either certain parts of the German secret service were working with the Intelligence Service, or else it could have been the result of the intervention of Coco Chanel, who was having an affair with the handsome German officer, Von D.

2

Louis made several trips to see John F. Hasey, who was the first Companion of the Liberation, and was convalescing in New York entirely at de Gaulle's expense. When he learned of Bellanger's role, Louis was torn between pride and worry; he knew that the Germans had bothered Jeanne, and they could now attack Jacques. Hasey and Jules Glaenzer reassured him: America was about to enter the war, and everything would move very fast.

Two years later, the notion 'America first' had changed, and America's neutrality was a mere formality. After the Havana Conference and the sending of 50 destroyers to England, America now had obligatory military service (the decision had been taken a week before the signing of the tripartite pact between Germany, Japan and Italy).

Japanese claims on Indo-China had been growing since the filtering through of Japanese troops into Tonkin; the United States had decided to prolong the duration of military service after the German invasion of Russia and, since promising to help Russia, the American Navy had been openly taking part in the Battle of the Atlantic (the law enabling merchant ships to supply Europe and North Africa had been voted in with a large majority).

On the 7th December, after the attack on Pearl Harbour, the United States and China entered the war against Germany and Japan, and, on the 10th December, Louis learned of the death of his brother Jacques from a telegram which came via Washington.

He was heartbroken at the thought that he could not go to his younger brother's funeral; such was the cruel and ironic destiny of the exiled citizen; he thought he could hear Jeanne's voice, and was comforted to know that she would go to the Basque Country. In death, Jacques was once again the vulnerable and sensitive adolescent whom he had guided, supported, helped and, yes, loved; the gentle Jacques, quintessentially an artist, yet he had achieved the stature of an international businessman in order to emulate his brothers.

The following day, a message was sent through the embassy to Biarritz, and coded orders reached Paris requesting one of Louis' colleagues to sail for New York as soon as possible.

Three-colour gold bangle.

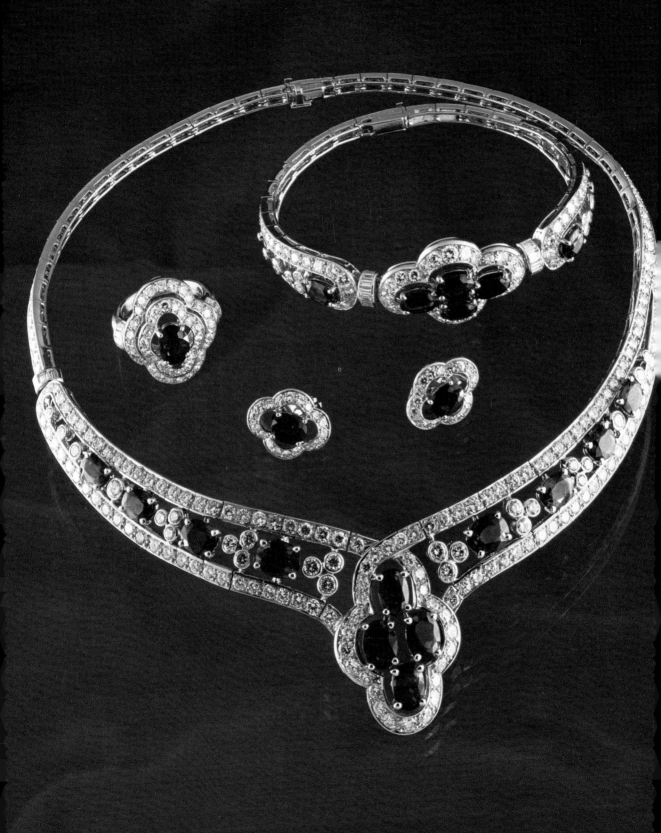

He arrived there 35 weeks later, after following the usual complicated itinerary via Madrid, Tangiers and a twelve-day crossing. Louis greeted him in person; he was shattered by the stuffy humidity of the July weather. The main aim of the interview concerned business and financial matters relating to Jacques' death; the 1921 agreement stipulated that, if one of the partnerships failed or the head of one of them was to die, the others became responsible; however, in July 1942, the future of the New Bond Street business, situated as it was in a capital living through the blitz, was a matter for conjecture.

Other reasons had motivated Louis to demand F.'s presence, the most important of which being to let him know the results of research carried out in collaboration with the Battell Institute in New York, which concerned the use of palladium in an alloy destined for use in setting; it was lighter than platinum and considerably less expensive. Louis showed F. a prototype with which he was not entirely satisfied, but he was convinced that he would soon overcome the problems caused by the softness of the alloy, adding that if he succeeded he would yet again have worked for the future.

F. said that his boss, at the age of 67, had not changed: he was disillusioned but always full of hope. Louis said that it would be his son's duty to use the lessons of the past to go into the future "as we have all done throughout the generations since 1847."

He talked to him at length about Claude who, at 17, was something of a dilettante, a top-class tennis player, a swimmer, a champion bobsleigh rider and mad about flying. He was also a very good draughtsman, but seemed to have little inclination for business. "Money which comes from work is vulgar; although my son is the descendant of Montorgueil craftsmen, he is also that of an aristocrat."

Louis was convinced that responsibilities would bring the necessary qualities to Claude, and that he would follow in his own footsteps. In a world agitated by wars, it was difficult to envisage the role of the fourth generation, but he was comforted to think of Claude reigning over Rue de la Paix, just as Marion and Pierre Claudel were doing on Fifth Avenue, while in London, Jacques' sons, Jean-Jacques and Harjes, were carrying on with the tradition. Tomorrow would always be better.

They chatted on about some of the extraordinary memories of a past rich in anecdotes, and F. recalled how, on a wet autumn evening, just as the metal shutters were being lowered, he had stopped the boy operating the handle, to let in a shady-looking character, wearing a soaking

'Rosace' parure.
Sapphires and diamonds
mounted in yellow gold
(1982, Cartier).

LE PRINCE CHARMANT
RUE DE LA PAIX.

*Cartoon illustrating a visit
by the Prince of Wales,
future King Edward VIII,
Duke of Windsor, to
Cartier in 1924 (by Sem).*

wet raincoat and a felt hat right down over his eyes, dripping with rain: it was Rockefeller himself, whom he had recognised under his unlikely appearance; that night the American placed orders worth millions.

. . . There was the Prince of Wales' visit in 1925, with all the girls in the street crowding before the shop, and Sem, the artist, who happened to be going past had made a quick sketch of 'Prince Charming visiting Rue de la Paix'. They recalled, too, the visits of the King of Siam and his wife, and the Jubilee . . . "Tell me the story of the Jubilee again," said Louis.

In 1938, the richest man in France had bought the diamond which had in former days been offered by Jagersfontein to Queen Victoria; the sale had been extremely difficult and required months of delicate discussions, until the memorable moment when Jacques Cartier, with four bodyguards, had brought to No. 13 one of the most famous diamonds in the world. The happy new owner had casually put the jewel in his pocket after signing a cheque carrying an impressive number of noughts. Once at the driving wheel of his car, he said: "I'll just go and change, I'm dining at Maxim's, I'm in a hurry to show the Jubilee to a few friends!"

The following morning when he woke up, the wealthiest man in France noticed that his dumb valet was empty; he could remember putting the historic gem in the inside pocket of his dinner-jacket, and in spite of his vast composure he had a moment of near panic when his majordomo told him that the butler had taken the dinner-jacket to clean a stain on the lapel "to the pantry, or perhaps he sent it to the cleaners."

The man, who was not only a first world war hero, an experienced aviator and a consummate businessman, who had multiplied the immense family fortune, could not lose his self-control, and with an even voice asked William: "Gaston did not mention a small box?"

"A small box? Sir means the jewel box? I do beg your pardon, he did give it to me a moment ago, I was called to the second floor, but here it is. Here you are, Sir."

William went and fetched the Jubilee from among the porcelain spice jars, and the richest man in France wondered whether Queen Victoria would have been amused.

Louis commented that F. was getting ever more daring when he told his stories. They were to go on reminiscing after dinner.

The master of the house was extremely annoyed to learn that the menu had been changed. He went bright red and took two pills. He was in a bad mood throughout the meal, and at the end of it the two men returned to the smoking-room. The boss asked his colleague how things were going. F. explained the new type of clients: black marketeers, traffickers, a few Germans. Goering himself had bought a watch: he had been very impressed by the royal testimonies and had suggested providing Cartier with a certificate from the Third Reich. "And now, tell me about . . ."

Suddenly, Louis' face turned puce, his eyes turned upwards, he brought his hand to his chest, his head shook and he collapsed. No pill could save him now from a death which occurred during a last moment of pleasure, while spending his exile with a close colleague from Paris.

A simple notice in *Aujourd'hui* dated 24th July 1942 said:

> *Louis Cartier, Director of Cartier Jewellers, died in New York yesterday after a long illness.*

The German authorities took no notice, but from Paris to Jersey, from San Sebastian to Rio de Janeiro, businessmen, lawyers and solicitors were studying the case of 'Loutier', a man of independent means, officially residing in Spain, who had died in New York. All this had to be done unofficially because of the Vichy decree which stated that any company whose directors had left the country would be commercially and administratively run by acting administrators, who would naturally be under the control of the German authorities.

It was therefore decided that the will would not be read until after the end of hostilities; if the war lasted beyond a year and a day, the case would establish a precedent.

During a meeting attended by family solicitors, L.D. (who had recently been freed), and the faithful Mademoiselle Decharbogne, Jeanne recalled what Louis had once said: "My destiny lacks simplicity, but I have lived through complications almost without noticing . . ."

So Louis died as he had lived, and he left his executors, his family and his friends to deal with an incredibly complicated judicial imbroglio, which was said by one lawyer to be without precedent: the 'Loutier' case, dealt with at the Liberation, included 101 typed pages, and in Paris and New York the official reading of the will was followed by nine months of proceedings and four trials.

Louis had written several wills, and the latest, dated 2nd February 1935, was the only valid one, revoking all previous wills, but it was contested by several members of the family. L.D. had to swear on oath

Her Highness the Empress of Siam on a visit to Cartier.

before an American tribunal that he had witnessed its writing and ratifying by an Hungarian solicitor.

On the 5th March 1945, Louis' widow told her brother-in-law, Pierre, in a surprisingly curt letter, that she was withdrawing all his powers concerning her husband's succession, as well as those concerning the running of the company:

> *As far as Claude Cartier's and my own rights are concerned, I acknowledge L.D.'s right to act as tutor according to the laws of the various countries concerned, and I will ask you in future to deal with him direct concerning any question relating to Louis Cartier's succession; he will have full powers to act in my name until Claude comes of age.*

Louis' appointed heirs were his daughter, Anne-Marie Révillon, and his son, Claude. Anne-Marie, who was being treated for a nervous breakdown, could not legally claim her rights before she had been declared by a tribunal capable of assuming her responsibilities, and the rights of her children would be dealt with by guardianship; her son, René-Louis, had come of age in 1943. By a cruel irony, two-thirds of the whole Cartier empire were in the hands of two widows, but Jacqueline was not the kind of woman to compromise with the family.

The family was indeed outraged when an article appeared in *Paris-Hebdo* – now *Ici-Paris* – headed:

FIRST THE CARTIER COLLECTION, THEN THE ASTOR COLLECTION: WHERE WILL THE TREASURE-HUNTING THIEVES STRIKE NOW?

> *Today, a double mystery is fascinating the English public and, in particular, art collectors: the disappearance of Louis Cartier's treasure . . . and Scotland Yard's attitude in this dramatic affair.*
>
> *At the beginning of the war, Cartier had placed jewellery worth some £50,000 in the cellars of Ingmire Hall, an old manor house far away from the blitz. The half burned-out house is situated near Sedbergh in West Yorkshire. Curious irony: Cartier was so confident that the hide-out was secure that he even had jewellery sent there from France.*
>
> *During the war, Ingmire Hall was requisitioned and, to this day, some of its buildings remain at the army's disposal. Louis Cartier died in the United States in 1942. The disappearance of his collection was noticed much later, in December 1945, when his executors came to Ingmire Hall to open the cellars. It then became clear that the crates, which were supposed to contain works of art and jewellery, were empty.*

This important theft is the source of a huge international enquiry, fraught with complications. The first surprising fact is that, although the theft of the Cartier collection was discovered over six months ago, Scotland Yard has up to this day not been told about it. On the other hand, if the enquiry had followed its normal course, the chief of Yorkshire police would have published in the police gazette a detailed description of the jewels and works of art stolen, as well as sending a list of the items to all pawn brokers in the United Kingdom, according to the usual procedure for important thefts. None of these measures were taken. However, the luxury magazine, Connoisseur, which is read by art collectors, published an item headed 'Wanted', giving a detailed list and description of all the valuable items in the collection, such as Persian carpets, china, silver, etc. It is known that the Cartier collection included such items. Until now, the advertisement had not caused any reaction.

Another disconcerting factor: there are no traces in Somerset House, where wills have to be registered, of Louis Cartier's last will. For any will to be legally valid, it has to be registered there, and, according to the police, the theft was discovered during the opening of the crates by so-called executors.

The following declaration by Mrs. Natter, one of Cartier's nieces living in Dorking, Surrey, sheds no further light on the matter: 'Neither my husband nor I know anything about this, but I don't understand the reason for all the fuss. Nothing in this business should be of any interest to the public.' A view all the more surprising when the matter is one concerning £50,000 worth of objects d'art which literally disappeared from the cellars of a military camp.

The lack of enthusiasm from the police for contacting pawn brokers and the public in general, seems to indicate that the thieves are in no hurry to sell their hoard. The present theory is that of an art theft: those who stole the collection would have done so for the 'love of art', and not to profit from any subsequent sales.

The most remarkable pieces in the collection were a XVIth century Ispahan carpet, two XVIIth century Yoshagan carpets and a silver dinner-service signed by Robert-Joseph Auguste (who was Louis XV's master silversmith), a dinner-service bearing the arms of King George III and an XVIIIth century Meissen china dinner-service.

Given the nature of the stolen pieces, and the circumstances of their disappearance, the business is the subject of considerable speculation. Specialists consider it to be one of the 'most disturbing of the century', and express the view that the stolen treasure is no longer in England where it would be too easily identifiable.

The whole affair can be compared with a strangely similar theft, that of the historic collection of Colonel J.J. Astor, which disappeared from his castle. It is thought that the two exploits are the work of the same group of gentlemen thieves, highly knowledgeable about art and very selective in their choice. All famous collections are under constant discreet surveillance. Scotland Yard is well aware of the proverb, 'bad luck always comes in threes'.

From Geneva to London to New York, gossip flourished and it was thought that certain inconsiderate comments made to a journalist were aimed at discrediting the family and could only be the work of either someone from within the organisation wishing to harm it, or from the Countess Almassy. What was the truth about the Ingmire Hall treasure? The items mentioned had indeed belonged to Louis, but was it certain that he had got them out of Budapest and San Sebastian in time? The mystery remains. The author actually conducted her own enquiry in Budapest – and it is undeniable that certain pieces of furniture have remained in Hungary. The journalist who wrote the article in London in 1945 "cannot quite remember" and refused an interview.

Louis Cartier's family and friends were convinced that Jacqueline Cartier had deliberately acted in order to harm them, and L.D. relinquished the powers with which she had entrusted him, as well as his role as tutor, which in any case was due to end with Claude's coming of age.

CHAPTER NINE

New Times

1

After an exciting period in the American air-force, which he had joined at the age of 20, Claude Cartier took over his father's office.

He was proud to be in power and yet worried about taking on the responsibility of an empire which had been ruled for seven years (and what years!) by fanatics who considered him a clumsy heir apparent. It was therefore natural that he should make mistakes, in spite of – or maybe because of – all the advice given him by Jeanne, who was now nearly 60 but more dynamic than ever, and by all the other people who sustained his father's image and aura.

Claude refused to wear the crown of the man who continued to fascinate him, even beyond death. There he was, clumsy, surprised, perplexed, looking for unknown facets of a father who was, at the same time, close and yet foreign to him. This strange feeling was at its strongest when he was told of the ceremony which had taken place after the return of Louis' body to France (organised by Jeanne down to the smallest detail), in which the funeral cortège, which included all the personnel of the firm, had had to stop on its way back from the funeral service outside 13 Rue de la Paix, all shut down, with the French flag flying at half-mast.

Jeanne told us: "I had wanted the ceremony to be a symbol, with the firm closed and all the personnel dispersing after the minute of silence in front of the firm for which he had lived and suffered – HIS firm."

Claude found it impossible to comprehend such worship of a dead man, and Louis' grandson (who was two years older than Claude) tried to help him by explaining the nature of the symbolism. It was a waste of time. The Hungarian blood of the Almassy ran in his veins and the idea of his father as head of Cartier was totally alien to him.

I leave to my son, Claude, in his own right and over and above his own rightful share, all the goods I own and will own in Hungary, and, still over and above his rightful share, I leave to my son, Claude, all the furniture and the entire contents of the said buildings situated in Hungary on condition that . . .

What had become of the part of Budapest where the palace had stood, successively bombed as it had been by the English, the Russians and the Americans? The palace which had sheltered the young Hungarian prince was nothing more than a heap of rubble; Claude missed his native Budapest, and Switzerland also, where he had lived an adolescence more full of fun than study. All in all, he didn't like Paris, at least not for work. Nevertheless, he tried to do his best in carrying out his duties, to prove to 'those in Paris' that he was a son worthy of his father, while at the same time remaining himself. He deliberately exaggerated his off-handedness, his American habits, and his contempt for decorum. In the end, he gave up, and decided to organise his life differently, dividing his time between Miami, New York, and Gstaad, and was rather put out to realise, each time he returned to Paris, that the organisation functioned perfectly well without him – if not better.

He could, therefore, see no point in restraining his enormous zest for living, particularly since he was convinced that his father had given up part of himself for the prestige of the family name. Talking to René-Louis Révillon, Claude confessed his intense thirst for pleasure, his frenzy for happiness in all its forms: sports contests, escapades, love affairs. So many aspirations for transgressing the immediate, that he felt there was a family curse. René-Louis told him that he was paying with his blood, that the spell had been broken: deprived of his father in the full flower of his adolescence, he could now see his mother gradually sinking into even deeper indifference for him, just as the Cartier forebears had done in previous times.

"So," said Claude, "I must live life to the full!"

He went from international championships to love affairs (some of these, involving famous actresses or models, were the subject of many newspaper headlines) and he travelled extensively, until one day an even more fascinating love affair persuaded him to settle in the United States. He decided to suggest to his uncle that they should swop Paris for New York; his cousins, Marion and Pierre Claudel, would assume his duties in Rue de la Paix, and he would reign over Fifth Avenue. The deal fitted the 1921 agreement and Louis' desires according to his will:

Claude Cartier (son of Louis), 1925–1975. In 1943 he volunteered to serve in the American Airforce.

Family divisions create ruin and misery, and I request my heirs to proceed as follows, in their own interests: should they decide to hand over their family claim, they should offer each other the shares in priority and they should then offer half each to my brothers or their direct heirs.

There was stock taking and exchange of deeds. Then finally a few months later Claude, on being told that he was now the head of the American organisation, uttered the following strange words: "I am at last going to free myself of Paris."

Paris, over which his father had ruled for a quarter of a century before his birth; Paris, where Louis had transformed the art of jewellery and reimposed the jewellery element in watch-making. The victor of former times had nothing in common with the father he remembered, the father who could tell his young son Claude about legendary characters moving across dream countries. Claude could still relive the slow march of royal elephants, their ears all covered with gems, bearing Oriental princes in solid gold palanquins.

He could see his father being welcomed as ambassador of French luxury and taste by the Grand Duchess Maria Pawlowna, and granted a private audience by the King of Bavaria, the extraordinary and enigmatic man, widely admired and feared, who was also the head of a disconcerting empire. Claude felt no inclination for acting the part of an extra in a play, the leading role of which had been so prestigiously carried off by Louis for many decades.

So Claude left No. 13 with no regrets. On his way to Le Havre he was involved in a car crash in which his chauffeur died, and he was prevented from getting on board; he joined the ship way out at sea, after hiring a motor-boat. The whole story made the headlines.

After fifteen years in the United States, Pierre Claudel and his wife settled in Paris. In seventeen years of married life, they had had five daughters, each with a Claudelian first name. It was not very easy for Marion to adapt to the French rhythm of life. To escape, she painted bright water colours. Jeanne liked them and encouraged her, saying, "it is the remedy for your innate anxiety." After helping Louis' son, she was now helping his niece. She recorded:

I sometimes felt that it was my privilege to help certain members of the family – no, not to help them, but to carry them – and with Louis gone, I was continuing my task.

Jeanne's naturalistic style was to inspire all jewellers, and two very different women, Princess Bibesco and Violette Leduc, expressed their admiration for the designer in the Rue de la Paix.

Violette Leduc, who did not yet know she was to achieve notoriety with *La Batarde*, wrote:

The panther has gone, the tiger is coming, the dragon-fly is still here, this is what is being said in Mademoiselle Toussaint's office on the first floor of Cartier. Animals are being covered with diamonds at the moment. I have a weakness for lighters, I would collect them gladly, but I daren't say so to Mademoiselle Toussaint while she is explaining to me how she converts the handle of a walking-stick, bought in an antique dealer's, or the tortoise, given to her by a young writer, into two surprising lighters. How very romantic her tapestry-covered cigarette case is! It is rare to see a study so full of originality. Mademoiselle Toussaint knows how to surround herself with objects d'art. In her office, we breathe the oxygen of courage and perseverance. Out of the blue, she explains that she feeds blackbirds on Gruyère cheese as they need fat in winter or else they die; is she trying to make me forget what is in my hand? It is a jewel which is also a bird – the body is an emerald, the wings and the beak are of diamonds. My favourite jewel is the one Mademoiselle Toussaint wears in her buttonhole: a bunch of tiny coral bells, faintly wilting with diamonds at once hidden and showing. Hurray for the lily of the valley if it inspired the designer! Gardenia is a word I find more precious than camelia; the gardenia which one used to buy in London at the time of the apotheoisis and fall of Wilde. Here it is, sheltered, lit up in a showcase, eternal and fragile with its ivory petals, insolent with an arrogant diamond at the heart of the flower. One night, a dragon-fly settled on the table in my huge cottage at Faucon, in the mean light of my paraffin lamp. For two hours I thought it was dead and dared not move it. Suddenly, it took off and disappeared, though it could not escape since all the windows and the door were closed. My comedian is now transformed into a summer jewel by Cartier. Its wings move, it carries diamonds and emeralds like ants carry loads. This metamorphosis is Mademoiselle Toussaint's business alone. 'I would like a tiger made out of daffodils.' Why did I not hear this sentence when I was ceaselessly picking white daisies in the Chevreuse valley? I would have dreamed of dangerous animals dressed up as flowers. There is a tiger at Cartier, but the daffodil is not a yellow diamond.

As for Princess Bibesco:

I knew there existed a stream which feeds the taste of the most famous jewellers of our time. This spring comes from Rue de la Paix, between the yellow and black pillars of a narrow temple devoted to Fortune. From Paris, this spring flows to London and New York, and from there goes on to shed its waters over all the continents. I knew that there existed a style for certain precious objects which, like roving stars, can be recognised throughout the world as Cartier jewels, but I did not yet know that it is the spirit of one woman which gives them their inimitable quality; that it is from her that they derive 'the beauty with which elegant gems are adorned,' as the poet says, 'a beauty without which the largest diamonds, the purest emeralds, the darkest sapphires, the deepest rubies and the heaviest pearls would be nothing more than rocks or vulgar currency.'

I wanted to know all the components of Paris' majesty, and, naturally, wished to know this woman; I liked to think that her imagination, her meanings, her judgement gave shape and colour and communicated the essence of life to these precious but lifeless stones. My wish was granted. I met the woman, who was silently acknowledged to be the artistic director of the firm. She appeared, holding in her hand a bunch of wisteria. Like an allegory, the delicate spring flower of French villages seemed part of her. She had just dipped it into the magical fountain to draw it out again as fresh and as soft and scented as if Fanny had just picked it from her window, but it had been transformed by its brief stay in the magical water into a bunch of diamonds. Who are you, you who give diamonds fragrance and turn wealth into poetry, whereas anywhere else it is so often ugly and heavy? That is what I wanted to ask . . . Who are you, Jeanne Toussaint?

Jeanne Toussaint's reply:

I was unpredictable, adored, adulated, blessed; a man entered my life when I was playing about with designing evening bags, everything moved fast, so very fast . . .

Such fame, such sudden renown made Jeanne better known abroad than in France, and might have transformed anyone else, but she knew that she was, under the Fourth Republic, a link in a chain which was first forged by François under Louis-Philippe. Jeanne's only pride was to see Louis' empire at work, not only as a perfect machine, but above all like a well-fed body, with a conscience and a soul. "When I have gone, the spirit will remain," he had said.

In the United States, Claude was doing his best to assume his responsibilities with the help of L.D. and Jules Glaenzer; in Britain, the fourth generation carried on the tradition under the direction of Jacques' son, Jean-Jacques, who was helped by his brother-in-law, Natter. During a trip to London, Jeanne was asked by a journalist whether Cartier did not mind adorning the wives of black marketeers, after having dealt with kings, and she replied that Cartier were proud to succeed in adorning black marketeers' wives with the same perfection they had formerly offered to kings. These words shocked the last survivor of the three brothers, who was living near Geneva and regularly entertained the cream of society.

While reading an account of Jeanne's interview, Pierre Cartier learned the news of his sister-in-law's death and simultaneously received a copy of the first draft of an explosive article for the *Washington Post*, in which the author discussed at length the affair between Countess Almassy and Alfonso XIII, an affair which he claimed had continued for some time after the marriage of the beautiful Hungarian to the King of jewellers.

Pierre immediately wired an order that the journalist must be bought out. There must be no hint of scandal involving the Pope's secret chamberlain, who he was preparing to receive on his yacht, *The Elma*, together with the wives of the three heads of the Peace Conference, Mrs. Eisenhower, Lucie Faure and Lady Eden, who had all been invited to a 'Peace Cruise' blessed by His Holiness. Pierre would have liked his daughter to receive the diplomats' wives at his side, but Marion declared outright that she would have nothing to do with social life any longer.

Suffering from the same fantasies as Louis' first wife, Marion felt – rightly or wrongly – that she was the victim of a family who had manipulated her in the name of ambition and prestige. She did not approve the exchange of Paris for New York, and took refuge in mysticism and in atheism, questioning her marital happiness. After living between New York and Switzerland, she found it difficult to get used to Paris. "We, the heirs of great families whose ancestors' sole aim was to succeed in their financial deals, are mere pawns on a chessboard."

On the 12th September 1956, Pierre Cartier and his wife announced to Paris and Geneva high society the wedding of their nephew, Claude Cartier, to the pretty Rita-Kate Salmona, daughter of an American industrialist. Among the invited guests were Baron and Baroness Hely d'Oissel. At 68, Jeanne had finally decided to marry the Baron. She had designed for Rita a ring which expressed to Louis' son's fiancée all the tenderness she had felt for his father.

Jeanne may have become Baronne Hely d'Oissel in the eyes of Paris society, but she remained 'Toussaint the panther' in her kingdom at Rue de la Paix, and she had recently been awarded the red ribbon of the *Legion d'Honneur* by the government, for her artistic achievements. Jeanne was now aware that what had been a privilege for a few people, was becoming more and more available to the general public. She was working on the notion of permanence and style with a different out-look; it was necessary to create, to innovate and to make use of all possible ideas.

Few tortoise sellers who had stalls along the Seine, could have had any idea that the gentleman, who periodically bought dead tortoises from them, was a colleague of the Panther who, that very evening would transform the animals with a scalpel, washing and cleaning them. The tortoise became an elegant table-top lighter, decorated with a ruffle of coral and lapis-lazuli: the mechanism was concealed inside the shell. Jeanne had launched a new fashion which was so successful that an infinity of tortoise-shaped jewels of gold or platinum, decorated with diamonds, emeralds and rubies, were produced in the following years.

"One of Jeanne Toussain's most spectacular successes," says Robert Thil, "was the miniature clock which was inserted into a scent bottle, that she submitted to us during a working session. She was fond of the crystal bottle which formed part of a travelling case that had belonged to Louis Cartier, and she said to me: 'Surely it must be possible to put something in there, I mean, something else but scent'."

Here again, the artist's will to alter an object, to change its original destiny, was at work; after thinking about it at length, Jeanne said: "Place a miniature clock in there!" These were precisely the words which the Master would have used.

When her colleagues objected, she replied, in a way which Louis would not have disapproved: "Nothing is ever totally impossible," adding that they could surely learn from the sailors who built sailing ships in bottles, the necks of which were narrower than her scent bottle.

A few weeks later, the clock-bottle emerged from the workshops, with its gold top enriched with a sapphire cabochon which served as a winder. "This is genius-like craftsmanship," she conceded.

Oval faceted Mystery Clock. Luzuli lapis and silver gilt. Garland motif and diamond leaves, carved emeralds and rubies. Carved sapphire bird. Hands of diamonds on yellow gold (1982, Cartier).

As well as creating unusual objects or jewellery in the medium price range, superb pieces were still being designed; there were still fairy-tales in a world where kings were becoming scarce, and the wedding of King Fouad of Egypt's son, Farouk, was an occasion of sumptuous festivities. Soon after the wedding, the King of Egypt commissioned a key-ring to add to his collection of erotica: it was an entwined couple, ready for the final act of love; the key-ring was delivered to Cairo at the same time as a clock made of lapis-lazuli and imperial jade, the face of which was made of gold and rubies and decorated with diamonds.

Eroticism was very much one of the components of the unusual requests of patrons looking for originality; such was the request of the wife of a very wealthy spirits trader, who loved to shock her friends by bringing out her highly phallic lipstick-holder or her 'specially created' powder-box with its secret spring below the mirror, which released minute animated characters indulging in group pleasures. "My darlings, I defy anyone in the world to possess a lipstick-holder and a powder-box similar to mine; they cost me a fortune, but no one else has anything like them!" she said proudly.

The most extraordinary erotic creation was made in 1924: it was a solid gold chastity belt, decorated with sapphires, emeralds, rubies and diamonds; R.G., who was 20 years old, had to go and fit it himself in the house of the young mistress of a lover, who was as perverse as he was jealous. P.G., who is R.G.'s son and a jeweller still working for Cartier, recorded:

> *My father used to tell us how, blushing with shame, he had to fit the object on the pretty lady, who was barely thirty. The fitting was delicate, and my father came out of the house with considerably more confidence in his masculinity than when he had gone, and I do believe that he had a duplicate key made.*

The anecdote would have amused Cocteau, for whom Cartier were just making their tenth Academician's sword. Among the close friends who were approached for the subscription where Francine Weissweiler, who donated rubies and diamonds, and Gabrielle Chanel (who had not as yet come to hate Cocteau), who offered the emerald which was to adorn Orpheus' lyre.

'Coquelicot' parure. Rubies and diamonds mounted in yellow gold (Cartier, 1982).

Jean Marais, who was with Cocteau throughout that memorable day, tells us how much the poet was moved by the simple beauty of his Academician's sword. He said: "You will place it by my side on my

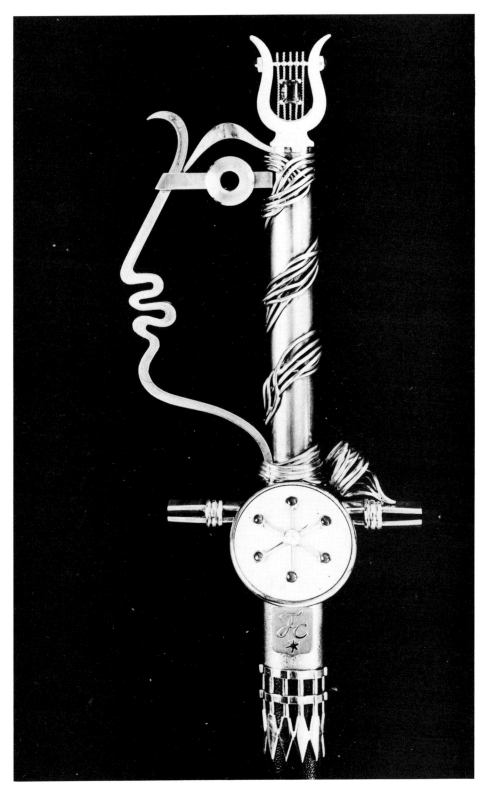

*The Academician's sword
of Jean Cocteau (Cartier,
1955).*

death bed, I am proud that it should be the most beautiful of them all."
And Jean Marais added:

> *He was so moved that I had to help him put on his green suit. I felt as if I*
> *was a father taking his son to a ceremony. He was rather like a young boy*
> *taking first communion, filled with faith, fear and scruples; before we left*
> *the flat, he talked again about the symbols on his sword, the profile and lyre*
> *of Orpheus, the five-point star, the draughtsman pencil-holder, the theatre*
> *curtains, the Palais Royal Gates and, at the very top, the minute bronze*
> *hand clasping the ivory snowball of* Les Enfants Terribles.

In the course of our discussion of one of the paradoxes about Cocteau,
there arose his contempt for honour and equally his love of it. Jean
Marais, who was looking at a detail of the sword, agreed that there may
have been a resurgence of Radiguet's influence on Cocteau when he was
accepting academic honours; the detail at the top of the scabbard
recalled the triple-ringed ring, for which they had started a fashion
many years earlier, at the Boeuf sur le Toit. Jean Marais remembered
that, after giving the emerald for the poet's sword, Coco Chanel, feeling
generous, offered the actor a handful of moonstones. "They are your
birthstones," she said.

The fashion for astrology was growing, and the symbolism of birthstones was all the rage; Marais was willing to be identified with moonstones. He was to learn, much later, that the birthstone for his own birth
sign, Sagittarius, was in fact the turquoise, and that Cocteau's birthstone was topaz. The stone for Aries was garnet, for Virgo, jasper,
Taurus' stone was agate, Gemini's aquamarine, Leo's was ruby, for
Libra, the diamond, Scorpio's was the cornelian, Capricorn's onyx,
Aquarius' sapphire and Pisces' stone was coral. When Jean Marais told
this to Coco, she replied with her customary bad humour: "You're the
one who claims that the moonstone isn't your birthstone! You can't
really expect me to offer you turquoises, those stones which are ruined
by scent!"*

---

* Turquoises are harmed by certain scents.

2

In London, New York and Paris, the three brothers' heirs were carrying on the business. In Paris, at Rue de la Paix, Jeanne pursued her task, taking refuge in her work with a vigour increased by sorrow: she had married late and soon became a widow. After the Baron's death, Cartier was her sole aim in life.

Despite her advancing years, Jeanne was electrifying her team, more the 'panther' than ever; the marvellous jewel for which she had found inspiration during her African trip became a fantastic success. Nina Dhier, former model and wife of the steel king, von Thyssen, had just ordered two bracelets, a brooch, a ring and hat-pin, all sporting the panther symbol.

As with royal romances in former days, people dreamed about the love-life of stage queens and princes of finance: such was the fairy-tale wedding of Josette Day, former Beauty to Marais-the-Beast in Cocteau's fantastic film, whose wealthy husband offered her a sixty carat emerald and a princely jewel collection.

So also was the fairy-tale destiny of Elizabeth Taylor, who had been famous since her first film at the age of 9, and whose third husband had just offered her a thirty carat diamond. Mike Todd, who followed Nick Helton and Michael Wilding in Liz's life, wanted his wife to possess the most fabulous collection of jewels in all Hollywood. Liz did not known then that Mike Todd, who died tragically, was to be succeeded by Eddie Fisher and then by Richard Burton, who was to make her the most bejewelled of all film stars. He offered her, among other pieces, an engraved diamond which had belonged to the mogol emperor, Shah Jahan, as well as the Cartier-Taylor-Burton pear-shaped diamond, which weighed 62 carats.

Another fairy-tale was the marriage of Grace Kelly – daughter of a millionaire and Hitchcock's favourite star – to Prince Rainier of Monaco. The sumptuousness of the royal wedding was somewhat sullied by the scandal surrounding the purchase of a necklace which caused the headline 'Monaco in grips of the Affair of the Necklace'. No one, from the humblest cottage in Central France to the remotest corner of Tennessee, was left in ignorance of the shady side of the discussions between the National Council of the Principality and Mr. M., who was the agent of a Paris jeweller who had sold, a few weeks before the wedding, a necklace costing thirty-nine million francs, for which the agent had paid 12 million francs on account.

Barbara Hutton (Princess Troubetzkoi).

When the Monaco experts looked at the necklace, they valued it at eighteen million, which was the sum for which it had been put up for sale (without success) in the auction room of the Hotel Drouot. The National Council, outraged by the size of the asking price, demanded the twelve million franc account back in exchange for the necklace. But the jeweller, who considered that the twelve million francs were a down payment, refused.

In a hurry, the National Council requested Cartier to design a new necklace, which was given to the Princess on her wedding day (among other jewels were a tiara made of platinum and diamonds, decorated with three ruby cabochons, and a bracelet made of platinum and diamonds, offered by the S.B.M. and Aristotle Onassis).

The Monaco councillors continued to worry about two necklaces being rather a lot for one neck, however pretty, and were still locked in discussions with the Parisian jeweller, who was threatening to block the New York bank accounts of Grace and Rainier.

'The Affair' was finally settled, and Princess Grace of Monaco always wore her Cartier necklace at public functions.

The fairy-tales which lit up the dreariness of daily life were fewer than before, and in order that Parisian luxury jewellery should remain the best in the world, it was essential to obey the rules laid down by Louis; the new age imposed the creation of jewellery which could be afforded by a wider range of clients, while at the same time maintaining tradition with sumptuous gems and prestigious objects.

Among the prestigious items were Academician's swords made for Daniel-Rops, Wladimir d'Ormesson and Jean Delay, as well as for Joseph Kessel; the latter received his sword from his friend, Pierre Lazareff, during a reception at the Ritz. Pierre Lazareff said at the reception:

I am using big words and everyone knows that you don't like them. But big words are necessary for a man of your stature. We are giving a knight's sword to a man who fought so many fights for freedom and for honour, a great writer who taught our generation the virtues of adventure and who has given so many examples of independence.

Kessel looked at his sword for a long time: on the handle was a gold lion's head; on the tang, the Pole star (symbol of Russia), a Southern Cross (recalling his Argentinian birth), the Star of David (his Jewish origins), the Lorraine Cross (he was one of the first Free French fighters) and a map of the world (he was a great reporter); on the guard, a wing symbolised the air force which he had joined, as well as his book *l'Equipage*. Joseph, smiling warmly to hide his emotion, replied:

> *Many weapons have gone through my hands, from the catapults of my childhood, yemeni daggers and mau-mau machettes; compared with those, this sword seems very light and harmless, and yet I know it will defend me well, because it symbolises friendship and friendship is the strongest.*

December 1962: all the French daily papers' headlines (across five columns in *l'Aurore*, three in *France-Soir*, two in *Paris-Presse*) proclaimed: 'SENSATION IN NEW YORK – END OF A FABULOUS ADVENTURE'; a leak, published in the *New York Times*, mentioned that Cartier-New York was being sold to Edward Goldstein, a director of the jewellery group, 'Black Star and Frost'.

René-Louis Révillon took the first plane for New York to try and dissuade Claude Cartier, and to remind him of the 1921 pact and also of the clauses in their father's and grandfather's wills:

> *Family divisions create ruin and misery, and I request my heirs to proceed as follows, in their own interests should they decide to hand over their family claim . . .*

It was a waste of time. Claude was tender and charming as usual, but inflexible, and Cartier-New York could not remain in the family – the 30% Paris shares held by Anne-Marie's son were derisory.

René-Louis returned by plane with tears in his eyes.

A few days later, Edward Goldstein's spokesmen announced that the deal was on, that Cartier would remain Cartier, and that Claude, son of the kings' jeweller, would be the president of the American empire.

> *The spirit remains, from Paulette Goddard to Rita Hayworth, from Dupont de Nemours and other Wall Street kings to 'dollar princesses' like Doris Duke and Barbara Hutton; the clientèle will remain faithful, since it is still true that for genuine collectors, a jewel which does not bear the Cartier signature is not a real jewel.*

Three months later, in acknowledgement of the spirit of the pact and of his grandfather's last wishes, René-Louis Révillon made over his shares to his uncle Pierre, and abandoned his post as administrator of Cartier-Paris.

The smallest watch in the world presented by the President of the French Republic to Her Majesty Queen Elizabeth II.

The repercussions of the take-over of Cartier-New York by a group outside the family were felt throughout the world. In Paris and London, however, as well as in the workshops on Fifth Avenue, a third generation of craftsmen continued to work within the spirit and the framework of the organisation, and so it was that the grandson of a craftsman, who had emigrated in 1909, and who had re-set the Hope Diamond in former days, was re-setting Shah Jahan's diamond pendant for Elizabeth Taylor.

Marion Cartier had given birth in 1957 to a severely retarded child, to whom she devoted most of her time, constantly on the look-out for a smile, for the ghost of a gesture or a word. She hardly ever went to the Rue de la Paix. In 1964, her father died at the age of 86, and, a few months later her only son, Pierre, died at the age of 7.

Marion banished from her painting the blues, pinks, greens and ochres which had delighted her in the past, and painted only in black, white and grey, and her barely figurative pictures blatantly exposed her loneliness.

Pierre Cartier's death enabled journalists to recall the extraordinary history of the dynasty, which spanned from Louis-Phillipe to the Fifth Republic, and to underline the remarkable resurgence of the heirs of the first Pierre, who had been an obscure creator of powder-flasks and gun butts, to his grandsons, who had reached international fame, and were also discerning collectors. Amongst them, Louis in particular, they had built up a superb library, which was being auctioned.

Looking through the sales catalogue, it is possible to measure the breadth of interest of the eldest son of the third generation, who had a collection of 288 rare volumes ranging from Apuleus to Verlaine and Colette, an Andreasi manuscript on vellum (with an Italian XVIth century binding dedicated to Isabella of Este, Marchioness of Mantua, sister-in-law of Lucretia Borgia and Ludovico the Moor), Ovid's *Metamorphoses* set in rondeaux by Benserade in an original edition bound for Louis XIV, a copy of the *Funeral Oration of Louis of Bourbon, Prince of Conde* in a mourning binding carrying Bossuet's arms, and also nineteenth- and twentieth-century books, first editions of *Madame Bovary* and of Victor Hugo's *Contemplations* . . .

And Jeanne, the only remaining witness of this past, followed her destiny along a road which linked the present with the past in which she had featured so many times, either by Louis' side, or alone, with or without the brothers who had formerly banned her from the family clan, only to recognise later that she was more Cartier than the Cartiers.

Deaths, suicides, auctions, so many news items which reminded Jeanne Toussaint of so many meetings, creations, negotiations, difficulties and victories.

Marilyn Monroe was dead. She who had loved the little diamond heart so much.

Nina Dhyer was dead – her suicide recalled Marilyn's tragedy; Nina, to whom Saddrudin Khan – following in von Thyssen's footsteps – had offered necklaces, bracelets, emeralds, diamonds and rubies.

Cocteau, too, was dead; the magician who loved and hated jewels in the same way as he both sought honours and despised them. Also – on the same day as the poet – Edith Piaf, who preferred to offer her lovers watches rather than buying jewels for herself, died. Her talisman had been the gold cross enhanced with rubies, given to her by Marlene Dietrich.

Ali Khan, who often used to amble through the rooms of No. 13, making saucy jokes for the sheer pleasure of shocking salesmen and smart clients, was dead.

And so, too, was President Kennedy, whose widow married Aristotle Onassis, who showered her with fabulous jewels . . .

Soon, de Gaulle was to die also. Always faithful to his first London headquarters, he had always gone to Cartier for his official presents (to the English and Greek royal families, and to Stalin and Mrs. Kruschev).

The road through life is littered with corpses. Was it fear or indifference to death which lead Jeanne, at the age of 80, to carry on spending a few hours every day in 'her' firm, happy in her office on the first floor, where many world leaders had come to see her?

A witness from the past, there she was, at the side of the company's president, during the elegant reception given for the international press to present the new Cartier gas lighter which was to be sold through a hundred sales outlets.

A necklace of Barbara Hutton's which converts into a tiara: on a gold mount, 7 emeralds weighing a total of 263 carats 47, the central hexagonal emerald 100 carats 15 (having once belonged to Catherine the Great of Russia), 379 diamonds, with a total of 36 carats 79.

A hundred sales outlets! This innovation rocked the closed milieu of the luxury jewellery business, and the reaction had been foreseen by Marion Claudel's financial advisers. Indeed, few clients or colleagues took any notice of the small newspaper announcement which appeared at the same time as the launching of the gas lighter:

> *Important changes at Cartier, creation of subsidiary companies in Japan, in the Middle East, and in the Common Market; each new agency represents an investment of a million dollars.*

At the end of the announcement, Marion Claudel added that she was about to increase the capital through a large contribution of Anglo-American capital, but that Cartier jewels would, nevertheless, continue to be created in Paris.

The discreet nature of the announcement – just fifteen lines – compensated for the international repercussions, seven years earlier, of the handing over of the American firm. In fact, Marion Claudel was abandoning her responsibilities, just as her cousin Claude had done, by disposing of her shares. From then on, only New Bond Street remained in the hands of Jacques Cartier's heirs.

3

It was in the nursing home where she had been operated on for a broken thigh bone, that Jeanne learned of the death of Coco Chanel. Recalling mutual memories of sixty years, she suddenly remembered Gabrielle's warning: "We are four years apart, our destinies are similar". But Jeanne refused to think about the present and the future, she immersed herself with intense pleasure in the mists and precious moments of an extraordinary past, which she alone was able to remember.

She was still convalescing when she learned through a friend and colleague, of the new developments taking place at No. 13: the group which had been directing the firm for the past four years was now handing over its shares to other shareholders, and Robert Hocq, who had created the luxury lighter, under licence from Cartier, was to become Chairman of the new company. "He is not even in our branch."

"He will learn!" commented Jeanne. "As long as he wants to, he will learn." Jeanne appeared for the feast of Saint-Eloi (the patron saint of jewellers) in 1973. She was delicate and distant, sometimes absent-minded, sometimes lively; she smiled at the old employees, and was surprised by the new faces; she told an admiring young girl:

I have lived through various periods during which divine women were covered with sumptuous jewels. You are inheriting from your father an empire which you will have to be worthy of, and I am sure you are capable of this.

She then placed her hand on Nathalie Hocq's shoulder, encouraging and protective.

To search among the memories Jeanne left behind, forces one to resuscitate the past and to evoke images of the times long gone. It is fascinating and moving to observe her immobile in her arm-chair, contemplating the bare branches of the trees outside followed by the first spring buds and, finally, the change from bright green to dark green to russet of the leaves. Remarkable also, to follow Jeanne through the seasons, inspired perhaps by a bird in flight, perhaps also thinking of diamonds, emeralds, sapphires, rubies. Such was this extraordinary woman, whose eyes would suddenly shine or grow dim, whose voice sometimes growled and then softly purred, and who, from time to time, at the age of more than eighty-five, would still enquire about the vast empire of Cartier, to whose glory she had devoted her life since the end of the First World War.

We took her to The Ritz for lunch – she had been looking forward to it for a week: "There's going to be a party, I love parties." It was then that we told her of the linking up of the London and Paris houses, and that soon New York would probably be placed under the same chairmanship.

"Just like the old days, Paris-London-New York? As in 1908?"

"Yes, as in the old days."

"I won't live long enough to see this, and believe you me, I am really sorry."

Jeanne was not able to see the retrospective exhibition organised at No. 13 to celebrate the centenary of Louis Cartier's birth: she had broken her thigh bone again. From her sick bed, she slowly looked at the photographs taken during the exhibition, making occasional comments: "Here is Réné-Louis Révillon, Annette and Roger Worth . . . This one looks like Jacques . . . is it his grandson? I am really a very old lady . . . and Claude? Claude was not present for this celebration in honour of his father?" It would not have been a good idea to tell her that Claude, who had remarried two years previously, was dying in atrocious pain of Charcot's nervous disease.

Three years earlier, he had bought, relatively cheaply, a superb flat in Manhattan and a friend had told him: "Be careful, the previous owner committed suicide, and there is an American superstition which says you should not live in a place still haunted by death for several months." Claude had laughed; in the old days, his family had feared superstitions and then refuted them – the whole thing was nonsense.

A few months after the centenary of his father's birth, Claude's body was taken to the Gonnards cemetery to join three generations of Cartiers in the family vault. From America, two fragile adolescents, Véronique and Alain, had accompanied their father's body; they were disconcerted by the mass of flowers, the unknown faces, and surprised by the freezing rain; they had just come from New York's Indian summer.

A few months later, Jeanne, without realising that four years had elapsed since Gabrielle's death, died too; as she had been forewarned, she joined the woman who had been sometimes her enemy, often her accomplice, but always her friend: Coco Chanel.

Jeanne died without learning that Robert Hocq had won his sentimental battle and united the American empire with London and Paris; nor did she learn that he was to give the name of Louis Cartier to the most beautiful diamond in the world, which weighed 107.07 carats.

Claude Cartier's son, Alain, aged twenty-two, was fascinated by art and was anxious to renew traditions. Meanwhile, in her office at No. 13 Rue de la Paix, having learned from the past, a young woman of twenty-eight was carrying on with the mission with which Jeanne had entrusted her, determined to maintain the preponderance of an organisation whose name has become a symbol since the turn of the century. Her name was Nathalie Hocq.

Cartier belongs to yesterday, today and tomorrow: an adventure in history and the story of a continuing adventure.